THE AMERICAN ERA

The murderous attacks of September 11, 2001, war and insurgency in Iraq, and the continuing dangers of terrorism have triggered profound concern about America's security and the nature of its role on the world stage. Yet much of the debate on foreign policy falls short because it fails to take into account the lethal realities of the post-9/11 world, and it often exhibits a "blame America first" attitude. Many academics and commentators dwell disproportionately on problems in the exercise of power, rather than the consequences if the United States fails to pursue an assertive foreign policy. Instead, *The American Era* makes a provocative argument in favor of superpower preeminence as both necessary and desirable, and based on three critical premises:

☆ First, militant Islamic terrorism and weapons of mass destruction (WMD) pose a threat of a wholly new magnitude that requires us to alter our thinking about preemptive and even preventive use of force.

☆ Second, wishful thinking aside, the U.N. and other international bodies are often incapable of acting on the most urgent and deadly problems of our time.

☆ Third, in an international system with no true central authority, other countries will inevitably look to the United States for leadership. America should seek to collaborate with others, but if it does not take the lead in confronting the most dangerous threats, no one else is likely to have the ability or the will to do so.

Thus in confronting the menace of terrorism and WMD, and when values such as human rights, liberty, and the rule of law cannot be guaranteed by institutions such as the U.N. and the European Union, American intervention becomes a necessity, not something about which to be apologetic. This understanding should inform our thinking not only about security, but about Europe, the Middle East, Asia, globalization, and anti-Americanism as well.

Robert J. Lieber is a professor of government and international affairs at Georgetown University. He is an expert on American foreign policy and U.S. relations with the Middle East and Europe and the author or editor of thirteen books on international relations and U.S. foreign policy. He has held fellowships from the Guggenheim, Rockefeller, and Ford Foundations; the Council on Foreign Relations; and the Woodrow Wilson International Center for Scholars. His most recently published book is an edited volume, *Eagle Rules? Foreign Policy and American Primacy in the 21st Century* (2002). His numerous authored works include *No Common Power: Understanding International Relations* (4th edition, 2001) and *The Oil Decade* (1986). His articles have appeared in scholarly and policy journals including *Foreign Policy, International Security, American Political Science Review*, the *Chronicle of Higher Education, Commentary*, the *International Journal of Politics, Culture and Society, International Affairs* (London), *Politique Etrangere* (Paris), and *Internationale Politik* (Berlin). His opeds have been published in the *New York Times, Washington Post, Los Angeles Times, Christian Science Monitor, Harper's, USA Today, Ha'aretz*, and *Asharq Al-Awsat*, and he has appeared on the PBS-TV *NewsHour*, ABC's *Nightline*, NBC network news, CNN's *Crossfire*, the *O'Reilly Factor*, Voice of America, BBC World Service, *Al-Jazeera*, and other radio and TV programs in Europe, the Arab world, and Israel.

D0322461

"An experienced scholar and writer with more than three decades of exemplary work to his credit, Robert Lieber has written a first-rate book, a 'cool' assessment of topics that normally come in for shrill treatments full of panic and exaggerations.... [He] knows the fields of energy and Euro-American relations and the play of things in the Middle East with intimacy and authority.... He is theoretically sophisticated, yet quite knowing of Washington ways and policy choices, [and he]... draws a realistic balance sheet of America standing in the world. Lieber writes with poise and calm: he has firm views of the world, but they are expressed with grace and appropriate reserve. He wears his learning lightly.... Lieber documents American pre-eminence but his book is free of triumphalism. He knows the weakness of European policies but does not succumb to Euro-bashing.... [His] reading of America's role in Asia... is subtle, informed by history, and shrewd in its reading of the Asian balance of power.... A work of scholarship, yet accessible to a wider readership, a work of judgment, yet anchored in the data and the objective world.... a book of quality by a scholar of genuine depth and authority."

Fouad Ajami, *Paul H. Nitze School of Advanced International Studies, Johns Hopkins University*

"This may be the best book on American foreign policy written since September 11. Robert Lieber is a scholar with deep insight, broad knowledge, and – what is lacking in most discussions of world affairs today – common sense. Anyone thinking seriously about global affairs today and in the coming years should begin with this smart and sober work."

Robert Kagan, author of *Paradise and Power: America and Europe in the New World Order*

"A powerful book with truly global scope. Lieber is not only a specialist on U.S. foreign policy, he has deep knowledge of Europe, the Middle East, global energy, and security affairs. The result is a book with range and depth, one that combines theoretical insights with practical policy recommendations."

Charles Lipson, *University of Chicago*

"With its powerful thesis and compelling arguments, Robert Lieber's *The American Era* is destined to become a key text in the global debate about American foreign policy."

Michael Mandelbaum, author of *The Ideas That Conquered the World: Peace, Democracy and Free Markets in the Twenty-First Century*

The American Era

POWER AND STRATEGY FOR THE 21ST CENTURY

Robert J. Lieber

Georgetown University

CAMBRIDGE
UNIVERSITY PRESS

CAMBRIDGE UNIVERSITY PRESS
Cambridge, New York, Melbourne, Madrid, Cape Town, Singapore, São Paulo

Cambridge University Press
32 Avenue of the Americas, New York, NY 10013-2473, USA

www.cambridge.org
Information on this title: www.cambridge.org/9780521857376

First published 2005
Reprinted 2006
First paperback edition with updates and a postscript 2007

Printed in the United States of America

A catalog record for this publication is available from the British Library.

Library of Congress Cataloging in Publication Data
Lieber, Robert J., 1941–
The American era : power and strategy for the 21st century /
Robert J. Lieber.
  p. cm.
Includes bibliographical references and index.
ISBN 0-521-85737-6 (hardback)
1. United States – Foreign relations – 21st century. 2. World politics – 21st century.
3. Balance of power. I. Title.
JZ1480.L54 2005
327.73′009′0511–dc22   2005008111

ISBN   978-0-521-85737-6 hardback
ISBN   978-0-521-69738-5 paperback

Contents

Preface

In recent years a lopsided and often unedifying debate has been taking place. Criticism of America's world role has been characterized by rhetorical excess, partisan acrimony, and ideologically driven assessments that fail to weigh the lethality of the threat we face in the post-9/11 world, the limits of international institutions, and the long-term implications for American strategy and policy. These shortcomings are evident not only in the policy and academic worlds in the United States, but even more so in Europe. Sterile debates about "empire," ad hominem denunciations of the Bush administration, ritual incantations about multilateralism, and an acrimonious climate of blame and counterblame over Iraq are rampant (a veritable *reductio ad Iraqum*). Conversely, on the part of those more favorable toward recent American policy, there has been some keen dissection of opposing arguments but also a substantial amount of stridency, partisanship, and self-satisfaction.

The recent past has demonstrated that problems of policy implementation and flawed diplomacy matter a great deal. It is also clear that American predominance or hegemony in itself can trigger resentment and even hostility. But legitimate expressions of concern about the exercise of American power ought not to make us lose sight of what can happen in the absence of such power. This is something often lost in the volley of charges and countercharges over Iraq, over flaws in American intelligence, and in relation to the dangers or virtues of primacy and preemption.

Some historical perspective is called for too. The 20th century witnessed the heinous crimes of Nazism and Stalinism, two world wars and the Holocaust, and mass murder in Cambodia. The end of the Cold War brought some respite, but even so, in the decade and a half since then we have seen genocide in Rwanda, ethnic cleansing in Bosnia, crimes against humanity in the Darfur region of Sudan, and widespread lawlessness and death in the ruins of failed states such as Liberia and the Congo. Now, in today's environment, despite unprecedented globalization, interdependence, and instant communication, we face what the official 9/11 Commission has termed the catastrophic threat of Islamist terrorism. In view of the fact that al-Qaeda's leader, Osama bin Laden, has called the acquisition of weapons of mass destruction a "duty," and one of his spokesmen has even claimed the right to kill four million Americans, half of them children, this is not the kind of peril that should be taken lightly. The threat is likely to remain with us for a considerable time to come, yet the implications of it often elude critics from both the world of affairs and the world of ideas.

In view of these dangers, and with a few praiseworthy exceptions (cited in chapter 1), what has been lacking is a serious treatment of the case for a grand strategy that both is cognizant of these realities and recognizes American preponderance as both necessary and desirable in coping with such threats. That is what I seek to do in this book. After setting out a general – and unapologetic – argument about American power and grand strategy, I turn to more specific treatments of Europe, globalization and culture, Iraq and the Middle East, Asia, and anti-Americanism. While recognizing that other regions and issues are important in their own right, I have not sought to provide a comprehensive treatment of foreign policy but have instead concentrated on those areas that now matter most. In doing so, I aim to inform and focus debate in the public realm, in the policy arena, and in academia. I hope that in the process, even those who do not share my conclusions or – for that matter – my basic assumptions will at least be challenged to reexamine their own ideas and suppositions.

As I have developed the ideas for this book, some of the material has appeared in articles and essays that I have published elsewhere. Where I have directly drawn on those writings, I have cited the specific references. Among these, I especially would like to take note here of three widely circulated essays written for the *Chronicle of Higher Education*. These include "Foreign Policy Realists Are Unrealistic on Iraq," "The Neoconservative Conspiracy Theory: Pure Myth," and "Rethinking America's Grand Strategy."* Portions of chapter 1 were published as "Die amerikanische Ära," in *Internationale Politik* (Berlin), October 2004. Sections of chapter 3 appeared in a paper written for the American Consortium on European Union Studies. Chapter 4 expands on a co-authored article originally published in the *International Journal of Politics, Culture and Society*.** And chapter 5 elaborates upon my essay, "The Folly of Containment," in the April 2003 issue of *Commentary*.

It is a pleasure to acknowledge those who have provided comments and suggestions on points large and small and from whose advice I have benefited in the writing of this book. Not all of them would agree with my arguments, and some hold points of view with which I have taken issue in this work. All the same, these exchanges of ideas have been without exception cordial and constructive – something that is by no means to be taken for granted in the worlds of policy and ideas. I thus have a real debt of gratitude to (in alphabetical order), Anthony Arend, Harley Balzer, Andrew Bennett, Peter Berkowitz, Steven Biddle, Philipp Bleek, Louise Branson, Michael Brown, Daniel Brumberg, Daniel Byman, Victor Cha, Benjamin J. Cohen, Sally Cowal, Dusko Doder, David Edelstein, Vera Fuchs, Robert Gallucci, Azar Gat, Thomas Helmstorf, Jeffrey Herf, Christopher Joyner, Sarah Kreps, Keir Lieber, Nancy Lieber, Joshua Mitchell, Tom Nichols, Robert Paarlberg, Yossi Shain, George Shambaugh, Raymond Tanter, Leslie Vinjamuri, Ruth Weisberg, and William Wohlforth, as well as two anonymous manuscript reviewers. Special thanks to my

* *Chronicle of Higher Education*, October 18, 2002; May 2, 2003; June 4, 2004.
** "Globalization, Culture, and Identities in Crisis," vol. 16, no. 2 (Winter 2002–3).

research assistant, William Josiger, and to the Department of Government, School of Foreign Service, and College of Arts and Sciences at Georgetown University. Finally, I am grateful for the advice and support of Lewis Bateman, an editor with the qualities of wisdom, judgment, and experience that now are all too rare in the publishing world.

Robert J. Lieber
Washington, D.C.

THE AMERICAN ERA

Introduction

Foreign affairs have captured (or recaptured) the attention of Americans. The murderous attacks of September 11, 2001, war in Afghanistan, war and insurgency in Iraq, and the continuing dangers of terrorism have triggered profound concern about threats to American security and the nature of America's role on the world stage. The end of the Cold War had ushered in a decade in which the public often appeared indifferent to the outside world and policymakers seemed unsure of the United States' mission in world affairs. To be sure, events sometimes rudely intruded – as in Kuwait, Somalia, Bosnia, Kosovo, and smaller scale terrorist attacks – but the sense of dire threat that pervaded the previous half-century had vanished with the collapse of the Soviet Union, and so did abiding concern over foreign policy.

The vacation from the wider world proved to be temporary, but while it lasted America cut its spending on international affairs and on defense as a proportion of gross domestic product (GDP), downplayed the subject in newspapers and on TV network news, and dwelled hardly at all on foreign and national security policy in election contests for President and Congress.

This was not a turning inward – globalization, trade, the Internet, and inexpensive travel connected Americans to other cultures – but foreign policy was far from most people's minds. As a sign of the times, in the first year of his presidency Bill Clinton was reluctant to devote sustained attention to the subject. In frustration, his secretary of state, secretary of defense, and national security adviser sent memos urging him to give them just one hour a week for foreign affairs. Clinton finally agreed, but to his "Yes" he added the words "when possible."[1]

In place of world affairs, a booming "new" economy, surging stock market, and fixation on the foibles of entertainment stars and politicians (O. J. Simpson, Princess Di, Monica and Bill) preoccupied the media and the public. But this holiday from history ended abruptly on 9/11, and in the years since that fateful morning, the claims of a troubled world have intruded into everyday American life. As a result, terrorism, weapons of mass destruction (WMD), Iraq, Iran, North Korea, tensions with Europe, problems of failed states, and seemingly endless turmoil in the Middle East now dominate the attention not only of policymakers and the media but of the wider public as well.[2] As a case in point, the 2004 presidential election was the first since the era of Vietnam in which voters accorded a higher priority to foreign affairs and national security than to the economy. The 2004 figure was 34 percent, whereas in 2000, only 12 percent reported that world affairs mattered most in deciding how they voted for President, and in 1996, just 5 percent did so.[3] In addition, substantial majorities continue to rank Iraq and terrorism as top priorities for the attention of the President and Congress.[4]

In view of this intense preoccupation, debates have erupted at home and abroad not only over specific policies, but also about the proper role of the United States. Urgent questions are now posed by politicians, journalists, ethicists, academics, and ordinary citizens: Has the United States become an empire on a scale surpassing even ancient Rome? Are the burdens of its engagement sustainable or do we risk overstretch? Will this unipolar moment endure? Has America become "Mars" to Europe's "Venus"? Should U.S. grand strategy dictate going it alone or acting only in concert with others? Is there a clash of civilizations? Why can't we bring peace to the Middle East? Why do foreigners have such ambivalent attitudes toward the United States? And given the problems and threats to world order and America's great power, how should we conduct ourselves on the world stage?

Such questions can seem disconnected and perplexing. Ultimately, they require serious thinking about threats, but also about values, historical continuities, and national identity. This book offers some provocative answers to such questions, and goes on to make an argument contrary to the conventional wisdom put forward by many academic experts and pundits. They tend to dwell disproportionately on problems in the exercise of power rather than on the dire consequences of retreat from an activist foreign policy. Some urge strategic disengagement,[5] while others assume that through multilateral cooperation or even "self-binding" to international institutions we can secure our vital interests and even remake the international system as we would like without either incurring serious costs or facing the realities of great power politics.[6] Commentators point to anti-Americanism abroad and frequently find the causes not in the stars but in ourselves, while observers in other countries tend to be more critical, even disdainful of United States policies and objectives. A number of foreign policy thinkers have assimilated the harsh lessons of September 11 in their thinking,[7] but many others – in part because of the overheated political atmosphere – have not. Much of the narrative about foreign policy thus falls short because it fails to take sufficiently into account the stubborn realities of the post-9/11 world.

The argument put forward in this book is, instead, based on three critical premises.[8] First, there is the meaning of 9/11 itself. The lessons of this event require us to alter fundamentally the way we think about the use of force and America's world role. In this sense it merits comparison with the Japanese attack at Pearl Harbor in December 1941 that plunged the United States into World War II.[9] The suicide terrorism of the nineteen hijackers embodies what has been termed "apocalyptic nihilism."[10] It is not something that can be wished away or dealt with primarily by treating "root causes." Instead, the combination of militant Islamic terrorism and WMD poses a threat of a wholly new magnitude. As the 9/11 Commission concluded in its final report, "[T]he enemy is not just 'terrorism', some generic evil.... The catastrophic threat at this moment in history is more specific. It is the threat

posed by Islamist terrorism – especially the al Qaeda network, its affil-
iates, and its ideology."[11] Moreover, the key underlying assumption of
deterrence – that one's adversary is a value-maximizing rational actor
who treasures his own survival – is not very useful in thinking about
countering such a menace. The scale of risk in the coming years, up
to and including that of a concealed nuclear weapon or "dirty" bomb
being detonated in an American city, is very likely to require a robust
defense policy that includes preemption.

Second, as much as we might wish for more effective means of cooperation in addressing common problems, the reality of the United
Nations and of other international institutions is that on the most
urgent and deadly problems, they are mostly incapable of acting or
inadequate to the task. The U.N.'s decision-making structure and institutional weaknesses, the makeup of the Security Council, failures in
Bosnia (1991–95) and Rwanda (1994), the massive corruption of the
oil-for-food program, the ability of terrorists to drive the organization out of Iraq with one blow,[12] and the feckless response to crimes
against humanity in the Darfur region of Sudan are evidence of these
grave shortcomings. Nor does the European Union, let alone weaker
regional bodies such as the Arab League, African Union, or Organization of American States, have much capacity to deal with the
deadliest threats. The U.N. has a significant role to play, not least in
burden-sharing and in contributing to the perceived legitimacy of collective action, but its weaknesses remain a fundamental constraint.
As Stanley Hoffmann, of Harvard's Center for European Studies, has
observed, the U.N. and other international organizations "are increasingly important as sources of legitimacy and stabilizing forces, but
often mismanaged and devoid of adequate means."[13]

Third, in an international system with no true central authority and
the United States as the preponderant power, other countries will continue to look to us for leadership. In this anarchic and unipolar system,
if America does not take action on the most dangerous perils, no one
else is likely to have the capacity or the will to do so.[14] Yet, in view
of U.S. primacy, it is not surprising that the onus for action falls on

its shoulders and that others may be tempted to act as free riders or "buck-passers" in a situation where security is a collective good.

In light of these premises, preemptive strategies in dealing with terrorism and WMD are, in my view, essential. In the face of lethal threats or imminent dangers, this use of force makes strategic sense. Indeed, under these circumstances, the use of preemption is supported by international law and the just war tradition. The maintenance of primacy – preponderance in the economic, military, technological, and cultural dimensions of power – is also in the national interest. And although the very fact of predominance can be a source of foreign resentment, a large disparity of power is more likely to deter challenges by other would-be powers than to provoke them.[15] American power is likely to remain robust and its costs are necessary and manageable provided we avoid disastrous miscalculations. Moreover, both primacy and active U.S. engagement are essential if we are to cooperate with others in the coming years to build a more stable, less dangerous, and more benign global order. Multilateral initiatives and institutions can be valuable in enhancing the effectiveness and legitimacy of foreign policy and in coping with common problems, but we must be both unsentimental about their weaknesses and cognizant of their strengths. At times, however, multilateralism becomes more tempting to others as a means of limiting or binding the United States, rather than achieving shared aims. In this regard, during the 2004 election campaign both George Bush and John Kerry were explicit in saying that America cannot wait for the consent of others when action is necessary to defend our national security.[16]

The United States thus has reason to follow specific policies in Europe, Iraq, the Middle East, East Asia, and elsewhere. For example, in Europe, consultation, cooperation, and joint action should be sought wherever possible, but freedom of action should not be limited only to those cases where there is prior approval by allies and by the U.N. Security Council. On terrorism, the United States should emphasize the fight against radical Islamist networks, work to prevent the proliferation of WMD, assert Western values, and seek to encourage liberalization and – where feasible – democratization. On Iraq itself, resort to force against Saddam Hussein was a lesser evil because of the dangerous long-term strategic threat he posed to the region and to U.S. national interests. The struggle there remains protracted and very difficult. Unprecedented free elections have shown that the majority of Iraqis do not want rule by radical Islamists or a return to Ba'athist tyranny, though insurgency and ethnic violence pose dire problems.

In the Middle East, the policy of supporting Israel, insisting on a Palestinian leadership not compromised by terrorism and corruption, and readiness to broker a peace process starting from the multilateral "road map" seemed to show progress, with an elected post-Arafat president, cease-fire, and cooperation with Jordan and Egypt in Israel's Gaza disengagement. However, electoral success by Hamas and its refusal to recognize Israel, accept prior agreements, and renounce terrorism pose severe obstacles to peace, as do policies of Hezbollah, Syria, and Iran.

In Asia, there has been alliance with South Korea and Japan, engagement with Vietnam, China, India, Pakistan, and other regional actors, nuanced support for Taiwan, and multilateral negotiations in efforts to deal with North Korea. As in other regions, this involvement is not without risk, but it contributes more to security and stability than would alternative courses of action including outright withdrawal.

Power, primacy, and a willingness to act decisively, including the use of force, are not the only relevant dimensions of foreign policy and grand strategy. *How* policy is conducted can sometimes be as important as the substance of policy, and consultation, adroit diplomacy, and tact in working with other countries and institutions are essential in assuaging the sensibilities of foreign leaders and in gaining political and material support for American objectives. Harsh language and hubris on the part of policymakers are almost always counterproductive. A suitable grand strategy can thus be undermined if it is poorly implemented, and – as John Lewis Gaddis has observed – the "grandness" of strategy does not ensure its success.[17] It is also necessary that American policymakers appreciate the limits and varieties of power and acknowledge the disparity between power and influence, in the sense that primacy itself does not guarantee desired outcomes. And there remains the question – as evident in the grueling experience with postwar Iraq – of whether the United States possesses the administrative and organizational capacity, the culture, and the national will to play the kind of role its size, position, and interests would appear to dictate. In any case, we ought not to berate ourselves nor entertain the idea of a radical reversal in our world role because of anti-Americanism. The roots of the phenomenon typically have more to do with what the United States is than what it does, and hostility often stems as much or more from reactions to globalization, modernity, and American preponderance than from U.S. policies themselves.

This book presents arguments supporting these propositions in some detail. It also considers the circumstances in which American primacy could be diminished by, for example, a grave economic crisis, a shattered domestic consensus, involvement in a Vietnam-style quagmire, or a mass casualty attack on the continental United States involving nuclear weapons or a viral biological agent. I also consider the implications for international order were the United States to play a far less engaged world role. I suggest that this would bring heightened instability and more dangerous competition and conflict among regional powers, for example, in East Asia (China, Japan, Korea), South Asia (India and Pakistan), and throughout the Middle East.

In sum, at a time when the threats from terrorism and weapons of mass destruction are no longer remote contingencies, and when the values of human rights, peace, and stability cannot be reliably assured by institutions such as the U.N. and the European Union, global activism on the part of the United States becomes a necessity, not something about which to be apologetic. In the urgent debate about America's place in the world, this book insists that we grasp the differences between the global arena as we might wish it to be and what it is, the ideals the U.N. was created to serve and why that institution so often falls dangerously short, the reasons why our European allies are often motivated to define their identity in contrast to ours but in the end remain tied to us, the cultural and societal causes of admiration and resentment, and the reasons why in the most dangerous regions of the world, the absence rather than presence of the United States is more likely to cause harm. Ultimately, it is the inevitable lack of global governance, the burdens of primacy, and the lethality of external threats that shape the requirements of the American era.

☆ ☆ ☆

The book is structured as follows. Chapter 1, "Caveat Empire: How to Think about American Power," examines the nature of U.S. power as well as its limits in achieving desired political outcomes, and considers contending views about America's world role. Chapter 2, "New (and Old) Grand Strategy," addresses the overall logic of U.S. policies toward the outside world, including the controversial ideas of primacy and preemption. Though these have been characterized as radical departures, there are in fact important precedents in U.S. history. This chapter also considers the dilemmas of grand strategy, threats to American predominance, and the reality that how a strategy is implemented can at times be as important as the strategy itself.

Chapter 3, "Europe: Symbolic Reactions and Common Threats," explores this country's single most important relationship: the troubled yet intimate tie with Europe. Despite predictions of a rupture and the emergence of an expanding European Union as a counterweight to the United States, there will be no divorce. Though the policies adopted by France and to some extent Germany in recent years have been described as an attempt to counterbalance the United States, it is at least equally significant that Europe itself remains deeply divided. Over the long term, Europe is likely to have only limited ability to provide for its own security and will continue to need the United States as a hedge against future threats. Despite the narcissism of small differences, we do share economic interests as well as the legacy of common institutions and values.

The American era cannot be understood only in geopolitical terms. Chapter 4, "Globalization, Culture, and Identities in Crisis," shows how the global diffusion of culture is bound up with U.S. primacy and why this results in a paradoxical blend of attraction and repulsion toward the United States to be found in many regions of the world. This chapter identifies both the material effects of globalization and American/Western values as triggers for cultural anxiety and turmoil, and finds that cultural and economic resentments, especially in countries where modern values do not prevail, are often deflected from domestic and systemic causes and redirected at the United States as a convenient symbolic target. In consequence, the root causes of anti-Americanism, like those of anti-Semitism, lie within the societies and identities of those who promote them.

Chapters 5 and 6 examine two of the most important theaters in which the United States is engaged: Iraq and East Asia. In each case, America's pivotal role is driven both by the lack of viable alternatives and by our national interest. No other country or international institution has a comparable capacity to deter threats to regional stability and to deal with terrorism and WMD, but this creates policy dilemmas. In the Middle East, the United States becomes a target for local actors aggravated by the failures of their own societies and because they often perceive the United States as guarantor for rulers they detest. Elsewhere, longer term great power challenges are at issue, and the gradual emergence of China as a true global competitor to the United States may ultimately present the single greatest source of opposition to American primacy.

In conclusion, chapter 7 addresses the simultaneous admiration and resentment directed toward the United States as a consequence of American primacy. Contradictory attitudes are both the product of the societies out of which they emerge and the inevitable result of that primacy. In a world where the demand for "global governance" greatly exceeds the supply, and in which U.S. power remains critical for coping with security threats as well as for resolving problems of cooperation, both attraction and backlash are unavoidable. More can be done to win "hearts and minds," but the beginning of wisdom is to know that these contradictory impulses and an accompanying anti-Americanism are inevitable as long as the United States exists as a great power.

1 Caveat Empire: How to Think about American Power

☆ ☆ ☆

Nothing has ever existed like this disparity of power; nothing. . . . Charlemagne's empire was merely Western European in its reach. The Roman empire stretched farther afield, but there was another great empire in Persia, and a larger one in China. There is therefore no comparison.

– Paul Kennedy[1]

I cannot succeed in pursuing my domestic objectives, economic or political; I cannot succeed in pursuing my regional objectives . . . and I cannot succeed in pursuing my global objectives . . . – be it on social issues, on arms control issues, on economic issues – without engaging America.

– Nabil Fahmy, Egyptian Ambassador to the United States[2]

It's strange for me to say it, but this process of change has started because of the American invasion of Iraq. . . . I was cynical about Iraq. But when I saw the Iraqi people voting . . . 8 million of them, it was the start of a new Arab world. . . .

– Lebanese Druze leader, Walid Jumblatt[3]

☆☆☆

H ow should we think about American power and America's place in the world?[4] An intense debate is under way that has the potential to alter the country's overall strategy for protecting and promoting its security, values, and national interests. This dialogue about grand strategy has had a long gestation period. Starting in the early 1940s, the United States faced lethal threats to its security, first in World War II and then from the Soviet Union under Stalin and his successors. Half a century later, with the end of the Cold War, American policymakers sought a new rationale for the country's international role. But for a dozen years, from 1989 to 2001, and despite numerous and largely unmemorable attempts at new blueprints, there seemed to be no single unambiguous peril that might serve as the focus for a new grand strategy.

The attacks of September 11, 2001, brought a violent end to that interlude. The vital national debate that it triggered, however, has been conducted in an acrimonious political environment. That atmosphere is in part a legacy of the bitter partisan divide over President Bill Clinton's impeachment in the late 1990s, the hotly contested outcome of the 2000 presidential election, and angry disagreement about the use of force in Iraq. It also reflects deep-seated social, cultural, and attitudinal differences that characterize the populations of "red" and "blue" America. Commentators and scholars have by no means been immune to that climate.

American and European analysts have offered various critiques of recent U.S. grand strategy.[5] Many of them characterize doctrines of primacy and preemption as ill advised and counterproductive, exacerbating the threats we face, alienating foreign leaders and publics, and isolating America from its erstwhile allies and others whose support we need to safeguard our security and tackle urgent global problems. The critics maintain that the unilateralism evident in the war on terror and the use of force in Iraq without the agreement of the United Nations break with half a century of multilateral cooperation and American commitment to institutions and alliances that we helped to create.

Many also condemn as simplistic the labeling of countries or groups as "evil," and they consider the goal of fostering democracy throughout the Middle East as overreaching. They argue that recent U.S. policies not only exhibit hubris but risk over-extension and are already galvanizing opposition to American power, especially through "soft balancing" (i.e., collaboration among other countries to oppose the United States through means other than direct military confrontation). We cannot pursue our own security and global interests, the argument goes, unless we mend our ways, return to habits of multilateral cooperation, and reintegrate ourselves within the expanding array of international institutions and agreements that represent a nascent form of global governance.

Although widely shared, such critiques stand on a shaky foundation. To begin with, they imply that the previous half-century was a halcyon era of multilateral cooperation among allies. But the Cold War years were marked by a long series of often bitter disputes, which were kept within bounds largely by the shared sense of Soviet threat.[6] Moreover, at the end of the Cold War, the administration of President George H. W. Bush pushed for immediate German unification without engaging in a process of consensus-building with major allies and "respectful give-and-take." In the words of an experienced diplomatic observer, the United States "opposed the major European powers (other than Germany, of course), ignored their views, got its way, and gave them almost nothing in return."[7]

In turn, during the post–Cold War decade of the 1990s and Bill Clinton's presidency, a number of major frictions with allies had already become apparent. They included, for example, bitter differences over NATO's response to ethnic conflict in Bosnia, and an inability to agree on a treaty to ban anti-personnel land mines, on terms for the International Criminal Court, and on the Kyoto Protocol on global warming. Moreover, French opposition to American predominance was increasingly evident. It was in 1999 that Foreign Minister Hubert Vedrine uttered his widely quoted complaint about American "hyperpuissance."

In recent years, much of the criticism has focused on the character and personalities of the Bush administration as the primary cause of European-American discord. However, that emphasis undervalues the structural dimension of the problem, especially the reality of America's unprecedented power and the inevitable foreign resentments that arise in reaction to it.[8] Nor is the idea that we can rejuvenate the Atlantic partnership by agreeing to a European veto over American policy likely to be feasible or desirable. It is hard to imagine that even a hypothetical John Kerry presidency would have been willing to cede such control.

Policy critics also tend to adopt a *reductio ad Iraqum*. As important as the war in Iraq and the subsequent insurgency have been, they are not the sum total of foreign policy, and exclusive focus on them can distort one's perspective. Not only are there other issues and regions to be considered, but the standard critique of policy implies that, apart from Britain's Tony Blair, America has become almost totally isolated in its Iraq policy. In reality, more than half of the governments of Europe originally endorsed or supported the U.S. position in the months leading up to the Iraq war, and some of the differences within Europe were as important as those between Europe and the United States. By the time sovereignty was restored to an interim Iraqi government, sixteen of the twenty-six NATO countries had at least token contingents of soldiers in Iraq.[9] In addition, the wider war on terror has seen close cooperation in intelligence and security (with exemplary U.S.-French collaboration) not only between European and American agencies but in other regions as well.

Indeed, real balancing against the United States has yet to occur.[10] Opposition at the United Nations, diplomatic wrangles, and public disagreements are in no way comparable to traditional power balancing in the form of arms races or the creation of competing alliances. European governments are by no means agreed in seeking to counterbalance the United States. Elsewhere, the United States actually received considerable, mostly unpublicized, cooperation from a number of Iraq's Arab neighbors, including Egypt, Saudi Arabia, Jordan, and the Gulf states, and Washington finds its interactions with many other regional powers to be at least satisfactory and often quite good. Russia under Putin has not followed a policy of confrontation. Relations with India are in better shape than they have been for half a century, and since 9/11 China, Japan, Indonesia, and Vietnam have conspicuously improved their ties with the United States.

In essence, much of the conventional wisdom about contemporary foreign policy falls short because it fails to take sufficiently into account the profound implications of the post-9/11 world. A few authors have assimilated those lessons, but others – in part because of the overheated political atmosphere – have not. It is essential to think clearly and without illusions about not only the nature of American power, but also the capabilities and limits of other countries and institutions in the face of the unique perils that now exist. The remainder of this chapter thus examines both the extent of U.S. power and its limits in achieving desired political outcomes, and then goes on to consider the most important competing views about America's international role and to indicate why they ultimately do not provide adequate guidelines for dealing with the world in which we now live.

I. AMERICAN PRIMACY: WHAT POWER CAN AND CAN'T DO

References to America's unmatched power have become commonplace, not only among those who welcome it, but especially by those who disdain it. The assessment made some years ago by a former French foreign minister is worth quoting, the more so because he spent so much of his time trying to stimulate a counterbalancing coalition, "The United States of America today predominates on the economic level, on the monetary level, on the military level, on the technological level, and in the cultural area in the broad sense of the word. It is not comparable, in terms of power and influence, to anything known in modern history."[11]

Primacy and Its Attributes

All the same, it is well worth contemplating what this preponderance means in practice. Consider, first, the military realm. In material terms, no other country or group of countries comes close to approaching America's capacity in warfare and in virtually every dimension of modern military technology. Nor does any other country have a comparable ability to project power and to deploy and sustain large and effective forces abroad.

Air power provides a compelling illustration. A single American aircraft carrier with its high technology and precision munitions is capable of striking 700 targets in a single day.[12] There are few, if any, air forces in the world that can muster such power, yet the United States possesses not one but twelve of these carriers and their battle groups. Military spending, too, dwarfs that of any other country and is roughly equivalent to that of the rest of the world combined. Yet at slightly more than 4 percent of GDP annually, this defense burden ought to be relatively manageable compared with levels during the Cold War. (At the height of the Reagan defense buildup in the mid-1980s, the figure was 6.6%, and at times during the 1950s and 1960s it was more than 10%.) Paul Kennedy has previously referred to America's ability to sustain the costs of its world role by observing, "Being Number One at great cost is one thing; being the world's single superpower on the cheap is astonishing."[13]

Other dimensions of American power are impressive in their own right. The most important of these is economic. The United States, with less than 5 percent of the world's population, accounts for more than 30 percent of world GDP. By contrast, in 1914 when Britain was widely regarded as the world's foremost imperial power, its economy amounted to approximately 8 percent of world GDP. In addition, the United States is responsible for more than 40 percent of the world's spending on research and development,[14] and – with Singapore and Finland – is consistently ranked as one of the top three countries in terms of global competitiveness.[15] Moreover, the United States possesses dozens of major research universities, produces the lion's share of Nobel prizewinners in science, medicine, and economics, and exerts a remarkable cultural influence that, for example, accounts for more than 80 percent of world movie box office receipts. The unique traits of American society make the United States adaptable, dynamic, and – despite the impact of post-9/11 visa regulations – a magnet for talented immigrants from around the world. In the words of the *Economist* magazine of London, "The clamour of Indians, Chinese, Guatemalans and millions more to go to America to work or be educated is not merely a mercenary reaction to its wealth. It is a reaction to the blend of opportunity, knowledge and freedom that America provides and that nowhere else comes close to matching."[16]

All in all, American primacy is both robust and unlikely to be challenged in the near future. It is robust because it rests on preponderance across all the realms – military, economic, technological, wealth, and size – by which we measure power. And with the possible exception of China, no other country or group of countries is likely to emerge as an effective global competitor in the coming decades. This unique status is evident when we consider other possible contenders.

The European Union (the subject of chapter 3), which some have argued will soon emerge as a counterweight to the United States,[17] has become an economic superpower but will not achieve the kind of foreign and security policy unity required to become a true challenger for decades to come, if ever. In material terms, Europe does have the capacity to do so, but the structure of its shared political institutions, differences among its twenty-five member countries, demographic and financial constraints, and the weight of competing budget priorities largely work against this.

China, with its 1.3 billion people and extraordinary economic dynamism, may one day prove a major regional or even global challenger to the United States, but it must cope with severe problems of rural unemployment and the transformation of its huge and uncompetitive state-owned enterprises. Moreover, so long as its political system remains a communist autocracy, China will not achieve the genuine rule of law, transparency, and liberty necessary for the fullest development of its economy. China also faces delicate problems in its region and has reasons to cooperate with the United States in dealing with North Korea as well as in seeking to discourage nuclear proliferation by Japan and its other Asian neighbors.

Russia, since the collapse of the Soviet Union, is a shadow of its former self. While it continues to possess strategic nuclear forces that could strike the United States with devastating effect, its conventional forces are in utter disarray and it is mired in an endless war in Chechnya. Russia's population is declining and is just half that of the United States, and it faces severe long-term demographic problems. As evidence of its economic limitations, Russia's GDP is less than that of Italy.[18] Strong export revenues from oil and natural gas sustain Russia's economy, but a chaotic legal system, cronyism, corruption, lack of transparency, and erosion of political freedoms continue to act as brakes on sustained economic modernization and investment. As a result, Russia's economic transformation has been halting and will take a very long time under even the best of circumstances. And despite a number of important policy disagreements with Washington, Russia under President Putin seems inclined to avoid overt confrontation.

Japan, not long ago described as the next great world power and one that was rapidly overtaking the United States, has since 1990 suffered from economic stagnation, a rapidly aging population, and intense competitive pressure from China. While it is recovering from the collapse of its stock market and real estate bubbles, it has not sought to become a major military power and in the post-9/11 world has actually intensified its alliance relationship with the United States.

India, with a population of more than one billion people, a dynamic high technology sector and a nuclear force with some fifty to seventy-five warheads, faces an ongoing and potentially explosive conflict with Pakistan over the disputed territory of Kashmir. It also sees its powerful neighbor, China, as a major regional rival; and it has far more reason to cooperate with America than to join others in balancing against it.

What Power Can't Do

Power and primacy bestow many advantages, and, all things considered, there are ample reasons to prefer the status these convey. But power does not automatically equal influence. That is, despite the preponderance that the United States enjoys in comparison with other countries, this does not necessarily mean that others will do what we wish them to do. The run-up to the Iraq War provided an obvious example. In the U.N. Security Council, diplomats from the United States and Britain were unable to gain the nine out of fifteen votes required for passage of a resolution that would have provided the world body's stamp of approval for the use of force. Not only was there opposition from France, Russia, and Germany – traditional powers whose views may have owed as much to status resentments as to the substance of the issue – but even countries more dependent on the United States, including Chile and Mexico, refused their support. In addition, Turkey, a longtime close ally, hindered American military operations by refusing to allow the Fourth Infantry Division to use its territory as a base for invading Iraq from the north.

No country can compete with the United States in conventional military power, but it is well to recall the dictum of Karl von Clausewitz that "war is the continuation of politics by other means." In other words, the ability to prevail militarily is a means to a political end and attaining it requires considerable acumen and diplomatic skill. But even in purely military terms, there are potential limitations. One of these is the classic problem of "friction," in that no plan ever survives initial contact with the enemy without some kind of surprise and need for adaptation. And some adversaries are able to adapt by shifting to asymmetrical warfare, for example, in the use of surprise attacks, urban warfare, concealed explosives, suicide bombings, terrorism, or other methods meant to offset the advantages of the superpower.

Wars in Afghanistan and Iraq exemplify both the impressive achievements of military power as well as some of its limits. In the case of Afghanistan, where U.S. aircraft and special forces began operations against the Taliban regime and al-Qaeda only weeks after September 11, 2001, the ability to prevail militarily faced an exacting test. Previous world powers – the British Empire in the 1830s and the Soviet Union in the 1980s – had come to grief in that country, and in the early weeks of the intervention, expressions of pessimism became increasingly common in Congress and the media. For example, in early November, a leading strategist wrote in the *New York Times* that "the moment for dramatic demonstration of American military power has passed" and that "[v]ictory in Afghanistan would probably require at least 500,000 troops."[19] Yet just nine days later, the American-supported Northern Alliance liberated the capital city of Kabul, and soon afterward, with the fall of Kandahar, the Taliban regime collapsed.

The victory was remarkable, not least because for eighteen days beginning in the last half of October, the entire U.S. special forces presence in Afghanistan had consisted of just seventy-eight men. These highly trained and adaptable units set the stage for the fall of the northern two-thirds of Afghanistan.[20] Using state-of-the-art technology, including laptop computers, laser range finders, satellite telephones, and global positioning systems, yet also at times operating on horseback, they could call in precision air strikes within minutes of locating enemy positions. In turn, aircraft overhead could hit multiple targets with typical accuracy, or CEP (circular error probable), of within three feet.[21] In comparison, as recently as the Gulf War of 1991, the CEP for precision guided weapons was thirty feet. And in the bombing campaigns of World War II, the figure was as much as half a mile.

Afghanistan was an impressive military success and it achieved a vital political objective in ending al-Qaeda's ability to use that country as a refuge and as its base for training and operations. Yet the success was incomplete. At the key Battle of Tora Bora in late November 2001, the decision was made to have Pakistani forces lead the assault. This spared American troops the likely casualties, but it may have allowed Osama bin Laden and other leaders of al-Qaeda to escape from eastern Afghanistan into the mountainous regions of northwestern Pakistan. In the months and years since that time, American and NATO forces (supported by U.N. resolutions) have faced an arduous nation-building task in sustaining the moderate Afghan regime of Hamid Karzai. While the government's legitimacy and effectiveness have been enhanced by unprecedented free elections, it does not fully control portions of its impoverished country, some of which remain under the domination of regional warlords. In addition, the United States and allied forces find themselves in a low-level but ongoing battle against al-Qaeda and Taliban insurgents who are difficult to root out in a vast and remote terrain.

Then there is the case of Iraq (the subject of chapter 5) where, in the months prior to the war, observers had warned of grave military dangers: heavy U.S. and allied casualties, sustained combat with Saddam Hussein's well-trained and -equipped Republican Guard and Special Republican Guard, Scud missile attacks aimed at neighboring countries, bloody urban warfare in the streets of Baghdad as the Iraqi capital became the Arab equivalent of Stalingrad, and vast numbers of civilian deaths as American and allied bombing pounded enemy forces. Within days of the March 19, 2003, outbreak of the conflict, assaults by Iraqi irregulars and a fierce sandstorm caused many observers to conclude that coalition forces were becoming bogged down, that they would need to await major reinforcements, and that war was likely to drag on for many months. Yet here, too, this phase of war was far more swift than almost anyone had dared to imagine. By April 9, after the most rapid armor advance in the history of modern warfare, U.S. forces captured Baghdad and were televised with local Iraqis as they toppled Saddam's statue, and on May 1, President Bush declared major combat operations at an end. However, the quick

victory and fall of Saddam's regime proved to be only the opening chapter in what would become a grueling experience.

In Iraq as well as Afghanistan, the force, speed, and precision of
America's military had allowed it to prevail at only modest human
cost. Initially, American combat deaths there totaled just 139, and an
additional sixty-nine in Afghanistan, but these numbers were soon
to rise. Iraq's cities and infrastructure were largely spared, and civilian deaths were far lower than had been feared. However, defeating
Saddam's army's proved to be only the beginning, not least because
the number of U.S. and coalition troops needed for modern warfare
was lower than the total that would have been required to assure the
security and stability for a successful political transition. The problem
was nicely illustrated in the remark of a U.S. Army gunner: "This has
become harder than we thought. Getting rid of Saddam Hussein, that's
one thing. Getting Iraqis to do what we want is another."[22]

While large portions of Iraq, especially in the Kurdish north and
much of the predominantly Shiite south were relatively secure, other
areas and major cities saw serious instability and a murderous insurgency organized by remnants of the Ba'athist regime and radical
Islamists. This form of conflict was more difficult to deal with. Though
not a truly national uprising, the insurgency resulted in a rising number of casualties to Americans and to Iraqi civilians and took place
amid a population increasingly impatient with and often hostile to the
occupation. Ultimately, the arduous task was both military, to quell the
insurgency, and political, so that a bona fide Iraqi government could
achieve sufficient control in conditions that would allow the United
States to withdraw without seeing Iraq once again become a significant strategic threat.

War and insurgency in Iraq stimulated domestic debate about
America's power and purpose in the region and even whether U.S.
forces should simply pull out of Iraq regardless of the consequences.
Two important elections, however, were instructive. First, the Bush
reelection in November 2004, after a campaign in which foreign policy was uppermost in the minds of voters, signaled that there would be

no early reversal of Iraq policy or of grand strategy. Then, on January 30, 2005, unprecedented free elections in Iraq, which saw 58 percent of the eligible voters defy intimidation and terrorism in order to cast their votes, showed that a substantial majority of the population supported the post-Saddam political transformation of their country. The significance of the Iraqi election not only eased some of the pressure for immediate policy change from within the United States and Europe, but also did not go unnoticed in the Arab world. There, the example of Iraqis, save for those in predominantly Sunni areas, being able freely to express their political preferences by voting not only encouraged the small but vocal group of those calling for political liberalization, but also seemed to have wider resonance as well. In the words of Lebanese Druze leader Walid Jumblatt, a central figure in Lebanese politics and a man who had previously been harshly critical of the United States, "The Syrian people, the Egyptian people, all say that something is changing. The Berlin wall has fallen. We can see it."[23]

Beyond the military and political challenges evident in Afghanistan and Iraq, there exist other limits to what power alone can achieve. One such factor is the beliefs of others, especially intensely held political, cultural, or religious ideas. The task of influencing these deeply held convictions is complex and difficult. Iraq is not Vietnam, but the American experience in Indo-China does provide one example of what can go wrong in the exercise of power. A generation ago in Vietnam, the United States possessed far greater military power than did North Vietnam, but the Communist government in Hanoi held sway over Vietnamese nationalism and was able to mobilize or coerce support, while the American-supported government of South Vietnam was less successful in gaining broad popular backing and in eliminating the communist-led insurgency. In 1973, though never defeated on the battlefield, the United States withdrew its forces. Two years later North Vietnam launched a large conventional military invasion and defeated the South Vietnamese forces, who could no longer count on American air power and military backing. The disparity between power and influence was later captured in an exchange between an American colonel and his North Vietnamese counterpart: "You know you never defeated us on the battlefield," said the American. The North Vietnamese replied, "That may be so, but it is also irrelevant."[24]

In the contemporary Arab and Muslim worlds, the impact of deeply held and fanatical beliefs of the kind put forward by the jihadists is quite evident. The official report of the 9/11 Commission takes note of this problem. It observes that humiliation from having fallen behind the West politically, economically, and militarily during the past three centuries and the paucity of attractive political models in the Muslim world create a ready audience for bin Laden's message, which gains active support from thousands of alienated young men and sympathy from a wider audience. Promoting the spread of a constructive alternative will take time, and in the words of the Report, "Tolerance, the rule of law, political and economic openness, the extension of greater opportunities to women – these cures must come from within Muslim societies themselves. The U.S. must support such developments.... But this process is likely to be measured in decades, not years."[25]

All the same, there is tangible evidence that positive change is possible. The views of Walid Jumblatt, cited above, are not unique and they are all the more worthy of attention because they come not from some courageous but embattled human rights advocate but from a highly skilled communal leader operating in a notoriously dangerous political environment. For a time, elections not only in Iraq but in Afghanistan, among Palestinians in Gaza and the West Bank, and in Ukraine seemed evidence that entrenched corrupt and authoritarian regimes can be replaced and that free elections may bring pragmatic leaders to power, but subsequent events have not been encouraging.

Yet another possible constraint on the exercise of power involves the administrative and organizational capacity of American government. The openness, flexibility, and traditions of limited government that have sustained the world's oldest representative democracy, and a robust and dynamic economy are not always the qualitites associated with the effective and sustained exercise of power. The United States does not possess the kind of strong and highly competent civil

service nor the history of an effective imperial bureaucracy comparable to those of Britain or France. The disparity between military and
administrative capacity is evident in comparing the early battlefield
triumphs against the forces of Saddam Hussein with the subsequent
problems of postwar occupation in Iraq.

Finally, to achieve many of its objectives, America requires the collaboration of others, whether measured in terms of financial and material contributions, personnel, or political support. Even at times of
maximum strength, American Presidents have taken note of this fact,
as in the wartime alliance policies of Franklin Roosevelt, the call for
Atlantic partnership by John F. Kennedy, or in the National Security
Strategy of George W. Bush, which acknowledged, "There is little
of lasting consequence that the United States can accomplish without the sustained cooperation of its allies and friends in Canada and
Europe."[26]

II. THINKING ABOUT AMERICAN GRAND STRATEGY

After the end of the Cold War, the absence of a single, overarching,
and unambiguous threat had the effect of relegating global concerns
to a low priority for most Americans, thus making it harder for any
administration to gain support for a coherent foreign policy or alloca-
tion of substantial resources for that purpose. Abroad, despite allied
collaboration in the 1991 Gulf War against Iraq and ultimately in dealing with the civil war in Bosnia and ethnic cleansing in Kosovo, the
collapse of the Soviet Union made cooperation more difficult because
there no longer seemed to be an imperative for collective action in the
face of a common enemy.

It is no exaggeration to describe September 11, 2001, as the start of
a new era in American strategic thinking. The attacks of that morning had an effect comparable to the Pearl Harbor attack on December 7, 1941, which propelled the United States into World War II.
In an instant, the events of September 11 transformed the international security environment. The threats from terrorism and weapons

of mass destruction that had seemed distant and hypothetical suddenly became a dominant reality, and responding to them necessitated a new grand strategy. Terrorism was no longer one among a number of assorted dangers to the United States but a fundamental threat to America, its way of life, and its vital interests. The al-Qaeda terrorists who masterminded the use of hijacked jumbo jets to attack the Pentagon and to destroy the twin towers of the World Trade Center were carrying out mass murder as a means of political intimidation.

The gravity of this danger was amplified by two additional factors. First, the cold-blooded willingness to slaughter thousands of innocent civilians without the slightest moral compunction raised fears about potential use of WMD. Given the terrorists' conduct and statements by their leaders, as well as evidence that state sponsors of terrorism were seeking to acquire chemical, biological, and nuclear weapons, there was a risk that WMD might be used directly against the United States as well as its friends and allies abroad.[27]

Second, in view of the fact that the nineteen terrorists in the four hijacked aircraft committed suicide in carrying out their attacks, the precepts of deterrence were now called into question. By contrast, even at the height of the Cold War, American strategists could make their calculations based on the assumed rationality of Soviet leaders and the knowledge that they would not willingly commit nuclear suicide by initiating a massive attack against the United States or its allies. September 11, however, undermined that key assumption. We thus live at a time when deterrence, which has often worked in confronting hostile states, cannot be relied on in facing non-state actors with millenarian aims and potentially equipped with devastating weapons. Though the threat had been developing for some time, 9/11 demonstrated that this peril is now quite real. Nor is the danger unique to America, as shown by the March 11, 2004, terrorist attack in Madrid – Spain's equivalent of 9/11.[28] As a result there is good reason to act decisively against the most lethal threats, rather than to hope to be able to deter them or to retaliate following a mass casualty attack.

Mechanisms of international law and organization can at times be effective, but international law is not self-enforcing. We continue to live not in a world of global governance, but in a world of states – some of which are benign, others malevolent or even failed. In reality, neither the U.N. nor other international institutions including the European Union are capable of intervening quickly and effectively on life and death matters. Thus, in its own interest, but also in terms of sustaining wider values of liberal democracy and economic openness, the United States can neither allow itself to be subject to an international veto nor disengage from the wider world. Nor should Americans be apologetic about the necessity or capacity of the United States to act.

Competing Views

Competing ideas and criticisms of American foreign policy have become a virtual growth industry and are widely evident both at home and abroad. For some, the inclination to blame America can seem relentless, even when a policy may have brought positive results. For example, during the peaceful popular uprising in Ukraine that resulted in reversing the results of a fraudulent election and bringing new free elections and a consolidation of democracy, there were complaints. On the political left, *The Nation* magazine criticized U.S. policy, writing, "Ukraine had been turned into a geostrategic matter not by Moscow but by Washington, which refuses to abandon its Cold War policy of encircling Russia." In turn, a prominent far-right conservative figure, Pat Buchanan, held that "Congress should investigate the N.E.D. [National Endowment for Democracy] and any organization that used clandestine cash or agents to fix the Ukrainian election, as the U.S. media appear to have gone into the tank for global democracy."[29]

One category of critics offers simplistic partisan attacks or outright diatribes against America and it will not warrant serious attention here.[30] Their world views are characteristically Manichean, in claiming to find the source of world problems either in the malfeasance of a specific administration or in the nature of the United States itself. On the extreme fringe of this group there can be found the conspiracy theorists, who lose touch with reality altogether but nevertheless find a ready audience (e.g., for the idea that the 9/11 attacks were carried out by the CIA or the Mossad or that the crash of the hijacked American

Airlines flight 77 into the Pentagon was faked).[31] Such notions rest on blatant distortions of fact and outright fabrications, but a number of works of this kind have become best-sellers abroad.[32]

More thoughtful critiques do deserve consideration. These contrasting viewpoints about American foreign policy address grand strategy as well as the content and conduct of policy. They incorporate assumptions not only about what a desired course of action should be, but also about how the world works and the underlying causes of the global problems and crises that policymakers necessarily must face. The analyses vary widely, but the most important of them embody themes drawn from the traditions of either realism or liberal internationalism.

Realists are attentive to the importance of power and appreciate the significance of military force. The realist tradition, with antecedents in the writings of Hobbes, Machiavelli, and some of the ancient philosophers, is not optimistic about human nature, rejects thinking that is excessively idealistic or legalistic, and sees conflict and war as durable features of world politics. Twentieth-century classical realists, among them Hans Morgenthau and Reinhold Niebuhr, found the root cause of conflict in the nature of men and states to dominate others. Contemporary realists (known as neorealists or structural realists) mostly focus instead on the structure of the international system, the absence of central authority above the level of the state (the problem of formal anarchy), and the distribution of power within that system. These features cause states to feel insecure and they behave accordingly, arming themselves and seeking to balance against more powerful states that might threaten them.[33]

Many realists judge an ambitious grand strategy as well as its implementation to be imprudent and argue that it poses the danger of over-commitment. This group, which includes prominent scholars as well as a number of senior policymakers who had been part of the administration of the elder George Bush, mostly opposed the war in Iraq and were skeptical about interventions elsewhere, for example, in Bosnia and Kosovo during the 1990s, preferring instead policies of retrenchment.

Ever since the end of the Cold War, a number of political realists have tended to argue for disengagement from Europe, the Middle East, and Asia, and one of the most influential figures in this group, Kenneth Waltz, has repeatedly predicted the breakup of NATO.[34] In the post-9/11 world, they have continued to prefer that the United States act as an offshore balancer rather than be actively engaged in major regional security alignments. They also anticipate that other countries will seek to balance against America as the sole superpower. Indeed, Benjamin Schwartz and Christopher Layne have argued that the 9/11 attacks were a violent reaction to American preeminence, and they call for a "clear-eyed realism" that rejects a strategy of preponderance and that specifically relegates the United States to the role of offshore balancer.[35] In turn, Andrew J. Bacevich wants the United States to reduce its commitments and scrap NATO.[36]

Realist views tend to rest on certain general assumptions about the nature of world politics, for example, that states with the capacity to use WMD or who make these weapons available to terrorists can be reliably deterred. And in the case of Iraq, realists believed Saddam Hussein could have been dissuaded from attacking his neighbors and that even if he eventually acquired nuclear weapons, he could have been deterred by the overwhelming power of the United States.[37] Some in this group, in comparing the United States with other dominant powers of the past, invoke the examples of great empires that came to grief through imperial overreach or through causing other powerful states to form coalitions against them.[38] And because of the emphasis on system-level explanations, some realists downplay the traits of especially violent and fanatical individual leaders or groups. However, as Richard Betts notes, although American primacy is one of the causes of the terror war, "There is no reason to assume that terrorist enemies would let America off the hook if it retreated."[39]

Realism constitutes a broad category, however, and in addition not all realists are academics. One strand of realism is identified with a number of figures who have held senior foreign policy positions in Washington. They include James Baker and Brent Scowcroft (respectively, the Secretary of State and national security adviser under President George H. W. Bush), as well as Zbigniew Brzezinski (President Jimmy Carter's national security adviser), and Dimitri K. Simes, president of the Nixon Center in Washington, D.C., and co-publisher of the *National Interest* journal. These realists are not averse to using power in America's national interest, but they are often reluctant to contemplate changes in the status quo. Simes, for example, has offered a sweeping critique of past interventions in Bosnia and Kosovo, has cautioned against ambitious objectives of regime change, and has urged that "we should learn to control our messianic instincts."[40] Realists of this type are skeptical about the possibility and importance of democratization and are cautious about humanitarian intervention. During the policy debates leading up to the 2003 Iraq War their reluctance about the preemptive or preventive use of force to oust Saddam Hussein put them at odds with former colleagues in the administration of President George W. Bush.[41]

There is much to be said for realist insights about world politics, especially in the willingness to think in a hard-headed and unsentimental way about contemporary realities. Nonetheless, the central predictions and policy prescriptions of many realists are open to serious challenge. The most important prediction, made some fifteen years ago at the end of the Cold War, that countries would seek to counterbalance America's preponderant power, has yet to be borne out, and often-cited historical analogies seem inapplicable. Unlike empires as well as hegemons of past eras, the United States does not seek to acquire territory. The realities of geography mean that America is not contiguous to countries other than Canada and Mexico, and thus does not present a proximate threat of the kind that would otherwise motivate a powerful country's neighbors to join together in an effort to balance against it. In addition, as compared to empires of the past four or five centuries (Spain, Napoleonic France, Britain, Germany, the Soviet Union), the United States has a much larger edge in terms of its power vis-à-vis other actors. William Wohlforth (himself a realist) has made a strong case for the proposition that American hegemony and unipolarity are likely to be stable and durable, given the huge margin of superiority the United States enjoys, the way this discourages competitors, and the advantages of geography.[42]

Realist policy prescriptions also are open to question. In a post-9/11 world, the argument that deterrence can be relied on with confidence and that leaders of terrorist groups or states hostile to the United States can be counted on to behave as value-maximizing rational actors is far from self-evident. For example, Saddam Hussein's record of dangerous miscalculation and rash behavior, as well as shoot-the-messenger attitude toward advice that contradicted his views, made such a calculation about Iraq highly debatable.[43] More broadly, the peril presented by the combination of terrorism and WMD increases the importance of a more risk-acceptant strategy, including the ability to act preemptively and, when necessary, unilaterally.

Equally important, realist advocacy of disengagement is problematic as well. In the past century, the United States found itself drawn back into Europe three times (in World Wars I and II and the Cold War) in order to prevent the Eurasian land mass from being dominated by a single hostile power. Both regional stability and American national interest are better served by ongoing engagement than by disengagement and the aspiration to act as an offshore balancer. In any case, such policies are difficult to apply in practice.

The imperatives for intervention are often compelling, despite the preferences of policymakers. For example, the administration of George H. W. Bush intervened in Somalia in late 1992, where the United States had no compelling national interest at stake, but where hundreds of thousands of people were facing death by starvation in the chaotic conditions of a failed state. For its part, the Clinton administration was reluctantly drawn into both Bosnia and Kosovo. And, in turn, the initially cautious foreign policy of the George W. Bush administration was radically transformed by the events of 9/11.

Liberal Internationalists: Among the most sophisticated alternative views are those of the liberal internationalists. They advocate multilateralism and reliance on international institutions and strongly oppose American unilateralism as well as strategies that emphasize preemption, the use of force, and the deliberate maintenance of primacy. They contend that emphasis in foreign policy must be placed on cooperation with other countries and in the crafting and reinforcement of international institutions. Multilateralists typically combine both a description of international politics as increasingly characterized by the role of international institutions and multilateral understandings[44] and a recommended course of action in line with their beliefs.[45] They prioritize collaboration via the United Nations and through other emerging areas of global governance to address common world problems,[46] as in the creation of the International Criminal Court and the Kyoto Treaty on global warming, the international treaty to ban anti-personnel land mines, and a host of other agreements.

In reality, there is a continuum of views among multilateralists. Many of those who emphasize collective approaches appear to make U.N. approval the *sine qua non* for American action.[47] On the most contentious issues involving the use of force, and especially the debate over Iraq, liberal internationalists were overwhelmingly opposed to the United States acting without the explicit authorization of the U.N. Security Council. (There is some inconsistency here, however, since many of those who hold these views favored the 1999 NATO intervention to halt ethnic cleansing in Kosovo, even though it took place without U.N. Security Council authorization.) Others, however, acknowledge the shortcomings of these and other multilateral efforts and are willing to contemplate national action when all else fails.[48]

Some liberal internationalists place much more weight on the autonomous capacity of international institutions and argue that the capacity and even relevance of states as actors in world affairs has been greatly diminished.[49] Others acknowledge the continuing importance and durability of states but argue that America's national interest and ideals are best served through prioritizing multilateral involvements.[50] For example, John Ikenberry pleads for emphasis on multilateralism and greater priority for working with others. He argues that American hegemony has benefited from a tradition of self-restraint and self-binding to international institutions and to an international order that has achieved constitutional characteristics. Along with other liberal internationalists, he is concerned about what he sees as aggressive and unilateralist policies and a lack of self-restraint that runs counter to a past tradition of liberal grand strategy.[51]

A more nuanced critique comes from Joseph S. Nye, a professor of international relations at Harvard University and a former assistant secretary of defense in the Clinton administration. Since the late 1980s, Nye has developed the idea of soft power, "the ability to get what we want through attraction rather than coercion or payments."[52] Soft power includes a country's culture, ideas, and policies, while hard power consists of military and economic might. Nye appreciates the need for both kinds of power but contends that seduction is more effective than coercion. He argues for "smart power" through the combination of both hard and soft, and he faults the Bush administration for its overemphasis on military might.

Few authors write more knowledgeably and thoughtfully than Nye, but he leaves unclear just how to apply soft power, especially because of the very broad nature of a term that encompasses culture, values, and civil society as whole. And there remains the question of whether any mix of U.S. policies, let alone soft power, can significantly influence the wider struggle that is taking place within Arab and Muslim civilization in circumstances where Western democratic values are abhorrent to the jihadists. Nonetheless, his criticism of the dangerous decline in American public diplomacy during the Clinton and Bush presidencies is very much on target. Indeed, an alarming sign is that especially in Europe the diatribes of Michael Moore (whose books have topped the best-seller lists in Germany)[53] and Noam Chomsky, and even the rantings of conspiracy theorists, are commonly read and cited as explanations of U.S. policy.

Labels do not fully capture the range of views among liberal internationalists, and the boundaries between them and others can overlap. The logic of these multilateral approaches varies, but even the most coherent and nuanced tend to give insufficient weight to the implications of 9/11 and tend to underestimate the robustness and durability of America's power and unipolar primacy. Multilateralists frequently do not come to grips with the weakness of the U.N. nor confront the stark choices that arise when it is all too often incapable of effective action. They also tend to minimize or overlook entirely the mixed motives of European states in their dispositions toward the United States and attribute to the European Union a coherence and capacity in foreign and security policy that is beyond the reach of that institution.

The multilateralist outlook faces other daunting problems too. One of these concerns who speaks for the world community. Officials of international institutions are not democratically accountable, and even less so are those who staff the organizations and implement their policies. However, the leaders of these bodies are at least responsible to the member governments who put them in place and provide their budgets. In contrast, non-governmental organizations do not have even that degree of accountability, yet they frequently claim to speak on behalf of the people of the developing world or the entire global community even when their preferred course of action may be ill-advised or self-serving.[54]

Another obstacle to the multilateralist ideal is that individuals continue to direct their loyalty to states, ethnic groups, or tribes, rather than toward any global citizenship. In addition, the U.N. itself is dependent on its member states, and especially the permanent members of the Security Council, for its authority and capacity to act. Enforcement too remains a grave problem. Often, U.N. members are reluctant to act, since, with a handful of exceptions, most put their own national interests above those of the world community or the U.N. as an organization. And even when the U.N. Security Council passes a formal resolution, compliance by individual countries, powerful national leaders, and armed movements is often spotty or nonexistent. Non-compliance has been especially evident in recent cases of civil wars and ethnic cleansing, as for example in western Sudan, the Congo, and Liberia.

An additional and perennial problem concerns the distortion of international ideals and the use of evasive or even Orwellian language. A conspicuous example is the United Nations Human Rights Commission (UNHRC), which has in recent years included among its members countries such as Algeria, China, Cuba, Saudi Arabia, Syria, Sudan, and Zimbabwe – all notorious for human rights abuses – and which at one point even elected Libya to a two-year term (2001–3) in the chairmanship. The UNHRC example would be less damning if it were anomalous; alas, it is simply one of the more visible manifestations of cynicism, ineptitude, and corruption[55] – as well as anti-Semitism[56] – that afflict the U.N. The phenomenon of virulent anti-Israeli bias accompanied by anti-Semitism has been described at length by former U.N. ambassadors Daniel Patrick Moynihan and Jeane Kirkpatrick and by former Assistant Secretary of State for Human Rights, Richard Schifter. This problem is one of long standing, and it often takes the form of a disproportionate emphasis on Israel's alleged abuses of human rights, while far more egregious cases are deliberately ignored. In 1975 the General Assembly passed a "Zionism is racism" resolution, which was not rescinded until 1991, and officially sponsored meetings have repeatedly equated Zionism with Nazism, as in the 2002 U.N. Conference against Racism, held in Durban, South Africa.

In the cases of the former Yugoslavia (1991–95), the Rwanda genocide (1994), and devastating civil wars in Sierra Leone, the Congo, Liberia, and Sudan, the consequences of the U.N.'s inability or unwillingness to act effectively can be deadly. The story of the Srebrenica massacre in a U.N. "safe zone" is an especially tragic case in point. The incident took place during the bloody civil war and ethnic cleansing in the former Yugoslav republic of Bosnia. Srebrenica, a Bosnian Muslim town, had been designated by the U.N. as a "safe area" where local inhabitants would be protected by the world body, but in July 1995, Serb militias overran the town while a Dutch army battalion in U.N. blue helmets stood by impotently. In the days that followed, the Serbs rounded up and systematically massacred some 7,000 Muslim men and boys.

International organizations can be important as sources of legitimacy and stability, but in view of their limitations there is often no global alternative to the U.S. role. No other country has both the ability and the will to deploy large forces abroad in order to cope with the most urgent and dangerous world problems. Nor is any regional or international organization able to do so. However, there are a number of negative consequences to the American role. For example, countries can avoid paying certain human or material costs that shared responsibility would otherwise entail because they believe the Americans will act regardless of whether or not they themselves contribute. And, not infrequently, other states may seek to use multilateral negotiations or institutions for the purpose of restraining the United States in a Gulliver-like web of constraints rather than for the purposes these bodies were meant to serve in the first place.

Implications

The unique situation in which America finds itself not only evokes ambivalent and often critical reactions abroad, but also prompts questioning at home about the wisdom of this role and the burdens it imposes. These obligations have been summed up in frank but sympathetic remarks to Congress by British Prime Minister Tony Blair:

And I know it's hard on America, and in some small corner of this vast country, out in Nevada or Idaho or these places I've never been to, but always wanted to go.

I know out there's a guy getting on with his life, perfectly happy, minding his own business, saying to you, the official leaders of this country. "Why me? And why us? And why America?"

And the only answer is, "Because destiny put you in this place in history, in this moment in time, and the task is yours to do."[57]

This unparalleled role is a consequence of the mortal threat posed by Islamist terrorism and WMD, the inadequacy of international means for confronting this danger, and the unique power of the United States. These realities shape the requirements of the American era, and it is to their foreign policy implications that the next chapter now turns.

2 New (and Old) Grand Strategy

☆ ☆ ☆

...[W]hen President George W. Bush warned, at West Point in June 2002, that Americans must be ready for pre-emptive action when necessary to defend our liberty and to defend our lives, he was echoing an old tradition rather than establishing a new one. Adams, Jackson, Polk, McKinley, Roosevelt, Taft, and Wilson would all have understood it perfectly well.

– John Lewis Gaddis[1]

[W]hen you see a rattlesnake poised to strike, you do not wait until he has struck before you crush him.

– President Franklin D. Roosevelt, September 1941[2]

[D]eterrence cannot work against an adversary with no territory to defend; and diplomacy does not work when the adversary rejects any limitation of objective and seeks the overthrow of societies.... In the world of privatized terror and proliferating weapons of mass destruction...survival [can be] threatened by deployments entirely within the borders of a sovereign state.

– Henry A. Kissinger[3]

☆☆☆

The post–September 11 world brought America face to face with a grave and long-term peril. This new and unprecedented threat forced a recasting of grand strategy, but the elements of that strategy have become embroiled in acrimonious debate at home and abroad. In this chapter I note the historical precedents of this strategy and find it a logical response to a deadly menace. I argue that, especially in a polarized climate of foreign policy debate, it is essential to accord an overriding priority to what the 9/11 Commission has termed "the threat posed specifically by Islamist terrorism."[4] However, I also take into account the difficulties and dilemmas the strategy poses, the circumstances in which the continuance of America's international predominance could be jeopardized, and the contrast between the doctrine itself and the actual conduct of policy.

Grand strategy is the term used to describe how a country will employ the various tools it possesses – military, economic, political, technological, ideological, and cultural – to protect its overall security, values, and national interests. Though traditionally the purview of academics and military strategists, the subject has gained much wider attention, first in the aftermath of 9/11, then with the publication of the presidential National Security Strategy (NSS) document in September 2002, and further stimulated by the intense controversies surrounding the use of force in Iraq followed by the occupation and insurgency in that country.

In the debates about strategic doctrine, many of the criticisms have overstated its historical uniqueness, focused on subsidiary issues, or even lost sight of the lethality of the threat we face. As noted in the previous chapter, there is also a tendency to overstate the will and the capacity of other countries and the United Nations in coping with such dangers. For example, a prominent historian has complained of post-9/11 grand strategy that "it smells of American arrogance" and that "it shows a great deal of disrespect to the UN."[5]

Much of the controversy centers on the element of preemption. This doctrine is said to risk embroiling the United States in unnecessary wars, to lack legitimacy in the absence of U.N. endorsement, to be perceived by other countries as threatening, and to be ill-advised if done without full allied support. The criticisms rest primarily on the idea that preemption and its accompanying unilateralism are unprecedented in American history and that they set a dangerous example for other countries to follow. Yet this suspicion is largely unexamined, and there are reasons to question the idea that these components of grand strategy are unique. Thus the eminent American historian John Lewis Gaddis rejects this notion and cites September 11 as actually the third major occasion in U.S. history in which a surprise attack has led American leaders to adopt strategies that involve preemption along with a commitment to the maintenance of primacy and a willingness to act unilaterally. The earlier events took place on August 24, 1814, when the British marched into Washington and burned the White House and Capitol, and December 7, 1941, when the Japanese attacked Pearl Harbor.[6]

The 1814 attack led John Quincy Adams, then the country's leading diplomat and later Secretary of State (1817–25) and President (1825–29), to articulate a strategy of achieving regional hegemony in North America through policies of unilateralism and even preemption. That strategy foreshadowed the Monroe Doctrine of 1823 and remained in place for more than a century, guiding the invasion of Spanish Florida in 1818, Andrew Jackson's brutal relocations of American Indians (which Adams came to regret), the annexation of Texas, the Mexican War, and the Spanish-American War, among other events.

More than a century later, with the attack on Pearl Harbor, it became evident that predominance in the Western Hemisphere was no longer sufficient to provide security because an attack could come from well beyond North America. President Franklin D. Roosevelt thus devised a new grand strategy, deemphasizing unilateralism and preemption but embedding unilateral priorities within a cooperative multilateral framework as a means of achieving primacy. Initially, this meant the wartime alliance with Britain and the Soviet Union. Planning for the postwar period led to the Bretton Woods agreements (establishing the World Bank, the International Monetary Fund, and the General Agreement on Tariffs and Trade), the U.N. Security Council veto, and, later, under President Harry Truman, the Marshall Plan. Together, these measures were meant to perpetuate American hegemony. Throughout the subsequent Cold War, American influence expanded with the consent of allies who had reason to fear "something worse," in the form of the Soviet Union.[7]

With the end of the Cold War and the Soviet collapse, academic and policy experts came to share a prevailing belief in the absence of security threats to the United States. In this environment, the Clinton administration was, as Gaddis notes, "closer to the examples of Harding and Coolidge than to those of Roosevelt and Truman" in allowing an illusion of safety to produce a laissez-faire foreign and national-security policy and in failing to grasp the implications of the diminishing power of states within the international system and the proliferation of weapons of mass destruction.[8]

I. GRAND STRATEGY AFTER 9/11 AND THE BUSH NATIONAL SECURITY STRATEGY

The terrorism of 9/11 dramatically altered the sense of complacency that had prevailed during the 1990s and provided the impetus for a new grand strategy.[9] In the wake of the attacks, President Bush and his administration were explicit in saying that the war against terror would not be completed quickly, and in January 2002, speaking to a joint session of Congress, Bush outlined what quickly became known as the Bush Doctrine:

[W]e will shut down terrorist camps, disrupt terrorist plans and bring terrorists to justice. And . . . we must prevent the terrorists and regimes who seek chemical, biological, or nuclear weapons from threatening the United States and the world. . . .

Yet time is not on our side. I will not wait on events while dangers gather. I will not stand by as peril draws closer and closer. *The United States of America will not permit the world's most dangerous regimes to threaten us with the world's most destructive weapons.*[10]

Two elements were crucial to the doctrine. The first was a sense of urgency, reflected in the words that "time is not on our side." The second was that the unique danger created by weapons of mass destruction required the United States to be prepared to take swift, decisive, and preemptive action. Both of these imperatives reflected the calculation that whatever the risks of acting, the risks of *not* acting were more ominous. These features foreshadowed the elaboration of a grand strategy, published just over a year after the September 11 attacks.

The National Security Strategy of the United States of America[11] (NSS) was released by the White House on September 17, 2002, and immediately attracted wide attention, including both praise as a determined and far-reaching response to the grave dangers America now faced and criticism as a radical and even dangerous departure from foreign policy tradition. In its thirty-two pages, the document provided a candid, ambitious, and far-reaching proclamation of national objectives. First, it called for preemptive military action against hostile states and terrorist groups seeking to develop weapons of mass destruction. Second, it announced that the United States would not allow its global military strength to be challenged by any hostile foreign power. Third, it expressed a commitment to multilateral international cooperation but made clear that the United States "will not hesitate to act alone, if necessary" to defend national interests and security. Fourth, it proclaimed the goal of spreading democracy and human rights around the globe, especially in the Muslim world. All four of these themes generated controversy, and each of them needs to be considered in turn.

Preemption

The NSS advocated the preemptive use of military force against terrorists or state sponsors of terrorism that attempt to gain or use WMD. These are the most lethal dangers facing the United States and, according to the document, "as a matter of common sense and self-defense, America will act against such emerging threats before they are fully formed." The preemptive use of force in the face of imminent attack makes strategic sense and is supported by international law and the *just war* tradition. This principle expressed by the NSS is highly controversial, however, as it broadens the meaning of preemption to encompass military action "even if uncertainty remains as to the time and place of the enemy's attack." Critics argue that this attempt to include *preventive* military action under the category of preemption has no legal or practical basis, and thus see the Bush doctrine as a worrisome break from tradition.

In practice, the United States has sometimes walked a fine line between preemption and prevention. The NSS declaration that "our best defense is a good offense" reflected a long-standing willingness to threaten the use of military action without an attack being imminent. In addition to a number of cases of U.S.-supported regime change during the Cold War, a prominent example is President Kennedy's naval quarantine of Cuba in 1962 to force the removal of Soviet nuclear missiles. In another case, the American campaign to oust Iraq from Kuwait in 1991 was partly justified among U.S. policymakers on the grounds of a future WMD danger from Iraq. In addition, the 1994 Agreed Framework with North Korea was negotiated under the implicit threat of American military action to prevent North Korea from developing a nuclear arsenal.

Some analysts believe that it is counterproductive to make explicit the conditions under which America will strike first, and there are reasons for blurring the line between preemption and prevention. The events of September 11 demonstrated that terrorist organizations such as al-Qaeda pose a real threat to the United States and are not deterred by the fear of U.S. retaliation. The nature of the attacks also suggests that the terrorists would probably seize the opportunity to kill millions of civilians if WMD could be used effectively on American soil. Indeed, al-Qaeda's spokesman has explicitly declared the organization's intent, saying, "We have the right to kill 4 million Americans – 2 million of them children.... Furthermore, it is our right to fight them with chemical and biological weapons...."[12] Thus a proactive campaign against terrorists is wise, and a doctrine holding state sponsors of terrorism responsible may deter those states from pursuing WMD or cooperating with terrorists in the first place.

Other critics have argued that the NSS went well beyond even the right to anticipatory self-defense that has been commonly interpreted to flow from Article 51 of the U.N. Charter, and hence the doctrine would undermine international law and lead other states to use U.S. policy as a pretext for aggression. They assert that too broad an interpretation of legitimate preemption could lead China to attack Taiwan, or India to attack Pakistan. This logic is not compelling, however, as there is little reason to believe that these states would be emboldened to take specific action merely because of a shift in U.S. policy that is as much rhetorical as doctrinal. In practice, Iraq (the subject of chapter 5) has been the sole case of post-9/11 preemption – though it can also be described as a preventive war – and the grueling experience there is likely to make any American administration leery of future preemptive wars unless there is compelling evidence of imminent threat. In addition, action against the two most prominent targets, Iran and North Korea, would almost certainly be even more difficult and dangerous than has been the case in Iraq. Finally, countries such as China and India have their own weighty lists of pros and cons in assessing whether to unleash the dogs of war, and in that calculation the precedent of American behavior is unlikely to be a decisive factor.

Military Primacy

The NSS cited this country's unparalleled position of power in the world and held that a fundamental goal of grand strategy should be to maintain American primacy by discouraging the rise of any challengers: "Today, the United States enjoys a position of unparalleled military strength and great economic and political influence. In keeping with our heritage and principles, we do not use our strength to press for unilateral advantage. We seek instead to create a balance of power that favors human freedom." And in a passage that has stimulated much discussion and debate, the document declared, "[O]ur forces will be strong enough to dissuade potential adversaries from pursuing a military build-up in hopes of surpassing, or equaling, the power of the United States."

Opponents saw in this proclamation a worrying move toward overconfidence and imperial overstretch. But the desire to maintain primacy by seeking to prevent the rise of a peer competitor has guided American foreign policy for the better part of a century. This basic strategic logic explains in large part why the United States intervened in both world wars and why the troops were brought home after World War I, but were recommitted to the defense of Europe not long after the end of World War II. The difference reflected the presence of a true great power rival in the latter case, but not the former. If the territory, population, and resources of the entire European continent had come to be dominated by a single major country hostile to the United States (Imperial Germany in World War I, Nazi Germany in World War II, the Soviet Union during the Cold War), that concentration of wealth and power would have constituted a major threat to the United States itself.

The objective of seeking to preserve American military predominance is not entirely new. In 1992, a leaked Department of Defense strategic planning document offered a blueprint for precluding the emergence of any peer competitor, using language strikingly similar to the 2002 NSS. The 1992 document language was subsequently disavowed by administration officials, but the basic concept was not abandoned.

While certainly controversial, there are valid reasons to think that U.S. military primacy is conducive to peace and stability. Perhaps the best evidence in support of this claim is the fact that a U.S. military presence is tolerated in many areas and welcomed in some others. Local motivations may range from free-riding under the American security umbrella to the deterrent or stabilizing effect of an American deployment to the urgent need for humanitarian intervention. Despite political tensions inherent in stationing U.S. forces abroad, many states see the presence of U.S. military forces as necessary for stability, especially in parts of southeastern Europe, East Asia, and the Persian Gulf.

Ultimately, however, the commitment to maintaining primacy is unlikely to reshape radically the contours of American foreign policy. For example, the United States is unlikely to take deliberate actions aimed at retarding the economic and military growth of potential great powers such as China. On the other hand, American defense spending has been rising with the war on terrorism, thus further widening the military gap with competitors. This may actually dissuade potential adversaries from seeking to challenge the U.S. militarily.

A New Multilateralism

The commitment to multilateralism has received the least attention, though the NSS contains a ringing commitment that "[w]e are guided by the conviction that no nation can build a safer, better world alone. Alliances and multilateral institutions can multiply the strength of freedom-loving nations. The United States is committed to lasting institutions." The document goes on to say, "While the United States will constantly strive to enlist the support of the international community, we will not hesitate to act alone."

Some interpreted this as a doctrine of unabashed unilateralism befitting a Lone Ranger, or as simply the rhetorical velvet glove covering the mailed fist of brute American power. While the NSS was clear about the benefits and necessity of cooperation, especially with other great powers, it set out a policy that in principle was often more multilateral than some of the Bush administration's own practice. Even so, prior to the Iraq War, and together with the British government of Prime Minister Tony Blair, the Bush administration spent considerable time and political capital working within the U.N. Security Council to secure passage of Resolution 1441[13] and an additional four months in an unsuccessful effort to obtain a resolution specifically authorizing use of force.

What is different is that the Bush administration appeared to reject the pursuit of multilateralism for its own sake; that is, as something inherently necessary for international legitimacy or morality. The document held that a basic willingness to "go it alone" was consistent with productive multilateral cooperation. Here again, the break from the past can be exaggerated. For example, at the end of the Cold War, the administration of President George H. W. Bush pursued rapid unification of Germany and in doing so "opposed the major European powers (other than Germany . . .), ignored their views, got its way, and gave them almost nothing in return."[14] Condoleezza Rice, who then served on the National Security Council, described these events in a well-received book.[15] She makes clear that at a time when François Mitterrand, Margaret Thatcher, and Mikhail Gorbachev had other ideas, American policy was based on pursuing "optimal goals" rather than delaying in the pursuit of an elusive consensus.

Even the Clinton administration, which was self-consciously committed to multilateralism, frequently subordinated its multilateral principles in the pursuit of more direct national interests when the two clashed. For example, President Clinton only belatedly signed the Kyoto Treaty on global warming, calling it a "work in progress," and did not submit it for Senate ratification. He could not reach agreement with other countries on the International Criminal Court treaty and complained about its "significant flaws," and though he later signed it, Clinton said he would not submit the treaty for ratification and recommended that Bush not do so either.[16] In addition, because of concern for U.S. forces in Korea, the Clinton administration refused to support the treaty to ban anti-personnel land mines.

The Spread of Democracy

The Bush NSS was not just about power and security. It also committed the United States to spread democracy worldwide and to promote the development of "free and open societies on every continent." To this end, the document called for a comprehensive public information campaign – "a struggle of ideas" – to help foreigners, especially in the Muslim world, learn about and understand America and the core ideas it stands for.

This aspiration embodied deep-seated themes within American history and evoked long-standing beliefs about foreign policy. In particular, the idea that the exercise of American power goes hand in hand with the promotion of democratic principles can be found in the policy pronouncements of U.S. Presidents from Woodrow Wilson to John F. Kennedy, Ronald Reagan, and Bill Clinton (whose 1993 inaugural address proclaimed, "Our hopes, our hearts, our hands, are with those on every continent who are building democracy and freedom. Their cause is America's cause"). This combination of values reflects both a belief in universal ideals ("The United States," the NSS declares, "must defend liberty and justice because these principles are right and true for all people everywhere") and a judgment that promoting these principles abroad not only benefits citizens of other countries, but also increases U.S. national security by making foreign conflicts less likely because democracies are unlikely to attack one another.

The National Security Strategy committed the United States to "actively work to bring the hope of democracy, development, free markets, and free trade to every corner of the world." This objective was driven by the belief that the fundamental cause of radical Islamic terrorism lies in the absence of democracy, the prevalence of authoritarianism, and the lack of freedom and opportunity in the Arab world. In the past, this idea might have been dismissed as political rhetoric. But after September 11, even the United Nations in its 2002 *Arab Human Development Report* and in subsequent reports in 2003 and 2005, defined the problem similarly and called for the extension of representative institutions and basic human freedoms to the Muslim Middle East. A Bush speech to the National Endowment for Democracy in November 2003 provided an elaboration that was both moral and strategic in its commitment to democratization, while criticizing half a century of policies that had failed to make this a priority: "Sixty years of Western nations excusing and accommodating the lack of freedom in the Middle East did nothing to make us safe, because in the long run stability cannot be purchased at the expense of liberty."[17]

The commitment to democratization was Wilsonian in its scope and ambition, but the practicality of this aspiration was daunting, The difficulties of reconstruction and political stabilization in Afghanistan and Iraq were sobering, and the American emphasis on democratization in the wider Middle East drew extensive criticism from domestic and European critics, who saw these efforts as overly ambitious and potentially destabilizing, and from Arab authoritarian governments, who depicted the approach as an imperialistic imposition of American and Western values. Media criticisms in the Arab world often struck similar notes, but a smaller number of Arab authors and political figures did speak up – often at great personal risk – to defend such initiatives as a means of breaking the tenacious hold of authoritarian rule throughout the region.

Conceptual and practical problems intrude as well. One of these concerns the distinction between democracy understood as elections and the much broader and far-reaching implementation of liberal democracy, with its elements of rule-of-law, freedom of the press and speech and of political opposition, minority rights, independent judiciary, accountability of elected and appointed officials, and the like. In countries with only limited elements of civil society and long years of powerful governmental repression by the dreaded *mukhabarat* security services, there is a risk that the major alternative to existing authoritarian regimes would be the violent and conspiratorial radical Islamist movements that have accustomed themselves to operating covertly. Indeed, regimes such as that of President Hosni Mubarak in Egypt emphasized this danger as a means of justifying their own entrenched rule.

The commitment to spread democracy "to every corner of the world" does remain an ideal and a long-term goal, one reiterated by President Bush in his second inaugural address, in acknowledging that the "great objective of ending tyranny" is "the concentrated work of generations."[18] Often, external encouragement of liberalization is likely to be the most feasible course of action, yet remarkable achievements have been evident in the Middle East, not only in countries where the United States has led military intervention, but elsewhere as well. In Afghanistan and Iraq, the first free elections have taken place, drawing large voter turnouts even in the face of violence and intimidation by those opposed to democratization. In Gaza and the West Bank, Palestinians voted to elect a president, and in Gaza they held genuinely free local elections. These are initial steps in the face of serious obstacles, but they are noteworthy achievements and there are signs of ferment elsewhere in the region, both on the part of those seeking change and by existing regimes feeling more pressure to liberalize.

II. DILEMMAS OF GRAND STRATEGY

The United States possesses the military and economic means to act assertively on a global basis, but *should* it do so, and if so, how? In short, if the United States conducts itself in this way, will the world be safer and more stable, and is such a role in America's national interest? Here, the anarchy problem is especially pertinent. The capacity of the United Nations to act, especially in coping with the most urgent and deadly problems, is severely limited, and in this sense, the demand for "global governance" far exceeds the supply. Since its inception in 1945, there have only been two occasions (Korea in 1950 and Kuwait in 1991) when the U.N. Security Council authorized the use of force, and in both instances the bulk of the forces were provided by the United States.

In the most serious cases, especially those involving international terrorism, the proliferation of weapons of mass destruction, ethnic cleansing, civil war, and mass murder, if America does not take the lead, no other country or organization is willing or able to respond effectively. The deadly cases of Bosnia (1991–95) and Rwanda (1994) make this clear. In their own way, so did the demonstrations by the people of Liberia calling for American intervention to save them from the ravages of predatory militias in a failed state. And the weakness of the international reaction to ethnic cleansing, rape, and widespread killing in the Darfur region of Western Sudan provides a more recent example.

International society, as Michael Walzer has observed, does not function in any way comparable to domestic society, whether in the use of force, rule of law, or effectiveness of its common institutions.[19] As cases in point, North Korean violations of the Nuclear Non-Proliferation Treaty, the funding by former Liberian President Charles Taylor of guerrilla armies in Sierra Leone and the Ivory Coast, and Saddam Hussein's violations of the U.N. sanctions and weapons inspections regime did not meet with effective enforcement by the international community. All too often, meaningful responses to challenges of this kind require ad hoc efforts, and for the most part that means leadership by a major power.

There is a damned-if-you-do, dammed-if-you-don't quality in the international reactions to U.S. interventions or the lack of them. On the one hand, American actions often elicit condemnation not only from those who are at the receiving end, but from foreign and domestic critics as well. Then too there are the human and material costs as well as the political hazards any administration faces when it commits troops and risks casualties. On the other hand, the absence of action also elicits criticism. The United States, has been widely blamed for its refusal to intervene during the 1994 Rwanda genocide and – along with the other permanent members of the Security Council – opposing U.N. action. Indeed, in June of the following year, American inaction in the face of the widening conflict in Bosnia led President Jacques

Chirac to utter the acid comment that "the position of the leader of the free world is vacant," implying that he was prepared to take on the task.[20]

Withdrawal from foreign commitments might seem to be a means of evading hostility toward the United States, but the consequences would almost certainly be harmful both to regional stability and to U.S. national interests. Although Europe would almost certainly not see the return to competitive balancing among regional powers (i.e., competition and even military rivalry between France and Germany) of the kind that some realist scholars of international relations have predicted,[21] elsewhere the dangers could increase. In Asia, Japan, South Korea, and Taiwan would have strong motivation to acquire nuclear weapons – which they have the technological capacity to do quite quickly. Instability and regional competition could also escalate, not only between India and Pakistan, but also in Southeast Asia involving Vietnam, Thailand, Indonesia, and possibly the Philippines. Risks in the Middle East would be likely to increase, with regional competition among the major countries of the Gulf region (Iran, Saudi Arabia, and Iraq) as well as Egypt, Syria, and Israel. Major regional wars, eventually involving the use of weapons of mass destruction plus human suffering on a vast scale, floods of refugees, economic disruption, and risks to oil supplies are all readily conceivable.

Based on past experience, the United States would almost certainly be drawn back into these areas, whether to defend friendly states, to cope with a humanitarian catastrophe, or to prevent a hostile power from dominating an entire region. Steven Peter Rosen has thus fittingly observed, "If the logic of American empire is unappealing, it is not at all clear that the alternatives are that much more attractive."[22] Similarly, Niall Ferguson has added that those who dislike American predominance ought to bear in mind that the alternative may not be a world of competing great powers, but one with no hegemon at all. Ferguson's warning may be hyperbolic, but it hints at the perils that the absence of a dominant power, "apolarity," could bring "an anarchic new Dark Age of waning empires and religious fanaticism;

of endemic plunder and pillage in the world's forgotten regions; of economic stagnation and civilization's retreat into a few fortified enclaves."[23]

III. THREATS TO PRIMACY

American preponderance is a fact of life by the criteria that are commonly used in measuring national power. But could this primacy prove to be short-lived? After all, there have been other periods in which judgments about the relative strength or weakness of the United States have proved to be overstated. For example, in the aftermath of the Cuban missile crisis of October 1962 and into the mid-1960s, foreign policymakers embraced overly ambitious notions of American power and influence. Conversely, during the late 1970s and early 1980s, in reaction to a series of adverse events (the loss of South Vietnam, fall of the American-supported Shah of Iran, Soviet advances in parts of Africa and in Afghanistan, energy crises, and lagging economic performance), talk of American decline became widespread but proved to be exaggerated. Instead, the decade of the 1990s saw the collapse of the Soviet Union and provided comprehensive evidence of American strength.

One of the most common contemporary warnings concerns imperial over-extension, in which a great power finds that the cost of maintaining its foreign commitments increasingly exceeds its resources. The process has been described elsewhere, most notably by Paul Kennedy, in his work on the rise and fall of great powers. And Robert Jervis has cautioned, "Avoiding this imperial temptation will be the greatest challenge that the United States faces."[24] Might this happen to the United States? Here it is worth pondering possibilities of military risk, entanglement in a foreign quagmire, erosion of domestic support, and economic decline.

Military risks. America dwarfs other states in military power, enjoys a huge lead in advanced military technology, and its relative advantage vis-à-vis other actors has actually been *increasing*, as demonstrated successively in Kuwait, Bosnia, Kosovo, Afghanistan, and Iraq. U.S. defense spending amounts to roughly 50 percent of that of the entire world, yet – in historical perspective – the burden remains relatively affordable as a share of GDP. On the other hand, troop commitments in Iraq have seriously stretched the capabilities of American forces, and large federal budget deficits caused by the imbalance between overall spending and tax revenue represent a potential constraint. Though the largest numbers of troops stationed abroad are in Iraq, with lesser numbers in Germany, Korea, Japan, and Afghanistan, deployments can be found in some 120 countries.[25] Because of the need to train, resupply, and refurbish units, this level of activity strains the army's capacity. An additional serious crisis or war would pose problems unless the forces themselves were enlarged – a costly and time-consuming process. There also remains the post-9/11 specter of unconventional attacks or asymmetrical warfare, in which U.S. forces, territory, or infrastructure are hit not by a state with conventional military means, but through a surprise attack, terrorism, or with weapons of mass destruction.

Quagmire. Could the United States find itself embroiled in another Vietnam, a bloody military stalemate where it was unable either to win or get out? The danger has been invoked repeatedly by opponents of the use of force in Iraq. In earlier cases (the Balkans, Kuwait), the concern proved unwarranted. However, the Iraq insurgency continues and troops are still needed in Afghanistan, hence these commitments serve as a constraint on additional military undertakings. A more diffuse and more stubborn problem concerns the difficulty of nation-building. Though the United States has demonstrated extraordinary success in its military interventions, the capacity to foster the development of stable institutions in defeated or failed states is both time consuming and a task for which U.S. power and expertise may be less readily suited. While such efforts are vital, and failed states pose risks involving terrorism and WMD, military forces are seldom sufficiently prepared let alone sufficiently numerous to carry out this kind of task on a long-term basis.

Domestic support. This may be the area of greatest long-term uncertainty. Decision-making ability is one factor. Washington's political and institutional capacity to manage multiple foreign commitments is limited. Intense crises such as those involving Iraq, Afghanistan, and North Korea command the attention of the President, his top advisers, and key cabinet members, but the ability to deal skillfully with several major foreign crises simultaneously puts exceptional burdens on those involved. This problem is not unique to the post-9/11 world. In the late 1970s, the administration of President Jimmy Carter had difficulty coping with nearly simultaneous crises involving Iran (the fall of the Shah, the Khomeini revolution, and the U.S. embassy hostage crisis), the Soviet invasion of Afghanistan, and the Sandinista revolution in Nicaragua. And in the early 1990s, Clinton foreign policymakers became preoccupied with the crisis in Bosnia to the detriment of priorities elsewhere.

In addition, popular discontent with costs or casualties can undercut the willingness and ability to exercise power abroad. Sophisticated analyses of public opinion have shown that the public will tolerate casualties if they perceive these to be in the cause of resisting aggression and protecting vital national interests, but far less so for the purposes of nation-building. The existence of an all-volunteer army provides some insulation from the Vietnam syndrome, but as negative reaction to the "Blackhawk Down" casualties in Somalia in September 1993 and more recently as the insurgency and its casualties in Iraq have demonstrated, a sense of purpose and the prospect of ultimate victory is essential in maintaining domestic confidence. A study of public reaction to American military interventions has found that domestic support has been greater when the purpose was to coerce restraint by an aggressor state, when there was a clear military strategy, and when the policy had been made a priority by the President and Congress.[26] In any case, the Bush reelection in November 2004 seemed to demonstrate sufficient public support for the administration to continue its Iraq policy.

Not only does public support remain crucial, but so does the broader phenomenon of social cohesion. Examples of the importance of broad domestic support for sustaining a great power's foreign role and the effectiveness of its forces can be traced all the way back to ancient Rome.[27] In addition, absence of foreign approval especially from allies, though not necessarily decisive in itself, can eventually undermine broader support within the United States itself.

Economic decline. An ever-increasing military burden could put significant strains on the U.S. economy. In itself, military spending is unlikely to be the cause of economic decline, but changing demographic patterns, especially with the aging of the "baby boom" generation, and the long-term costs of entitlement programs (Social Security, Medicare, Medicaid) could affect the overall economy. More important, growing domestic budget imbalances and a balance of payments deficit amounting to nearly 6 percent of GDP create serious financial vulnerabilities. Here, it is important to note that in the five-year period following the 1999 adoption of the euro by twelve member countries of the European Union, that currency accounted for 47 percent of international bonds issued, compared with 44 percent for the dollar.[28] The dollar does remain the dominant reserve currency, making up some two-thirds of global foreign exchange reserves. However, were there to be an accelerating shift away from the dollar, in which foreign central banks begin shedding some of the $2.3 trillion of treasury securities and other dollar assets they now hold,[29] this flight from the dollar could cause a sudden increase in interest rates or even trigger a serious recession and a steep rise in unemployment. These factors would almost certainly create strong economic and political pressures to cut defense spending and foreign commitments.

Other developments that are unpredictable but have the potential to weigh on the economy might include, for example, a severe and prolonged interruption of oil imports or terrorist attacks with WMD that result in serious economic disruption and loss of life. Possible longer term causes over the course of a generation or more could

include serious deterioration of public primary and secondary education, curtailment in the flow of foreign scientists, engineers, and
students working or studying in the United States,[30] difficulty in coping with the steeply rising costs of retirement, disability, and medical
benefits, or an unexpected erosion in society's ability to absorb large
immigrant populations. However, other than China, which has the
potential to become a formidable challenger, the U.S. economy is likely
to maintain its edge over Japan, Russia, and Europe, all of whom lag
behind the United States in competitiveness and face far more serious
demographic pressures involving low birth rates, aging populations,
and a declining ratio of those in the active work force compared with
retirees.

IV. FOREIGN POLICY WHERE IT COUNTS

How a grand strategy is put into practice can be as important as the
substance of that strategy. Here, the interplay between power and
diplomacy is crucial. As Stanley Hoffmann has observed, diplomacy
without power is impotent, but power without diplomacy is blind. A
wise choice of priorities is equally essential, since the range of possible
foreign commitments is vast.

Critics of an assertive grand strategy incorporate varying assumptions. Realists overstate the likelihood of other countries effectively
balancing against American power and are too sanguine about what
would occur if the United States really did disengage from its principal foreign commitments. Liberal internationalists, on the other hand,
often exaggerate the effectiveness and cohesion of international institutions and idealize the motives of other countries who actually seek to
use international organizations to constrain the United States rather
than to achieve collective goals. And ultimately, neither realists nor
liberal internationalists give sufficient weight to the implications of
9/11 and the gravity of the threats to American national security that
it represents.

All the same, the risks of over-commitment are real. In the mid-1960s, when both the power and purpose of the United States seemed unparalleled, the Kennedy and Johnson administrations found themselves drawn into Vietnam. At the time, a sense of benign invincibility shaped foreign policymaking in an atmosphere where our purposes seemed noble and our capacity to achieve those purposes unlimited. Decisions about the American role in Indochina thus unfolded without sufficient regard to priorities and limits. In the end, the United States was unable to achieve its objectives and withdrew after costly expenditures of lives, material resources, political capital, and domestic consensus. This experience means not that intervention and the use of force must not be undertaken, but that decisions about these issues need to be prioritized, carefully weighed, and skillfully implemented.

The United States today possesses unique strengths, but its ability to achieve desired outcomes is not infinite. It is thus essential that the application of power, including political commitments and military engagement, be focused on those cases in which American national interest is most squarely at stake.[31] This dictates a focus on those places where nuclear proliferation and radical Islamist terrorism pose particular threats, and hence American grand strategy must be framed with such compelling priorities in mind.

3 Europe: Symbolic Reactions and Common Threats

☆ ☆ ☆

Any community with only one dominant power is always a dangerous one and provokes reactions. That's why I favor a multipolar world in which Europe obviously has its place.

– French President Jacques Chirac[1]

[T]his superpower, by its unbearable potency, has roused all the world's innate violence, and thus (without knowing it) the terrorist imagination that dwells in all of us.

– Jean Baudrillard[2]

The current [American] stereotype of Europeans is easily summarized. Europeans are wimps, petulant, hypocritical, disunited, duplicitous, sometimes anti-Semitic, and often anti-American appeasers.

– Timothy Garton Ash[3]

☆☆☆

Europe's relationship with America is intimate and yet troubled. Some have predicted that the expanded European Union (E.U.) of twenty-five countries, reaching from the Atlantic to the Russian border and with a population of 460 million people, a common currency, and aspirations for a common foreign and defense policy, will emerge as a powerful competitor to the United States. European resentment of American political, economic, and military predominance is real, and disputes have multiplied over a wide range of issues, from Iraq to the International Criminal Court to genetically modified foods. Many foreign journalists, authors, and politicians offer strident criticism of American policy, and it is by no means excessive to ask whether the United States and Europe may now be on the verge of a divorce in which their alliance of more than half a century collapses or they even become great power rivals.

A number of European leaders have proclaimed their vision of an E.U. comparable to the United States and – in the view of some – one that can act to counterbalance America. The former head of the European Commission, Romano Prodi, observed that one of the E.U.'s chief goals is to create "a superpower on the European continent that stands equal to the United States." For his part, French President Jacques Chirac has said that "we need a means to struggle against American hegemony."[4] Germany and France, in cooperation with Russia, not only opposed the United States on the use of force against Saddam Hussein's Iraq, but Chirac and his then Foreign Minister Dominique de Villepin took the lead at the United Nations in opposing the American policy and in organizing an international coalition against it.

This opposition came as no surprise to those who, since the end of the Cold War, had been predicting an imminent rupture of the U.S.-European relationship and the demise of NATO. For many observers, the removal of the Soviet threat presaged a new era and with it the unraveling of an alliance created in response to a Soviet Union that no longer existed. They expected this distancing to occur not only in security policy but across a range of economic issues, since the end of the Cold War removed the imperative to contain international commercial or financial conflicts for the sake of preserving the anti-communist alliance.[5] European states would thus cease their collaborative bandwagoning behavior and instead begin to balance against one another or even against American power.[6] In the words of Kenneth Waltz in 1990, even before the Soviet Union had ceased to exist, "NATO is a disappearing thing. It is a question of how long it is going to remain as a significant institution even though its name may linger on."[7]

Predictions such as these were made in the months and years immediately following the end of the Cold War. But by the mid- to late 1990s, they seemed less relevant in the face of U.S.-led efforts to end the fighting in Bosnia (1995), the allied air war to stop ethnic cleansing in Kosovo (1999), and the enlargement of NATO. In turn, the September 11 terror attacks on New York and Washington seemed to represent a new and much more ominous shared threat. Nonetheless, with the passage of time and with the eruption of bitter debates about Iraq and extensive European criticism of American unilateralism on a broad range of issues, the specter of an Atlantic rupture reemerged. Robert Kagan, in his widely quoted assessment, attributes the growing divergence to a profound difference in attitudes, in which America is now "Mars" to Europe's "Venus":

It is time to stop pretending that Europeans and Americans share a common view of the world, or even that they occupy the same world. On the all-important question of power . . . American and European perspectives are diverging. Europe is turning away from power. It is entering a post-historical paradise of peace and relative prosperity, the realization of Kant's "Perpetual Peace." The United States, meanwhile, remains mired in history, exercising power in the anarchic Hobbesian world where international laws and rules are unreliable and where true security and the defense and promotion of a liberal order still depend on the possession and use of military might. *That is why on major strategic and international questions today, Americans are from Mars and Europeans are from Venus*: They agree on little and understand one another less and less....When it comes to setting national priorities, determining threats, defining challenges, and fashioning and implementing foreign and defense policies, the United States and Europe have parted ways.[8]

From a very different perspective, Charles Kupchan also concludes that America and Europe are fundamentally diverging, adding that "NATO, far from being in the midst of rejuvenation, is soon to be defunct."[9] Kupchan bases his prediction on what he perceives as a shift in American strategic priorities away from Europe, an increasing political divide between the United States and the European Union, and a Europe at peace no longer needing its "American pacifier."[10]

Notwithstanding a long list of disputes and numerous predictions of political divorce, it remains premature to write the epitaph for the European-American partnership. Despite its historic expansion, the E.U. is not about to emerge as a formidable superpower, let alone take on the role of balancer against the United States. The enlarged E.U. lacks sufficient central authority and the military capacity for an effective common defense policy. In addition, a community of twenty-five countries now includes member states from Eastern Europe, whose history provides strong motivation for maintaining close ties with the United States. This perspective was evident in the support of the ten governments of the Vilnius group for American policy toward Iraq. Indeed, the intra-European divide over Iraq policy provided evidence that the member states of the E.U. will not reach a consensus on balancing against the United States. Moreover, domestic politics, economic problems, and the demographic profile of aging populations are much more likely to produce reductions in defense spending than the increases that would be required to provide the E.U. with the military capability of a major world power.

In sum, Europe's lack of unanimity on foreign and security policy, the inability to provide for its own security, and shared interests in trans-Atlantic economic cooperation and institutions require a continuing partnership with America. Moreover, despite what Freud called the narcissism of small differences, the legacy of common values remains fundamental. Europe has neither the will nor the capability for a real break, and the interests of the United States work against a divorce as well. Nonetheless, the sources of disagreement are deep-seated and have been increasing, and they deserve close attention.

I. SOURCES OF CONFLICT

If, as Lord Acton famously said, power corrupts, then lack of power may also do so. For today's Europe, and especially for counties once accustomed to a true international great power status, the disparity with the United States is especially painful. During the Cold War, sheltering under the American security umbrella was an unavoidable imperative, though under de Gaulle and his successors the French quest for autonomy repeatedly pushed the Atlantic relationship to its limits.

These problems were not exclusively of Parisian origin. Virtually from the time of its inception in 1949, the Atlantic alliance weathered a wide range of disputes, concerning not only strategy, but economics and politics as well. One of the earliest crises erupted over German rearmament and the 1954 rejection of a proposed European Defense Community by the French National Assembly. The controversy was serious enough for Secretary of State John Foster Dulles to threaten an "agonizing reappraisal" of America's relationship with Europe. Two years later, in 1956, the Eisenhower administration found itself at loggerheads with France and Britain when it joined with Moscow to condemn the Anglo-French expedition to retake the Suez

Canal from Egypt. A more subtle but far-reaching problem arose after the October 1957 Soviet launch of Sputnik, the world's first orbiting space satellite. With the American homeland potentially vulnerable to Soviet intercontinental ballistic missiles, how could an American President credibly sustain the commitment to Europe if defending Paris or West Berlin now meant exposing Chicago or New York to a potential Russian nuclear attack? Intra-alliance conflicts continued with the French withdrawal from NATO's integrated military command structure in 1966. Symptomatic of disputes at the time was the title of a book by Henry Kissinger, *The Troubled Partnership*.[11]

Out-of-area disagreements also developed over France's desperate and ultimately futile efforts to keep control in Indochina (1946–54) and Algeria (1954–62), and subsequently over U.S. intervention in Vietnam. A severe crisis erupted after the October 1973 Yom Kippur War, with the accompanying Arab oil embargo against the United States and the Netherlands and the French-led tilt toward the oil-producing countries in contrast to American support for Israel. Oil and energy-related issues continued to reverberate in policies toward Iran after its 1979 revolution and in disputes over the construction of a pipeline to carry natural gas from Russia to the West. In the early 1980s, an intense crisis developed over the U.S. and NATO decision to station intermediate-range nuclear forces in Europe in order to counter Soviet SS-20 missiles, and prior to the November 1983 deployment of Pershing missiles, more than two million Europeans demonstrated against it. Multiple examples could be added to the list: trade frictions, economic competition, agricultural protectionism, cultural clashes, and disagreements about policy toward the Israeli-Palestinian conflict, among other issues.

While these disputes were often intense, the underlying mutual security imperative caused Western Europe to remain closely allied with the United States in order to preserve an unambiguous American guarantee. In recent years, however, and without Cold War concerns, the possibilities for fragmentation have increased. Among the Europeans, France has become the most strident critic of American power and the most avid in seeking ways to increase its own autonomy and to steer the European Union toward an independent course. Near the end of his life, President François Mitterrand gave vent to a deep antagonism, declaring, "France does not know it, but we are at war with America. Yes, a permanent war, a vital war, an economic war, a war without death. Yes, they are very hard, the Americans, they are voracious, they want undivided power over the world."[12] Subsequently, the then French foreign minister Hubert Vedrine proclaimed, "We cannot accept...the unilateralism of a single hyperpower," and President Jacques Chirac called for a "more balanced...distribution of power in the world."[13]

Note that Mitterrand, Vedrine, and Chirac expressed these resentments during the mid- and late 1990s, while the Clinton-Gore administration guided American foreign policy, and well before the 2000 election and the coming to office of George W. Bush. Indeed, under Clinton, tensions had emerged over Bosnia and Kosovo, the treaty to ban anti-personnel land mines, the Kyoto Treaty on global warming, the International Criminal Court, the ABM Treaty, enforcement of U.N. sanctions against Iraq and Iran, and the Israeli-Palestinian conflict. This list serves as a reminder that serious disagreements, including complaints about American hegemony and unilateralism, have emerged under both Democratic and Republican administrations and under Presidents with very different leadership styles and policies.

Reactions to the Bush Doctrine

With the start of the George W. Bush presidency in January 2001, European-American relations became increasingly acrimonious. An important reason was the disputed outcome of the November 2000 election and the fact that the then Texas governor was largely unknown abroad. European political leaders, as well as journalists, commentators, and foreign policy analysts, displayed the anxiety that occurs when the White House suddenly is occupied by a chief executive unfamiliar to elites in Paris, Berlin, London, and Brussels. Many took cues from their American counterparts, most of whom had preferred Gore for President, and expressed strong antipathy to the new administration. European first impressions thus became lopsidedly negative, and there was not only an immediate uneasiness but increasingly inflammatory press coverage of the new President. Despite taking office with an experienced foreign policy team, Bush was frequently derided as a primitive, a Texas cowboy, and even, in the words of one prominent British columnist, a "global vandal" and "reckless brigand."[14]

In the wake of the September 11 terror attacks, European criticism of the Bush administration subsided and political leaders, the media, and the public embraced the United States in the presence of what seemed a threat not only to America but to the entire modern world and its values. Despite an undercurrent of smug satisfaction that even the seemingly omnipotent United States was not invulnerable or that America might somehow have deserved the attacks, there was widespread solidarity. This was evident in public opinion polls and took the form of political support and active cooperation in intelligence and anti-terrorism measures.

Indeed, just one day after the attack, on September 12, 2001, the nineteen members of NATO invoked Article V of the North Atlantic Treaty for the first time in the history of the Alliance. Article V treats an attack on one member state as an attack on all and requires that they take action under their respective constitutional procedures. Ultimately, sixteen of the then nineteen member countries contributed personnel to the Afghan campaign. In the ensuing months, American air power and special forces, working with the Afghan opposition, quickly defeated the Taliban regime and its al-Qaeda allies. The victory occurred far more rapidly and with far fewer casualties than many observers had expected,[15] but in order to retain tight control of the operation, the Bush administration opted not to conduct the Afghan war as a NATO operation. The decision made sense militarily, but it contributed to European resentments about unilateralism.

These reactions increased in response to the President's January 2002 State of the Union address to the Congress in which he spelled out what became known as the Bush Doctrine ("The United States of America will not permit the world's most dangerous regimes to threaten us with the world's most destructive weapons") and especially Bush's use of the term "axis of evil" to describe Iraq, Iran, and North Korea. During the following year, with the growing divide over the impending use of force against Iraq and the September 2002 release of the President's National Security Strategy (NSS) document,[16] European criticisms of American policy intensified. The change in attitude marked a shift away from the solidarity expressed by the allies in the initial days after September 11, and it occurred for reasons specific not only to the United States, but also to Europe itself.

First, American policymakers together with a substantial part of the public saw September 11 as a watershed, and in their view the country now found itself in a war against terrorism. By contrast, with the passage of time, Europeans were less inclined to share this understanding. For example, an opinion poll conducted by the German magazine *Der Spiegel* eight months after the attacks found that by a 3:1 margin Europeans saw September 11 as an attack on America, but not on Europe or the world.[17] Though the analogy was misplaced, they tended to equate September 11 with their own experiences of domestic terrorism during prior decades. Indeed, in France, a sizable minority even saw the United States as a threat. In response to an April 2002 opinion poll asking respondents to choose from a list of France's principal adversaries in the world, 31 percent pointed to the United States, ranking it the third greatest threat, after international terrorism (63%), and Islam (34%), and just ahead of small countries armed with nuclear weapons (30%).[18]

Second, there was a reaction against America's willingness and ability to employ its formidable power without the agreement of the United Nations Security Council or deference to the expressed views of European leaders themselves, particularly those of France and Germany. In addition, foreign as well as domestic critics seized on two features of the NSS: preemptive military action against hostile states and terrorist groups seeking to develop weapons of mass destruction, and the determination to maintain primacy by dissuading the rise of great power challengers. Some even expressed the view that the United States itself was becoming a rogue nation.

Third, much of the European reaction was directed against the American-led effort to disarm Iraq and oust the regime of Saddam Hussein. Policy differences had existed before, but in this case the intensity of German and especially French opposition and the way in which more animus seemed directed against a democratic ally, the United States, than at the tyrannical regime in Iraq, with its record of aggressive wars against its neighbors and flagrant defiance of binding UN Security Council resolutions, suggested an entirely different attitude. Yet European governments were by no means unanimous in opposition, and the leaders of eight countries signed a letter by Prime Ministers Blair of Britain and Aznar of Spain supporting the United States. (The other signers represented the Czech Republic, Denmark, Hungary, Italy, Poland, and Portugal.[19]) Shortly thereafter, ten countries of the Eastern European Vilnius group signed their own letter of support. On the eve of the Iraq war, the Bush administration could thus claim backing from the leaders of four of the six largest countries in Europe (Britain, Italy, Spain, and Poland) and from the leaders of at least eighteen European countries.

This official support masked the problem that by the time the war began on March 19, 2003, European public opinion, with the partial exception of Britain and a number of Eastern European states, had become increasingly opposed to the use of force against Iraq. Between July 2002 and March 2003, there was a strongly adverse shift in European attitudes toward the United States. In Germany, for example, where 61 percent of the public had held a favorable view of the United States versus 34 percent unfavorable, the numbers shifted to just 25 percent favorable and 71 percent unfavorable. In France there was a similar swing, from a favorable 63 percent versus 34 percent unfavorable to a negative 31 percent versus 67 percent, and during the war, one-fourth of the French public wanted Saddam to win.[20] Even in Poland and Britain, where the public remained sympathetic to the United States, there was an erosion of support. Britain saw a decline from 75 percent favorable versus 16 percent unfavorable, to 48 percent versus 40 percent, and in Poland there was a comparable shift from 79 percent versus 11 percent to 50 percent versus 44 percent.[21] These views reflected the heated political climate and often intense public opposition to the war, but even a year after the war, in March 2004, only 37 percent of the Germans and 38 percent of the French expressed a favorable view of the United States.[22]

European Attitudes and Structures

On both sides of the Atlantic, it has become commonplace to depict "Europe" as a single entity with shared attitudes and policy predispositions increasingly at odds with those of the United States. This has been apparent in the words of European critics of America, as well as in the complaints by American critics of Europe. But Europe is not monolithic, as evident not only on controversial foreign policy issues but on wider questions of European unity and on whether an enlarged and increasingly institutionalized E.U. should plot its course as a counterweight to the United States or in partnership with it. Britain and France have frequently been at odds over these issues, but other cleavages exist as well. The smaller and medium-sized countries (Austria, Belgium, Denmark, Finland, Greece, Ireland, Luxembourg, the Netherlands, Spain, Sweden, Portugal) and many of the new member states of Eastern Europe have often differed with the largest ones (Germany, France, Britain, Italy) over the extent to which decision-making authority within the E.U. should be based on the size of each state. And historically, there have been disagreements among those who seek a truly federal United States of Europe versus those insisting on limiting the transfer of sovereignty. These internal differences limit the extent to which Europe can take on an adversarial role vis-à-vis America. Nonetheless, there *are* commonalities that transcend the E.U.'s internal divisions.

Even countries that sided with the United States on the use of force in Iraq and that favor a close Atlantic partnership do see multilateral institutions in a more favorable light than does Washington. On support for the Kyoto Treaty, the International Criminal Court, the Comprehensive Test Ban Treaty, and the role of the United Nations as a fundamental source of international legitimacy, European policymakers and publics mostly agree. These shared views also exist on sensitive cultural and life-style issues. One in particular is the death penalty, where European governments now uniformly oppose capital punishment, though popular attitudes have sometimes been less uniform. Countries applying for E.U. membership are required to have abolished the death penalty, and the issue has become a source of friction with the United States.

Europe's receptivity to multilateralism and to international institutions has been shaped by experiences of the past half-century in which the continental countries have finally transcended centuries of conflict and war. Together, they have achieved steadily expanding cooperation and integration, the codification of agreed rules and procedures, and the transfer of previously sovereign state powers to the E.U. As a consequence, Europeans tend to draw lessons from their specific regional experience and transpose these to a global level.

This perspective can create tensions with the United States, as does a structural trait of the E.U. itself. As the E.U.'s original institutions (the European Coal and Steel Community, followed by the Common Market and European Community) expanded from six member states (France, Germany, Italy, and the Benelux countries) to nine, then twelve, fifteen, and now twenty-five, agreement on European policies has become an ever more cumbersome task. Though provision for decision by weighted majorities has steadily increased, unanimity is still required on the most important issues, including foreign and defense policy. Thus, when the E.U. does manage to overcome coordination problems and succeed in hammering out positions on specific issues, the policy stance often becomes inflexible. As a result, negotiations between Europe and the United States become fraught with difficulty, since the opportunities for compromise and adjustment that would ordinarily exist between two large countries, each with its own central authority, are much less likely to be available on the European side.

Two other structural problems create obstacles to cooperation. One is reflected in a widely quoted comment attributed to Henry Kissinger: "When I want to call Europe, whom do I call?"[23] In some instances, the E.U. does have a single individual empowered to negotiate on its behalf, and the constitutional treaty agreed on in October 2004 attempted to address this problem by providing for a President and a single representative for foreign policy. However, even if a modified constitution is ratified, it is hard to imagine that countries such as France, Britain, or Germany will be content to abdicate their own foreign policy roles. Another difficulty is political as well as structural. In establishing their common identity, European states face a temptation to do so by defining their own position as distinct from that of the United States. This creates an incentive for disagreement almost regardless of the substance of the issue at hand.

Then there remains the disparity of power. The disproportion between the capacities of the United States and those of the individual European countries is so great that the latter often embrace multilateral institutions and rules as a means of limiting their superpower ally's freedom of maneuver. This impulse is intrinsic to disparities of size and influence, regardless of specific policies. Indeed, a former French foreign minister once observed that were France to possess the kind of power that the United States now enjoys, Paris would be even more cavalier in its exercise. The power disparity also contributes to a free-rider problem. Achievements such as security represent a form of collective or public goods for all the countries of the alliance, in the sense that they are able to benefit from it whether or not the Europeans contribute. As Michael Mandelbaum has noted, peace in Europe, nuclear nonproliferation, and access to Persian Gulf oil are examples of international public goods.[24] Not surprisingly, there is a temptation to evade responsibility because participants know that the United States is likely to pay the cost of dealing with potential threats (including economic ones), whether or not they contribute.

Note, however, that this kind of tension has been a feature of long standing and that it existed well before the end of the Cold War and the emergence of the United States as the world's sole superpower. A graphic example of free riding, and of the accompanying buck-passing, in which a costly or dangerous task is avoided, whether through inaction or deliberate evasion, was for many years evident in French policy toward terrorist groups operating in Europe. During much of the 1970s and 1980s, Paris applied the "sanctuary doctrine," in tolerating the presence of terrorist groups provided they did not carry out operations against French interests.[25] An egregious case of this behavior took place following the 1977 arrest in Paris of Daoud Oudeh, known as Abu Daoud, a founder of the Palestinian terrorist group Black September. His group had been responsible for the Munich Olympic massacre of Israeli athletes in 1972 and for the murder of the American ambassador to Sudan, Cleo Noel, in 1973. Ignoring extradition requests from Israel and Germany, the government of President Valery Giscard d'Estaing instead deported him to Algeria.[26] During the 1980s and '90s, however, as the groups became more violent and in some instances took actions within France, the policy began to break down and intelligence cooperation with the United States and other European countries significantly improved.

Policy Conflicts

On issues large and small, European and American differences have multiplied, and they are by no means confined to foreign policy. In trade policy, for example, there have been continual frictions, for example, over governmental subsidies to aircraft manufacturers Airbus and Boeing. In another case, the E.U. filed a complaint against the United States in the World Trade Organization (WTO), challenging a policy that allowed major American corporations to establish foreign subsidiaries in tax havens as a means of reducing taxes on exports. The WTO ruled against the American policy, and the judgment temporarily allowed the E.U. to impose punitive tariffs on $4 billion worth of U.S. exports until Congress passed legislation changing the law.

In a case that combined trade, culture, and politics, the United States and twelve other countries, including Argentina, Canada, Egypt,

Mexico, and Chile, filed suit against the E.U. for its five-year moratorium that had blocked exports of genetically modified agricultural
products, even though no scientific evidence of health risks had been
found. American officials also criticized European policies for causing unwarranted fears in famine-stricken African countries that have
a pressing need for food aid as well as for the improved yields of these
crops. In turn, Europeans faulted the United States for refusing to join
100 other countries in ratifying the Convention on Biological Diversity,
or the Cartagena Protocol on Biosafety, an agreement for importers
and exporters of genetically modified crops.[27] However, the protocol
itself was drafted in the face of U.S. objections about allowing import-
ing countries to reject genetically modified crops even without scientific evidence of risk – a provision that American negotiators saw as
unduly restrictive.[28]

European critics of the United States sometimes convey the impres-
sion that the E.U. countries are far more altruistic and cooperative in
their global relationships and in helping other countries to develop.
However, the E.U., along with America and Japan, shares a pattern
of protecting domestic agriculture in ways that are harmful not only
to consumers and taxpayers, but also to agricultural exporters in the
developing world who find it harder to compete against these subsi-
dized products. Indeed, the E.U.'s agricultural protectionism has been
especially egregious (a tribute to the political effectiveness of French
farmers), and Oxfam, the international aid organization, reports that
the E.U. has higher barriers to imports from the developing world than
any other large industrial economy.[29]

On many of these issues, the domestic structure of European
economies and political systems makes cooperation harder, not only
with the United States but with other countries as well. Historically
high levels of unemployment, demographic pressures from an aging
population, and rising costs to maintain generous social services and
pension benefits, coupled with relatively higher taxes and rigidities
in the mobility of labor and in regulatory policies, tend to undercut
Europe's competitiveness with America and Asia. These conditions

foster restrictive economic and trade policies and thus greater friction with the United States and other countries. In addition, European parliamentary systems, with the exception of Britain, mostly produce coalition governments that are seriously constrained by the demands of their component groups.

American Exceptionalism

The sources of transatlantic conflict are evident on the American side as well. The U.S. political system can complicate the efforts of administrations of either party to implement coherent foreign policy strategies and to bargain pragmatically with others. At times, divided government, in which the opposition party controls one or both houses of the Congress, has been a feature of contemporary political life, as for example was often the case between 1981 and 2002. Under those circumstances, a president may have to compromise on much of his foreign policy agenda, especially on appropriations, confirmation of appointees, treaty ratification, trade policy, and economic sanctions. For example, the Clinton administration, after its first two years in office, had to deal with a Senate Foreign Relations Committee chaired by the formidable Jesse Helms, who saw the world in very different terms. As a result, administration policies on such issues as arms control, trade, the environment, and multilateral institutions were more at odds with European preferences than might otherwise have been the case.

Even when the executive and legislative branches of government are controlled by the same party, as with Republican dominance during most of the Bush presidency, serious problems in foreign policymaking often exist. For example, legislation in response to the WTO ruling on foreign sales corporations took a long time to pass because of partisan disputes among legislators. The structure of Congress also tends to magnify protectionist pressures, as evident for example in the web of subsidies and other non-tariff barriers that shield domestic producers of steel, sugar, and cotton from foreign competition.

American exceptionalism, the unique character of the ethos, society, and culture in the United States, also sets this country apart from

Europe. For nearly two centuries, observers of America, from Alexis de Tocqueville writing in the 1830s to contemporary social scientist Seymour Martin Lipset, have identified fundamental factors shaping the American character. These include the absence of a feudal past, a "nonconformist" religious tradition, and the manner in which, during the 19th century, the legacy of the American Revolution evolved into a liberalism that emphasized individualism and anti-statism. An early 20th-century American author, Mark Sullivan, provided a similar list of "distinctive characteristics." These included individual freedom of opportunity, zeal for universal education, faith in representative democracy, adaptability, responsiveness to idealism, and "independence of spirit."[30] As Lipset later observed, Americans prefer a competitive, individualist society with equality of opportunity and effective but weak government.[31] In contemporary terms, these traits often take on a form almost guaranteed to antagonize European elites who, in the words of Walter Russell Mead, find American society "too unilateralist, too religious, too warlike, too laissez faire, too fond of guns and the death penalty, and too addicted to simple solutions for complex problems."[32]

American idealism also comes into play in ways that can influence foreign policy, as, for example, in the language of the Bush second inaugural in January 2005:

[I]t is the policy of the United States to seek and support the growth of democratic movements and institutions in every nation and culture, with the ultimate goal of ending tyranny in our world. ...

We will continue to promote freedom, hope and democracy in the broader Middle East – and by doing so, defeat the despair, hopelessness and resentments that feed terror.[33]

The President's emphasis on freedom and liberty caused some uneasiness among Europeans, who feared an excess of crusading zeal to impose democracy by force. But the inaugural speech echoed themes with deep roots in American life, and precedents for it can be found in the language of Presidents Woodrow Wilson, Franklin Roosevelt,

John Kennedy, and Ronald Reagan. The Bush language was tempered with assurances that this was "not primarily the task of arms" and that "America will not impose our style of government on the unwilling." Nonetheless, there remained transatlantic differences of emphasis and belief, as evident in contrasting U.S. and European approaches toward dealing with past and present leaders such as Saddam Hussein, the late Yasir Arafat, and the rulers of Iran and North Korea. That contrast was evident in the words of Condoleezza Rice to a British audience on her first trip as Secretary of State: "There cannot be absence of moral content on American foreign policy. Europeans giggle at this, but we are not European, we are American, and we have different principles."[34]

Diverging attitudes also are reflected in differing understandings about modern society and world affairs. In foreign policy, the most salient of these competing notions concerns nationalism and the use of force. Robert Kagan, David Brooks, Walter Russell Mead, and others have written eloquently about the diverging 20th-century experiences of Europeans and Americans.[35] For Europeans, nationalism brought repeated and catastrophic wars, and the use of force did not prevent most of their societies from being ravaged by war. By contrast, with the exception of the Civil War and the terrorist attacks of September 11, 2001, Americans have been largely insulated from such devastation, and 20th-century military campaigns, with the exception of Vietnam, have been mostly successful and often laudable in moral terms. Intervention against Germany in World War I, liberation of Western Europe from Nazi occupation in World War II, defense of Europe from Stalin and his successors during the Cold War, and liberation of Kuwait are among the major cases, but even a number of recent smaller scale interventions (Panama, Bosnia, Kosovo, Haiti) can be seen in a positive light.

World War II experiences also help to explain differences between Britain and the continental Europeans. Almost all the European powers were either defeated and occupied by Nazi Germany in the early years of the war or, in the case of the Axis powers (Germany, Austria, Italy), ultimately defeated and occupied by the allies. By contrast,

England managed to stand alone after the fall of France in 1940 and ultimately emerged at the end of the war with America and the Soviet Union as one of the victorious Big Three allies. Britain did share the 1956 Suez debacle with France, but it did not suffer the kind of disastrous colonial wars that Paris fought in Indochina and Algeria from 1946 to 1962. These experiences help to explain why Britain delayed so long in seeking Common Market entry and why it has typically been the least willing among E.U. member countries to relinquish sovereignty.[36]

II. SOURCES OF SOLIDARITY

Based on the above wide-ranging causes for a parting of ways – the end of the Cold War, differences of structure, attitude, experience, and policy – it would seem logical to begin writing the epitaph for the European-American relationship. Indeed, not a few students of the subject have been doing exactly that. Nonetheless, the conclusion is almost certainly mistaken. Instead, practical experience not only of the Cold War decades but of the years since 1989 suggests an entirely different lesson. The E.U.'s capacity in the realm of foreign policy and defense remains limited, and on issues including proliferation, terrorism, international trade, financial stability, the environment, foreign aid, and disease, the evidence again and again is that there simply is no alternative to cooperation with the United States. Overall, the sources of Atlantic solidarity are grounded in the deep structure of the world in which Europe and America live, and they are at least as durable as the stubborn problems the Western world continues to face.

Europe in the International System

European aspirations to a certain high-mindedness are often evident in the rhetoric of its leaders. By addressing the outside world as though the European experience of the past half-century was somehow universal, they imply the Kantian categorical imperative, "Act as if the maxim from which you act were to become through your will a universal law."[37] But Latin America (viz. Cuba, Venezuela, Columbia), East Asia (North Korea), and South Asia (Kashmir, Pakistan, India) are not well understood through the E.U. lens, and even less is this optic useful in viewing the brutal realities of the Middle East (Iraq, Iran, terrorism, al-Qaeda, the Israeli-Palestinian conflict), let alone Africa (Sudan, Congo, Liberia, Ivory Coast). In this sense, the precepts and practices that now prevail on the continent, especially peace, domestic stability, the rule of law, cooperation, the transcending of national sovereignty, and agreed means for nonviolent resolution of disputes, are noble as ideals but often beleaguered or irrelevant in troubled parts of the world. Indeed, insofar as portions of the Balkans are concerned, even Europe itself does not enjoy uniform cooperation, tranquility, and the rule of law.

At the international level, the basic reality remains that of *anarchy*, meaning the absence of effective and binding sovereign authority above the level of the state. In other words, there is no government of governments. This feature has been repeatedly cited by contemporary scholars as well as in the classic writing of Thucydides and later in the work of thinkers such as Machiavelli and Hobbes. The anarchy problem gives rise to security anxieties. Realist scholars describe a *self-help* system, in which states fear for their security and are ultimately dependent on their own efforts. This in turn leads to a *security dilemma*, as states' efforts to provide for their own security tend to make other states feel insecure. This insecurity has been neatly expressed by John Mearsheimer, who has observed that "because there is no higher authority to come to their rescue when they dial 911, states cannot depend on others for their own security."[38]

Of course, there exist important realms in which multilateral institutions and even international law do operate successfully. Examples abound in economics, trade, communications, air and sea travel, health, and other areas. But on the most urgent and lethal dangers, existing law and institutions as well as the United Nations itself are frequently without the capacity or political will to act. Evidence from recent decades provides numerous examples: Iraq's invasions of Iran in 1980 and Kuwait in 1990; Saddam Hussein's flagrant defiance of U.N. Security Council resolutions; genocide in Rwanda; ethnic cleansing in Bosnia and Kosovo; North Korea's violations of the Nuclear Non-Proliferation Treaty (NPT); Iran's pursuit of nuclear weapons; contraband trade by countries knowingly engaged in violating U.N. sanctions; state complicity in drug-running, money-laundering, and terrorism; and the desperate problems created for their own populations and their neighbors by failed states (as in the Congo, Liberia, Sudan, and elsewhere.)

In cases such as these, the use of state power and of military force by the United States or by other countries that have the ability to act is often the sine qua non. For example in the Kuwait crisis of 1990–91, without American leadership the U.N. Security Council Resolutions and sanctions would have been unable to prevent Iraq's incorporation of that U.N. member state as Iraq's nineteenth province. In the case of Bosnia, weapons embargoes, Security Council resolutions, the creation of U.N.-protected "safe areas," and European intervention under U.N. auspices proved ineffective in halting murderous ethnic violence. Only after three years and 200,000 dead did the United States finally take the lead in ending the killing.

Impressive as it is, the E.U.'s experience of cooperation, law, and institution-building as a means to end conflict and war does not by itself explain how Europe managed to reach its present state. While the miracle of Franco-German rapprochement and European unity had multiple causes, the central factors in ending three centuries of balance of power rivalry in Western and Central Europe included World War II, the Cold War, and the role of the United States. Among these were the devastating military defeat of Germany and the Axis powers, which discredited fascism and aggressive nationalism; the occupation of Germany and Italy by U.S. and Allied forces; the threat posed by the Soviet Union, which required a large American military presence for the purposes of deterrence and defense; and the need for states that had previously been rivals (France, Germany, Britain, Italy, and others) to cooperate within the American-led NATO alliance.

World War II and the Cold War were critical factors in creating the conditions for European unity, and the American security umbrella had the effect of solving the anarchy problem on a regional basis. As a result, European states no longer needed to fear or balance against one another.

Beginning with Marshall Plan aid in the late 1940s, the United States also provided crucial support for the development of European economic and political integration. This was motivated by the desire to strengthen Europe in the face of Cold War challenges and to ward off the kind of economic and political instability that had afflicted much of Europe during the 1920s and 1930s. Of course, the ideals, passions, energy, and institutions that went into creating the E.U. were necessary conditions, but by themselves they would not have been sufficient. The relevant comparison can be found a generation earlier in the aftermath of World War I. Then too, there was revulsion against the destruction and carnage of war, widespread expression of idealistic hopes for doing away with armed conflict, the creation of new institutions, most notably the League of Nations in 1919, as well as solemn international agreements such as the 1928 Kellogg-Briand Pact to outlaw war. But none of these prevented the downward spiral that saw Hitler and the Nazis take power in Germany and unleash the events that led to World War II and the Holocaust.

Europe's Foreign and Defense Policy Vacuum

With the enlargement and deepening of the E.U., efforts to develop a truly European foreign and defense policy have intensified. This is not altogether new. Since at least the 1992 Maastricht Treaty, the E.U. countries have been formally committed to a common foreign policy and since 1999 to important elements of a shared defense policy. Yet Europe's quest has delivered limited results, and progress toward a European defense has proved elusive. This lack of achievement is no mere failure of policy or leadership. The obstacles are deep-seated and are unlikely to be overcome for the foreseeable future. They stem from two fundamental European deficits: the inability to reach internal political agreement and the inability to mount a common defense even if such agreement did exist.

Foreign and defense policies exist in a sphere of high politics and national sovereignty in which states are reluctant to relinquish autonomy. Decisions about the use of force, with their life and death implications, are not readily delegated. Indeed, for all its insistence on a European identity separate from America, France has been the most assertive of its own foreign policy autonomy, even when this contradicts the positions of its European partners. French unilateralism has been evident in numerous cases ranging from the oil shocks of the 1970s to interventions in Africa to policies toward the former Yugoslavia, Iraq, and China. British leaders, too, have long been outspoken on not ceding control of foreign policy, considering it a core prerogative of sovereignty.

Prior to the 2004 drafting of the constitutional treaty, the E.U. had not just one but two senior foreign policy representatives empowered to speak on its behalf. One of these, Chris Patten, was a representative of the European Commission, the other, Javier Solana, a spokesman for the European Council, which brings together the leaders of the member governments. Yet in the immediate aftermath of September 11, it was neither of these figures but the individual leaders of Britain, France, Spain, and Germany who flew to Washington in order to meet individually with President Bush at a time of grave crisis. Not surprisingly, the E.U. constitution envisaged a single individual with authority to represent Europe as a whole in foreign policy, yet on the most important policy matters the limits of both will and capability are likely to persist.

Another serious obstacle to a common E.U. foreign policy is that differences among the member countries have sometimes been as great as those between Europe and the United States. Political differences, such as those on Iraq, are not new. For example, in May 1991, responding to the increasing turmoil in Yugoslavia and the unwillingness of the United States to intervene in another crisis in the immediate aftermath of the Gulf War, the president of the European Council, foreign minister Jacques Poos of Luxembourg, proclaimed that "the hour of Europe has dawned."[39] But a lack of political agreement and of capability left the E.U. unable to act effectively, thus compounding Yugoslavia's tragedy. Kosovo was another case in point, with Britain more assertive than the United States in advocating the use of force, while Greece (historically sympathetic to the Serbs) opposed the action.

The expansion of the EU widens these differences even as it adds to the number of countries supportive of close ties with the United States. The Czech Republic, Hungary, and especially Poland have painful historical memories of their treatment at the hands of their powerful neighbors, Germany and Russia, and they have good reason to look to the United States for credible security guarantees. The Baltic states of Lithuania, Latvia, and Estonia have even stronger motivation. After signing a statement supporting the U.S. use of force against Iraq, these countries found themselves the target of intense pressure from France. President Chirac uttered the condescending words "Ce n'est pas très bien élève"[40] ("This does not show good upbringing"), and implied that East European dissent could adversely affect their pending E.U. membership. As another example, Lithuania complained that France had failed to consult it during delicate E.U. negotiations over Russian transit access to the territorial enclave of Kaliningrad.[41]

These incidents illustrate a larger point about the conduct not only of France but of other leading member states of the E.U. For all their rhetorical embrace of European solidarity, fidelity to multilateralism, and commitment to international institutions and laws, when they believe their national interests are at stake, they are capable of acting unilaterally, regardless of these stated principles. France's protection of its agricultural interests, its refusal to allow the import of British beef despite E.U. clearance, its arm-twisting of the East Europeans, and its indulgent position on Iraqi sanctions in the years from 1992 to 2001 (not entirely unrelated to Iraq's large debts for purchases of French arms) are cases in point. But France is not alone, and whether in dealing with terrorism, national security, powerful domestic lobbies, or sensitive matters of national sovereignty, Britain, Germany, Italy, Spain, and others have been capable of acting with lesser regard for lofty ideals.[42] As an example, Chancellor Schroeder actively sought a permanent U.N. Security Council seat for Germany without regard to E.U. priorities. Moreover, in the face of stubborn economic problems, including lagging growth rates and historically high levels of unemployment, France and Germany, as well as a number of other smaller countries, have defied the E.U.'s limit on domestic budget deficits. These countries incurred deficits that broke the E.U.-imposed ceiling of 3 percent of GDP. Indeed, Germany exceeded that limit in the years from 2002 through 2005, even though its own government had played a major role in writing the rules for the E.U.'s "stability pact," created to coincide with adoption of the euro.

Even if the countries of the E.U. were to find themselves in complete policy agreement and to relinquish sovereignty concerns, their incapacity remains a stubborn obstacle to the emergence of a credible European defense. In the aftermath of wars in Afghanistan and Iraq, the United States devotes more than $400 billion annually to defense. In absolute terms this dwarfs the spending of all likely competitors combined, yet it amounts to just 4 percent of GDP, a figure well below the 6.6 percent peak during the Reagan buildup of the mid-1980s and much less than the double-digit levels of the early Cold War years. In contrast, the twenty-five countries of the E.U. spend just 55 percent of the U.S. figure,[43] yet even that amount gives them far less capability because the effort is divided among separate national defense budgets and much is wasted in duplication.

Europe has more men and women in uniform than the United States, yet its large forces (many of them reliant on conscripts) are mostly more suited to traditional land warfare than to the specialized foreign interventions and high-technology weaponry characteristic of 21st-century conflict. Until recently, the capabilities have remained remarkably limited. For example, in the Kosovo crisis of 1999, despite the Europeans having nearly two million men and women in uniform, it took "an heroic effort" (in the words of the British Foreign Secretary)

merely to deploy 2 percent of them as part of a peace-keeping force.[44]
In contrast, as manifested in a series of stunningly successful military
campaigns (Kuwait, Kosovo, Afghanistan, Iraq), the United States has
capabilities that no other country can match.

In material terms, the E.U. does have the ability to organize a significant and effective defense. The creation of a new European Defense
Agency (EDA) for the purpose of coordinating military research and
spending reflects the aspiration to improve capabilities and prepare
for global security threats. Nonetheless, the EDA is a very modest
undertaking, and the structure of the E.U.'s political institutions, differences among its twenty-five member countries, demographic and
financial constraints, and the weight of competing budget priorities
largely work against fundamental change.

As if these were not sufficient obstacles to Europe's going it
alone, there remains the problem of fragmented European defense
industries. The larger states seek to protect their own corporate cham-
pions while often excluding more efficient foreign producers. Even
when Europeans have cooperated to acquire military equipment, they
often face disproportionate costs or other limitations. For example,
a consortium of European countries is building the "Galileo" system
of space satellites for its own global positioning system. Though this
gives them a capability of their own, it does so at a cost of more
than $3 billion and largely duplicates what is already available from
the United States. As another example, seven European countries
(Belgium, Britain, France, Germany, Luxembourg, Spain, and Turkey)
finally agreed in May 2003 to purchase 180 large military transport
planes from the European aerospace consortium Airbus at a cost of
$24 billion. In opting for European manufacture rather than buying
existing and less costly American models, they purchased an aircraft
(the A400M) that does not yet exist and the initial delivery of which
will not begin until the year 2009. As another example of added costs
in buying European, the $3.6 billion contract to build the engines for
this aircraft went to a French-British consortium, despite a bid by an
American manufacturer, Pratt & Whitney, for 20 percent less.[45]

Even with the new transport plane and the Meteor air-to-air missile system being developed by an Anglo-French consortium,[46] Europe will remain far behind the United States in air warfare capabilities. Though the quality of European weaponry in air-to-air and air-to-ground systems actually meets or exceeds that of the United States, air superiority requires the integration of the most modern high-performance aircraft and avionics, weapons systems, surveillance, satellites, real-time intelligence, communications, targeting information, sophisticated radar, and battle-management systems. In the absence of this complete package, the impact of any one component is limited.

The types of military systems required for Europe to achieve effective modern capabilities demand not only a much more rational use of existing funds but a higher level of funding altogether. Although France spends 2.6 percent of GDP on defense and Britain 2.4 percent, Germany, the European country with the largest population and economy, spends less than 1.5 percent.[47] Moreover, the imperatives of subsidies for east Germany, high unemployment, budget deficits, an aging population, and the political dynamics of coalition government, as well as cultural and historical factors, create pressures for lower rather than higher defense spending.

Elsewhere in Europe, comparable political, economic, and societal constraints also tend to cause downward pressure on defense budgets. The consequences are evident in the difficulty Europe has encountered in creating an effective Rapid Reaction Force. The idea for such a body was conceived in 1999, in the aftermath of the American-led Kosovo action and in reaction to Europe's limits (with the partial exception of Britain) in contributing either to the modern precision air war there or to a prospective land force intervention. European governments, led by France and Britain, sought to create by 2003 a force of 60,000 troops capable of being deployed within sixty days and sustained in action for up to one year. This force was to be available for action in cases where NATO opted not to intervene, and to carry out the so-called Petersberg tasks, that is, largely humanitarian missions. However, even this capacity, directed mainly at peace-*keeping* – not the much more difficult requirement of peace-*making* – remained at least temporarily out of reach. The Europeans lacked not only the overall number of 180,000 designated troops (required for training and rotation purposes, in order to sustain the 60,000-member force in the field), but also the transportation, surveillance systems, precision guided weapons, and other modern equipment that such a force would require.[48]

Given its population, modern technology, and wealth, the E.U. does possess certain kinds of military potential. Britain maintains well-trained forces available for deployment in combat outside Europe, and its military personnel played active roles in the 1991 war to oust Iraq from Kuwait and again in the 2003 campaign to defeat Saddam Hussein. British aircraft also took part in the Bosnia and Kosovo campaigns of 1995 and 1999, and in enforcing the no-fly zones in northern and southern Iraq (1991–2003). France has somewhat less capacity, but has intervened periodically in Africa in times of chaos or civil war, as in Ivory Coast and the Congo, and French generals took command of the NATO peace-keeping forces in Afghanistan in August 2004 and in Kosovo in September 2004. Nonetheless, the achievement of a true European military capability in the foreseeable future will fall well short of the robust, independent force originally envisaged, and the E.U. will remain without the military capacity of a real world power.

American Capabilities and European Insecurity

Given its limitations in foreign and defense policy, Europe has fundamental reasons to rely on America as a hedge against future threats. Though Russia appears considerably less chaotic than in the immediate aftermath of the breakup of the Soviet Union, even its future behavior cannot be assured. Important parts of the old USSR remain troubled, and the long-term stability of the central Asian republics (Uzbekistan, Tajikistan, Kazakhstan), the Caucasus (Georgia, Armenia, Azerbaijan), and the large East European Republics (Ukraine, Belarus) appears far from certain. Elsewhere, instability throughout parts of the former Yugoslavia, internal problems within the countries of the southern Mediterranean, and dangers stemming from the Middle East and Persian Gulf all represent potential risks. Upheaval along the European continent's eastern or southern periphery, whether from economic collapse, ethnic conflict, or interstate war, also could send waves of refugees flooding into Europe.

As evident in the cases of Pakistan, Iran, and North Korea, the actual or potential diffusion of weapons of mass destruction, including missile technology and nuclear, chemical, and biological weapons, poses significant dangers for Europe. While these threats are more diffuse and conjectural than the Soviet threat during the Cold War, they are not negligible and provide a reason for European countries to retain their alliance with the United States as a form of insurance. Consistent with these concerns, the E.U. heads of state and government in December 2003 endorsed a European Security Strategy based on a proposal by Javier Solana, their High Representative for Common Foreign and Security Policy, for facing five security threats: terrorism, proliferation of WMD, regional conflict, failed states, and organized crime. Although the European Council deleted a reference in the original Solana strategy paper implying support for the preemptive use of force, it did retain language referring to robust intervention, preventive engagement, and a crucial role for the United States ("Acting together, the EU and the U.S. can be a formidable force for good in the world").[49]

Closely connected to Europe's need for an American security partnership is the fact of U.S. primacy. Only the United States possesses the means to project power abroad in a decisive and compelling manner. Since the end of the Cold War, American might has been apparent both when it was deployed (as in Kuwait in 1990–91, Bosnia in 1995, Kosovo in 1999, Afghanistan in 2002, and Iraq in 2003) and when it was absent (Rwanda in 1994, Bosnia prior to 1995, Darfur). With time, the relative margin of U.S. power vis-à-vis other actors appears to be increasing rather than decreasing. Not only does the United States possess the ability to move large forces by sea and air across great distances on a timely basis, but it also enjoys wide advantages in precision-guided munitions, stealth technology, satellite communication, command, and control, and the whole panoply of forces and technologies needed to prevail in the air and on the modern battlefield.

Despite the unusually harsh and vindictive rhetoric leading up to the Iraq war in 2003, even those governments most adamant in their criticisms of Washington still took pains to cite the overriding importance of the American security tie. Thus Germany's Foreign Minister Joschka Fischer observed, "As anyone with any sense of history realizes, the transatlantic relationship is the crucial cornerstone of global security, of peace and stability not just in Europe, not just in the United States, but around the whole world. To call this cornerstone into question would be worse than folly."[50] Indeed, just one week after the start of the Iraq war, then French Foreign Minister Dominique de Villepin, who had been the most strident critic of the United States, nonetheless proclaimed, "Because they share common values, the U.S. and France will reestablish close cooperation in complete solidarity."[51] The German defense minister was even more direct in observing that there could be no security in and for Europe without America.[52] Despite continuing tensions after the Iraq War, Foreign Minister Fischer was explicit in expressing a sense of the common threat to regional and global security from "destructive jihadist terrorism with its totalitarian ideology."[53] And in the aftermath of the Bush reelection, Chirac told British journalists that "constructing Europe in opposition to the United States makes no sense."[54]

In this context, the countries of the E.U. do have a security contribution to make, not only in intelligence and anti-terrorism cooperation, but also in peace-keeping, policing, and nation-building, tasks for which U.S. forces have often been less well suited. Such activity mostly takes the form of cooperation with NATO, which is the organization by far the best suited for coordinating large-scale multinational engagements. As France's minister of defense has observed, the European defense capabilities are meant to work as part of NATO, in relief of NATO, and on their own without NATO.[55] The E.U. took a small practical step in March 2003, when it assumed command of what had been a NATO peace-keeping mission in Macedonia and deployed slightly more than 300 troops there in a non-combat role. Subsequently, the E.U. took over peace-keeping responsibilities in Bosnia in late 2004. European forces also have played leading roles in Kosovo, with the NATO-led international force (KFOR) responsible for establishing and maintaining security,[56] and in Afghanistan where NATO's International Security Assistance Force (IFOR) operates primarily in and around the capital of Kabul.

Shared Interests and Values

Not only do security imperatives underpin the European-American connection, but despite disparaging words hurled across the Atlantic, so too do shared interests and values. Euro-American economic relations are simultaneously cooperative and competitive. They are competitive in their rivalry for export markets and commercial advantage, but they remain cooperative insofar as all parties share a deep interest in preserving the successful functioning of existing arrangements for trade, investment, financial flows, and the international economic institutions that sustain them. Europe and the United States find themselves needing to cooperate through the International Monetary Fund, Group of Eight (G-8), WTO, and other groupings, not only to resolve mutual problems but to cope with global financial and economic dangers. Europe and the United States are one another's top trading partner, and they have a huge stake in each other's economic health, as demonstrated by vast two-way flows of investment and transatlantic mergers in many industries.

Shared experiences and values complement these material interests. Although the Western leaders who founded the great postwar institutions have long since passed from the scene and the events of the Cold War are a rapidly receding memory, other factors tend to sustain cooperation among policy elites, including easy familiarity with each other's culture and, in the case of most Europeans, a broad knowledge of American English. The information revolution, the Internet, and the media have also fostered increasing communication and contact across a wide range of activities. To be sure, not all these contacts are positive, as reflected in complaints about mass culture, "Disneyfied" entertainment, McDonald's, and the like. Resentment about American predominance in these spheres is very real, but complaints have been expressed in some form throughout the past half-century, often as much by cultural critics in America as those in Europe. Moreover, at the popular level (discussed in the following chapter), attraction to or at least fascination with American mass culture, clothing styles, music, entertainment, leisure, and language has spread throughout Europe, especially among younger generations.

Perhaps most important, however, is the fact that Europe and the United States continue to share basic values, including liberal democracy, open economies (albeit in different variations), the rule of law, the dignity of the individual, and Western notions of morality and rationality. This underlying commonality remains fundamental, even (or especially) in an era of globalization. Regardless of highly publicized differences, Europe and America continue to have far more in common with each other than with any other regions of the world.

III. RADICAL CHANGE?

Could Europe and the United States nonetheless one day come to an irreversible parting of the ways and even become great power antagonists? Momentous events often arrive by surprise, so the question deserves attention. In essence, a fundamental rupture would require the combination of two elements. One of these is *capability*, the capacity of Europe to act as a great power opponent of the United States. The other is *will* – that is, whether Europeans or Americans desire this to happen and seek to bring it about. Despite the rhetoric of conflict, neither of these elements now exists nor seems likely, but under what conditions could they ultimately occur?

In terms of capability, the E.U. would need to achieve an unprecedented breakthrough in which member countries did not just talk about relinquishing fundamental political sovereignty, but actually did so. But the existing ability of each of the twenty-five members to exercise a veto necessarily limits E.U. foreign policy. In contrast, a true European federation, a United States of Europe, would possess the institutional prerequisites for acting as a single great power in defense and foreign policy. Even then, the E.U. countries would also need to make the politically difficult decision to allocate scarce resources in order to build a powerful military and to choose competition rather than partnership with the United States. French leaders have tended to favor such a course of action, but theirs is not the prevailing view. Could these changes ever take place? Theoretically, the answer is yes, though the likelihood remains remote. Some scholars of international relations and history argue that reaction to America's extraordinary predominance will lead to such an outcome, but for the combination of reasons cited above, there is little reason to anticipate such a transformation.

Motivation and will also are key. Were the Europeans to find themselves facing some unprecedented threat to their survival in circumstances where the United States was no longer able or willing to provide security, then the political impetus for Europe to provide its own security could emerge. On the other hand, the alternative of E.U. political fragmentation or breakdown cannot be ruled out, either. By itself, a growing European-American divergence in values and beliefs of the kind to which Robert Kagan and others have pointed is unlikely to sustain this kind of change. Instead, a steadily worsening climate of political dispute that finally reached a breaking point on both sides of the Atlantic would have to occur, and with it a collapse in either the will or ability of the United States to sustain its own world role, for example, in reaction to a military quagmire or some devastating series of attacks on a scale far greater than those of September 11.

IV. EXPLAINING THE LACK OF BALANCING

Just as it has been said that Britain and America are two countries divided by a common language, so it is tempting to add that Europe and the United States are divided by their shared history, interests, and values. Though some European leaders, most notably those of France, have proclaimed the need for Europe to counterbalance American power and indeed had sought to do so over Iraq, it remains highly unlikely that any sustained balancing will take place. At the time, leaders such as President Chirac and Foreign Minister de Villepin seemed to become intoxicated with the accolades they received in heading the opposition to America's use of force in Iraq. Their efforts went well beyond the boundaries that their predecessors – de Gaulle, Pompidou, Giscard, and Mitterrand – had observed, in that they were acting no longer as allies who disagreed with a policy but as leaders of a putative coalition of adversaries. Their efforts ultimately failed, not only in stopping the United States from undertaking the Iraq campaign, but also because the controversy highlighted the deep divisions within Europe as well as the shortcomings of the U.N. and the limitations on the role of France itself.

For the foreseeable future, Europe does not have a viable alternative. The United States is too preponderant, the countries of the E.U. are too divided, Europe lacks the means of its own defense, and there is no real alternative to the security tie with the United States. At the same time, Europe does possess a comparative advantage in postwar peace-keeping and nation-building. Both Europe and the United States have a vital interest in the viability and institutions of the existing economic order, and only through their cooperation can they have any possibility of addressing broader world problems. In addition, they share far more in common than appears from the cacophony of Atlantic debate. In sum, however ardently it may be predicted or desired by disgruntled critics, divorce is not on the horizon.

4 Globalization, Culture, and Identities in Crisis

☆ ☆ ☆

[America-hating] has become too useful a smokescreen for Muslim nations' many defects – their corruption, their incompetence, their oppression of their citizens, their economic, scientific and cultural stagnation. America-hating has become a badge of identity, making possible a chest-beating, flag-burning rhetoric of word and deed that makes men feel good. It contains a strong streak of hypocrisy, hating most of what it desires most, and elements of self-loathing. ("We hate America because it has made of itself what we cannot make of ourselves.") What America is accused of – closed-mindedness, stereotyping, ignorance – is also what its accusers would see if they looked into a mirror.

– Salman Rushdie[1]

Resistance to the hegemonic pretense of hamburgers is, above all, a cultural imperative.

– *Le Monde*[2]

We know our lives are linked more than ever to an international presence, and if you can't speak English, you can't sell and you can't learn.

– Sergio Bitar, Chilean Minister of Education[3]

☆☆☆

The American era conjures up images of military might and political power, but from abroad the most immediate and pervasive point of contact with the United States is often at the intersection of globalization and culture.* While globalization and culture both stem from multiple sources, and much of what is commonly described as "Americanization" incorporates significant foreign influences, nonetheless the end product has come to be closely identified with the United States. Indeed, the rapid development of an integrated international economic system, accelerated by the information revolution, has brought the global diffusion of American movies, television, popular music, mass media, fast food, and trends in clothing, recreation, and life-style. As a result, people throughout the world have been massively exposed to both the material effects of globalization and the accompanying values they embody.

Culture, in the broadest sense, can evoke deeply emotional responses because of the way in which it encompasses both identity and beliefs. Contact with American culture and Western values often serves as a trigger for societal resentments, especially in troubled regions where modernity is suspect and suppressed. At times, these bitter feelings are deflected from domestic and systemic causes and redirected at

---

* This chapter is based on an updating and revision of Robert J. Lieber and R. E. Weisberg, "Globalization, Culture and Identities in Crisis," *International Journal of Politics, Culture and Society* 16, no. 2 (Winter 2002–3): 273–96, included here with kind permission of Springer Science and Business Media.

the United States as a convenient symbolic target. Under these circumstances, the root causes of anti-Americanism, like those of anti-Semitism, lie within the societies and identities of those who promote them.

Focusing on the intersection of culture and politics can provide insights that an emphasis on either culture or politics alone cannot offer. An apt analogy exists with the study of political economy, which explores the interplay of politics and economics.[4] While treatments of globalization and of foreign policy have occasionally cited culture, they have tended to focus on politics and economics. A partial exception is Samuel Huntington, who in his writing on the "Clash of Civilizations,"[5] argued that with the end of the Cold War and its contest of ideologies, and as a result of disruptions brought by modernization, urbanization, and mass communications, the fundamental source of international conflict would be not primarily ideological or economic but cultural. However, Huntington was emphasizing what he referred to as civilizations rather than what is commonly understood as culture.

Cultural backlash can be triggered by both globalization and American primacy. However, the effect is very different in modern societies than in regions where traditional ways of life are fading but modern values do not yet prevail. In effect, two distinct causes of cultural anxiety and turmoil – and of reaction against "Americanization" – exist. One of these, the material effects of globalization, includes the consumer economy, the information revolution, and the mass media. These provide a window to the wider world and a challenge to age-old structures and relationships. The other, Western values, such as freedom of speech and inquiry, the rule of law, religious toleration, equal rights for women, and liberalized social and sexual mores, exerts an even more profound impact because it touches on the most basic elements of human identity and aspirations.

In consequence, cultural expression in its many forms becomes a means by which individuals and societies convey their problems and conflicts. The more intense these reactions, the more likely they are to be manifested in conspiracy theories, scapegoating, and transference.

These virulent forms emerge when cultural and economic resentments are deflected from systemic causes, such as modernization, urbanization, and economic rationalization, to the convenient symbolic targets evident in anti-Americanism and anti-Semitism. Both phenomena attribute societal problems to an all-powerful alien source, evade local responsibility, and redirect frustration and anger externally.

To the extent that foreign repercussions stem from indigenous causes, the ability of the United States to exert influence is necessarily limited, and no amount of fine tuning is likely to produce a fundamental shift among America's most fanatical adversaries. A graphic illustration of this can be found in the words of a radical Islamist leader in Lebanon: "We don't want to change your mind. We want to destroy you."[6]

I. GLOBALIZATION AND ITS DISCONTENTS

Definitions of globalization abound, but for practical purposes it can be described as the increasing worldwide integration of economies, information technology, popular culture, and other forms of human interaction.[7] In an increasingly polarized discussion of the subject, one side tended to be relentlessly optimistic in character, and – at least until the 9/11 attack – enthusiasm about globalization as a whole was sometimes accompanied by an almost blissful naïveté about the information revolution as an unalloyed blessing. Illustratively, in the words of Bill Clinton, "In the new century, liberty will be spread by cell phone and cable modem."[8] Among the optimists, globalization's impact on culture has been viewed primarily as a side effect. For example, one observer has asserted that "globalization promotes integration and the removal not only of cultural barriers but many of the negative dimensions of culture. Globalization is a vital step toward both a more stable world and better lives for the people within it."[9]

On the other hand, there have been dire warnings about globalization's disruptive effects and the economic and social inequities it is said to exacerbate. Critics have treated globalization of culture as an evil, while expressing their fears about the power and duplicity of multinational corporations and of international institutions such as the International Monetary Fund and the World Bank. This reaction has been manifest in organized protests and in sometimes violent demonstrations in recent years when the leaders of the world's richest countries have held their annual meetings (e.g., the G-8, the European Union) – as evident in the streets of Seattle, Washington, and Genoa.

And who would not be disturbed by, for example, the echo of rap music in an old Barcelona neighborhood, the demise of local food products and neighborhood shops, accompanied by the proliferation of the same brands and chain stores from San Francisco to Santiago to Shanghai? Yet beyond the unwarranted optimism or the equally exaggerated negativity, there exists an underlying dynamic that drives the strong but often contradictory reactions to the cultural effects of globalization. Culture takes on this pivotal position, not only because of its intrinsic significance, but because it has become so bound up with the fundamental dimensions of human identity. As a result, controversies about culture often have less to do with surface level phenomena – McDonald's, American tastes in music, language, art, and life-style – than with deeper forms of alienation that owe more to the disruptions brought by modernization and globalization.

In the Western world and in more prosperous regions of East Asia and Latin America, cultural reaction tends to be more symbolic and less extreme and is based primarily on an uneasiness about the ubiquity of American influence as well as on U.S. primacy more generally. These preoccupations are less those of the general public than of intellectual elites, who perceive cultural intrusions into their own established prerogatives. At times, the responses can approach the level of parody, as in French denunciations of EuroDisney as a "cultural Chernobyl."[10] Specific criticisms thus can have more to do with what the United States seems to symbolize than with any specific characteristic of American culture or policy in itself.

In large areas of the developing world, however, and especially in many Muslim countries, reactions to globalization and to the United States as the embodiment of capitalism, modernity, and mass culture tend to be much more intense. In these cases, radically different notions of society, identity, religion, women's roles, and authority are played out in the cultural realm. For example, Sayid Qutb, the leading ideologue of modern Islamism and whose ideas deeply influenced al-Qaeda, was scandalized by the nature of relationships between the sexes that he encountered while studying in the United States from 1948 to 1950, and in his writing denounced what he viewed as America's sinfulness and degeneracy.[11]

Much of the critical impetus stems from anger at corrupt regimes and failed societies, which with the breakdown of older traditional social, political, and economic relationships have failed to meet the needs of their own people. In these regions, negative expressions about modernity, the West, or America are often a sublimation of deep-rooted personal and societal resentments that are then redirected. Intense cultural resentments thus come to be focused on outsiders who bear little relationship to the problems at hand yet provide convenient scapegoats.

II. CULTURE AND AMERICAN PRIMACY

In the 21st century, the United States possesses a degree of international preponderance that has rarely been seen in any era. Historians, strategists, journalists, and cultural observers have called attention to the phenomenon in increasingly hyperbolic terms. In the words of one recent observer, "We dominate every field of human endeavor from fashion to film to finance. We rule the world culturally, economically, diplomatically and militarily as no one has since the Roman Empire."[12] The United States, with less than 5 percent of the world's population, produces more than one-fourth of its economic activity and possibly as much as 32 percent.[13] It leads in the information revolution, accounts for some 75 percent of the Nobel prizewinners in science, medicine, and economics,[14] predominates in business and banking and in the number and quality of its research universities, and funds a defense budget larger than those of the next fifteen countries combined. And there are few signs that any other international actor will become a true peer competitor of the United States anytime soon.

Primacy and influence in the cultural arena are more difficult to gauge than in the economic or military realms. Many of the criteria are less specific and more subjective, but here too American preponderance is evident. An astute German official, Karsten Voigt, long acquainted with the United States, has aptly characterized the impact of this influence in the cultural realm:

The USA has long been setting standards on a worldwide basis, not just for the general populace, but has been leading the field in the classic cultural spheres, for example in research and teaching, or film and modern art. Its global role is rooted in a hitherto unknown blend of economic power, the ability to set the global cultural agenda and military superiority.[15]

Moreover, this influence is evident not only in what Voigt refers to as the classic cultural spheres, but even more so at the level of mass culture. Evidence of this can even be seen in the reported habits of Iraq's ex-dictator, Saddam Hussein, who was reported to have been fond of watching *The Godfather* and listening to "Strangers in the Night" by Frank Sinatra.[16]

One feature that confers enormous influence is the spread of American English as an international *lingua franca*. A century ago, French served as the language of diplomacy, German was a leading scientific language as well as the common denominator in Central and Eastern Europe, and by mid-century Russian dominated throughout the Soviet sphere in Central Asia and in Eastern Europe. Now, however, it is English that prevails. For example, at the United Nations, 120 countries specify English as the language in which correspondence to their missions should be addressed. By contrast, some forty countries (mostly former French colonies) choose French, while twenty designate Spanish.[17] In much of the world, English has become the dominant second language and the choice for those who aspire to communicate outside their own locality. English is the language shared by the different communities of India (or at least by their educated, commercial, or political elites), is overwhelmingly the second language in China, and is often taught as a required subject in primary or secondary schools throughout Europe and Asia. Nor does the push to learn English show any signs of diminishing. In South Korea, the number of school children sent abroad to study English over the past five years has increased by a factor of ten, and in Chile a recently established government program aims to make the country's entire population fluent within a generation.[18] Stories abound of bilateral meetings of foreign leaders who are not fluent in each other's languages conversing in English, which they share as a second tongue.

The inroads made by American English have been growing with globalization and as a consequence of America's power and influence. Among native speakers worldwide, English ranks third, slightly behind Spanish. Mandarin Chinese is first.[19] Approximately 380 million people use English as their first language and another 250 million as their second language. More important, a billion people are learning English, and approximately one-third of the world's population have some exposure to it. In addition, over 85 percent of international organizations employ it as one of their official languages, and English is the predominant language used within the European Union.[20] Among the E.U.'s non–English-speaking countries, more than 92 percent of secondary school students are learning English, while only 33 percent study French as a second language and a mere 13 percent take German.

To the intense irritation of France's cultural and political elites, and despite annual expenditures of some $1 billion per year to promote that country's language and culture, French is now ranked only ninth among the world's most widely spoken tongues. In reaction, a senior French official of the European Commission expresses alarm about whether "it is possible to speak English without thinking

American."[21] Such concerns have not, however, slowed the growth of English as the predominant language of world business, and four of France's most important and dynamic international companies, Alcatel, Total-FinaElf, Airbus, and Vivendi, have made English their official language.[22]

The growing linguistic globalization based on English as the common international language not only poses cultural questions, but also provides intrinsic advantages to the United States and other English-speaking countries. For example, the most skilled individuals from lands where the national language is not English tend to look abroad for education, career advancement, and better pay, and America has benefited from this "brain drain."[23] Ironically, though, immigration security measures taken since 9/11 to prevent the entry of terrorists have had the unintended consequence of making it harder for legitimate students and professionals to come to the United States. For example, in 2004, foreign enrollments in American graduate schools dropped by 6 percent and the number of foreign applicants by 26 percent.[24]

Entertainment is another cultural realm in which American influence is omnipresent. This takes various forms. Hollywood films capture more than 70 percent of the Western European audience and have a huge market share elsewhere, in some cases as much as 90 percent.[25] Here too, France has sought to stem the tide through regulations and subsidies. Paris has ardently asserted a "cultural exception" in trade negotiations, and under prevailing international agreements the countries of the European Union can impose quotas on imported American music and television programs as well as movies. France itself requires that at least 40 percent of TV and radio programs be made domestically and maintains an elaborate system for subsidizing its movie industry.[26]

The results, however, are modest. American movies take in approximately 65 percent of French box office revenues,[27] and the most popular films are quite often Hollywood productions.[28] Moreover, the heyday of French cinema in the 1930s and again in the late 1950s and the

1960s, when its directors, actors, and films were a significant presence in world cinema, is a fading memory. To the extent that French films have been at all competitive, this is mostly a result of embracing those features for which Hollywood has been criticized. In the words of one French critic:

French cinema is allowing itself everything American cinema used to be blamed for: sex, violence, epic-scale historical reconstruction. All that distinguishes France's biggest hits of 2000 from some American B-movie is that the car chase is happening in Marseille, not Los Angeles, among Peugeots, not Chryslers. And the repetitiveness we once condemned in such hit film series as *Rocky, Rambo,* and *Halloween,* is becoming a more French practice too....[29]

Elsewhere in Europe, the pervasiveness of American films is even more evident. For example, in Berlin, following the opening of a huge business and entertainment complex at the Potsdamer Platz, a multiplex cinema there featured Hollywood films on eight of its nine screens. The sole exception was a German-based film with an English title, *Crazy*, a subtle coming-of-age story based on a German bestselling novel of the same title.[30] Overall, in five leading countries of the E.U., the U.S. market share of the cinema audience has recently ranged from just under 54 percent in Italy to 76 percent in Germany and 86 percent in the United Kingdom.[31]

Beyond Europe, the dominance of American movies is often even more pronounced. Though India is an exception, with a large film industry of its own, turning out many hundreds of commercial movies for domestic consumption each year, the overall U.S. share amounts to some 85 percent of world film audiences.[32] This can be a mixed blessing, however. In the words of an astute observer of the industry, treatment of popular culture in film "portrays a world that is far more violent, dangerous and sexually indulgent... than everyday America reality."[33] For audiences who have not had the opportunity of wider exposure through travel or study, these impressions contribute to a highly distorted notion of the United States.

III. CULTURE AND POLITICAL CONFLICT

Whether defined as popular, folk, or high art, culture provides an arena in which clashes of nationalism, ethnicity, religion, and ideology often play out. Underlying such conflicts are two sets of competing impulses: One set involves the tension between attraction and repression, the other concerns differentiation and assimilation.

A graphic illustration of repression was evident in the deliberate destruction of two 5th- to 7th-century giant cliff-side carvings of the Buddha by the former Taliban regime in Afghanistan. These had been designated a world historic monument by the U.N., yet in the spring of 2001 the Taliban and other Islamic militants used artillery and explosives to demolish them, and they also smashed with sledgehammers much of the Buddhist patrimony stored in Afghan museums.[34] According to notes from a meeting between Taliban officials and Islamic militants, "The Taliban authorities agreed the destruction of [the statues] is an Islamic act that would make the Islamic world happy."[35] In its nihilistic rage, the act also foreshadows the destruction of the twin towers of the World Trade Center.

These actions were shocking for contemporary Westerners, who tend to value cultural artifacts very highly. However, 20th-century Western history does contain haunting episodes of the symbolic destruction of culture, as in the book burnings in Nazi Germany during the 1930s. And in an East Asian example, there was widespread smashing of ancient artifacts during the Chinese Cultural Revolution of the late 1960s.

The spectrum of responses to cultural phenomena is very broad. It ranges, at one end, from the extremes cited above through hostility to toleration and attraction at the other end. In fact, attraction and repression can happen simultaneously. Human nature seems to respond to a number of siren songs in this area: enforced rarity, the exotic, the transgressive, and the forbidden, among others. Foreign and domestic subcultures can affect a dominant culture, especially in the cycling of styles and artifacts of subcultures into the mainstream.[36]

A dynamic of attraction/repulsion periodically emerges, so that a forbidden subculture sometimes has a certain appeal to the mainstream.
For example, in the late 19th century, the demimonde in Paris had
a huge influence on popular culture and the Impressionist and Post-
Impressionist art movements, while in recent decades in America, the
fad for rap music with its "gangsta" lyrics and clothing paraphernalia
became widespread.

What is the mechanism at work here in the competing pulls of attraction and repulsion? Reason may argue for one set of choices and emo-
tion, or a deep-seated sense of identity may press for another. Samuel
Huntington has written that "cultural characteristics and differences
are less mutable and hence less easily compromised and resolved than
political and economic ones."[37] This may help to explain why nations
and ethnic and religious groups as well as individuals sometimes make
choices that appear so irrational and against their best interests.

The other pair of often simultaneous cultural tendencies involves
impulses toward differentiation and assimilation. Societies constantly
borrow and incorporate, just as they may also seek to set themselves
apart. Yet the rhetoric about cultural adaptation can be highly charged,
so that the globalization of mass culture is often roundly condemned
as vulgarizing or ruining the diversity of human civilizations or even
as "cultural genocide."[38]

This is similar to the argument of anti-globalization advocates about
American corporate interests destroying biodiversity. In the words of
such critics, part of the richness of human culture is its variety, its
trueness to its own cultural roots, yet a global popular culture increasingly dominated by American products and ideas is eroding a valued
cultural diversity. Thus there is a backlash against what is viewed as a
sweeping homogenization or Disneyfication of culture. For example,
Iran's president, Mohammed Khatami, labeled globalization as a form
of "neocolonialism," describing it as:

a destructive force threatening dialogue between cultures. The new world
order and globalization that certain powers are trying to make us accept,
in which the culture of the entire world is ignored, looks like a kind

of neocolonialism. This imperialism threatens mutual understanding between nations and communication and dialogue between cultures.[39]

IV. POPULAR, FOLK, AND HIGH CULTURE

As an assessment of globalization, Khatami's condemnation is overblown, but rather than advocating or condemning the globalization of culture, it is more useful here to identify the underlying historical and political causes that make culture a major subject of dispute. To do so, it helps to examine the three partially overlapping arenas of popular culture, folk or indigenous culture, and high art.

Popular culture is the most obvious realm to explore because of the pervasive influence of American music, fashion, food, movies, and television, all of which are associated with open markets and global consumerism. Such products have enormous popularity and consumer attraction, and although U.S. firms have the advantage of well-capitalized production and distribution, as Richard Pells points out, "global culture is hardly a monolithic entity foisted on the world by the American media."[40] Instead, Americans have excelled at absorbing and repackaging foreign cultural products and successfully retransmitting them to the rest of the world. For example, fast food, amusement parks, and the movies were not invented in America, and their antecedents can be found in English fish and chips, the Danish Tivoli Gardens, and the early European cinema. Yet our history as a nation of immigrants has taught us to synthesize and incorporate the cultural and popular expressions of a wide range of nationalities and ethnicities. We are the consumers of foreign intellectual and artistic influences par excellence.

As a result, not everything "American" really is truly American, and many products have been shaped by foreign influence or made elsewhere. American movies do have a huge influence abroad, but the action films that dominate international markets also are manifestations of the reciprocal phenomenon in which the global market significantly affects the production of films. Approximately 60 percent of Hollywood's profits come from overseas.[41] As a consequence, and because younger moviegoers make up a disproportionate share of the audience, Hollywood action movies, especially those aimed at Asian markets, are characterized more by their violence or explosiveness (which require little translation) than by their dialogue. This de-emphasis on language and the tendency toward highly demarcated good and evil is appealing across many societies.

Folk or indigenous culture is another arena where observers lament the effects of globalization as damaging to indigenous production. Yet the concerned parties are often not from the cultures in question, and the criticism incorporates a great deal of idealization in its underlying assumption that traditional folkways are pure, authentic, and unchanging. But folk art has never been pure. Rather, it provides an excellent example of the dynamics of assimilation and differentiation, as it is usually a mixture of local production and aesthetics with outside influences. Two examples from the Navajo illustrate this point. The rugs we view as so characteristic were greatly influenced by the Navajos' late 19th-century discovery of German aniline dyes. If we were to look at the rugs made before the use of these dyes was adopted, they would not even look like Navajo artifacts to us because of their subdued appearance, as the Native Americans were limited to colors obtained by dying the wool with vegetable matter. Another example is the bifurcation of design in Navajo jewelry, which was heavily influenced by native aesthetics, on one hand, and tourist preferences, on the other. What Navajos did for themselves tended to be heavy and bold because they were designing jewelry emblematic of power. By contrast, more delicate jewelry was created to satisfy the taste of tourists. The Navajos willingly adopted two modes of production geared to two different audiences, which is a sophisticated marketing technique. These are clear examples of cultural output influenced by foreign technology and tourist preferences. We thus ought to view folk art as more complex and more calculated than is generally understood.

While popular culture dominates public discourse about the cultural impact of globalization, high culture also deserves attention in its own right. Moreover, in any given country it is usually the elites who are involved in high culture and it is they who are most likely to have influence abroad. There are numerous focal points for international presentation, exchange, and collaboration. They include biennials, festivals, exhibitions, and architectural competitions. One of the most visible sites for global high culture is the museum, which has traditionally been seen as an aid to civic, national, or ethnic identity. Typically, museums came into being through the secularization of royal or church collections, which were then made public in national or municipal forums often in the 19th century.

The history of the Bilbao Museum in the Basque region of northern Spain exemplifies a number of these issues. In the late 19th century the elites of Bilbao were in an intellectual ferment concerning their local folkloric legacy in relation to late 19th-century cosmopolitan culture. At the time, similar scenarios played themselves out in many different locales. Nations were becoming much more aware of their folkloric heritage and the field of ethnography was born. Germany in particular established ethnographic collections, and collectors began to value folk material, which became a point of identification for local or ethnic pride. Because of a number of different phenomena, including world fairs, there was a growing sense of positive identification with national production. Yet at the same time a cosmopolitan art world was coming into being. One result of this more international awareness and diffusion of information was the rapid spread, for instance, of Impressionism as it came to permeate American, English, and Italian art in less than twenty years.

Note that there are at least three pertinent terms that seem to overlap in meaning but have slightly different connotations. They are the words "cosmopolitanism," "internationalism," and "globalization." They can all be applied to culture but carry somewhat different baggage. The term *cosmopolitan*, arising in the second half of the 19th century, had a kind of worldly, urbane, sophisticated sense to it. It was associated with fine arts and particularly with things French. Cosmopolitanism in Iran, Russia, and the United States in the 19th century embodied French cultural influence. *Internationalism*, however, while identified with Western culture, was less identified with one particular country. It is also a word more applicable to the 20th century. In the art world it referred to whichever was the elite style of the period. In architecture, the "international style" was a manifestation of 20th-century modernism, and abstract expressionism exemplified the international style in the immediate post–World War II period. *Globalization*, in turn, has recently acquired more negative connotations and is less strictly tied to high culture, as it has come to be identified with consumerism and Disneyfication.

The Basque situation was, and still is, a particular blend of ethnicity, cosmopolitanism, anti-Spanish, and anti-Madrid sentiments. The Basques are a very distinctive cultural entity and they possess a unique language. Their choice in the late 19th century was between a strong ethnic identity and a more cosmopolitan one, and oscillation between those two poles has characterized their situation throughout the 20th and into the 21st century. In the 1990s, a core group of industrial and civic leaders from Bilbao had concluded that internationalism was their best choice, and they were receptive to having their city become the site for a European Guggenheim Museum. The facility had originally been proposed for Frankfurt, a very well-established art center. However, when Frankfurt and the Guggenheim failed to reach agreement, Thomas Krens, the museum's director, mounted a sophisticated campaign in Bilbao in order to gain the necessary wider consensus there. Art historian Selma Holo describes how the strategy coupled internationalism with local identity:

It would enable the civic leaders, with the assistance of a small group of advocates to convince enough of the elite population of the city that rejection of the Guggenheim Museum Bilbao, would be tantamount to scuttling any chance for Bilbao to assume a modern identity or protect the regional identity. These new institutions were meant to prove that the intent of the politicians to support internationalism would not preclude their aggressive support for Basque cultural identity reinforcement.[42]

So Basque identity and a modern identity became linked. The museum would solve both problems. As in the 19th century, much of this was fueled by a rejection of Madrid and Spanish identity. Ironically, Basque elites traded off centralist Spain for centralist New York. In the end the idea that the Guggenheim would promote Basque cultural identity was forgotten once the spectacular Frank Gehry–designed building became a reality. Despite attracting wide attention, the new facility reinforced an almost exclusively internationalist program and cast of characters. The work of regional artists was not exhibited in the museum, and though that obstacle has eased slightly in recent years, these regional figures have not enjoyed the prominence the Guggenheim might have provided.

The payoff, however, has been an extraordinary surge in cultural tourism. Bilbao thus provides a perfect illustration of the late 20th- and early 21st-century importance of museums as branding a city or a culture and, in this case, giving it a global presence. This was also part of an aggressive, deliberate campaign on the part of the Guggenheim to create a global brand for itself. The Guggenheim with its various branches worldwide had three million visitors in 2001, which compared favorably with giants such as the Louvre, with six million visitors. Thomas Krens has said that he was "constantly approached by cities wanting to share in the so-called Bilbao effect." New projects are under consideration in Guadalajara, Singapore, Rio de Janeiro, and Hong Kong, as well as an extension of Russia's Hermitage museum with a Guggenheim component in St. Petersburg. The sense of an American enterprise with global ambitions is evident in Krens's observation about the Guggenheim: "It is an international museum whose home is in New York."[43]

Biennials are another way that nations or cities project themselves into the world art market. Biennials are typically international exhibitions held every other year. Most of the really big ones are truly global: Sao Paolo, Venice, Dusseldorf, and even Havana, for example. They are very widely dispersed geographically and constitute a deliberate strategy for achieving prominence in the world high culture arena. The flavor of these exhibitions has changed over the last decade. The new directions tend to reinforce the value of spectacle rather than authenticity or a profound engagement with the art. The elements of a world style circulate very quickly. Over a century ago, it took French Impressionism some twenty years to permeate art circles in other major cultural centers. Now with the Internet and the information revolution, the latest trend in Berlin will hit Tokyo in a matter of minutes and it might be assimilated and repackaged in Japan in a matter of days or weeks.

In addition to the jockeying for position among cultural elites of many countries, who seek to promote their regions (and themselves), there exist more radical and destructive forms of contestation. For example, the Taliban banned all music and visual culture that didn't conform to their fanatically restrictive standards, and they severely punished transgressors. They burned more than 1,000 reels of Afghan films, and a prominent musician who was caught playing his instrument was warned that if he was ever caught again, they would cut off his hands.[44] In the case of Iraq, after American forces had defeated the armies of Saddam Hussein, the destructive looting of archeological sites by local groups was driven not by a religious or cultural impetus but by the lure of financial gain without regard to their country's ancient heritage.

V. CULTURE AS A PROBLEM OF IDENTITY

As noted in the introduction to this chapter, both globalization and American primacy evoke cultural backlash. But the character and magnitude of the reaction take forms in the West and in other modern societies very different from those in the developing world and especially in Muslim countries. In portions of the Islamic world, as one widely respected observer has commented, the result is an "intractable confrontation between a theistic, land-based and traditional culture, in places little different from the Europe of the Middle Ages, and the secular material values of the Enlightenment."[45]

In Europe, Canada, Japan, and other societies, where modern values are for the most part widely prevalent, cultural reactions tend to be more nuanced. Intellectual, literary, artistic, and political elites often seek ways to define or reassert their own identities and importance as well as their national cultures by confronting the policies and the material and cultural influences of the United States. In part, these reactions have less to do with Washington's policies than with the imbalance of power and influence between their own countries and America. The critiques can become heated, but they remain largely symbolic and are often ephemeral.

More broadly, reactions to globalization take a wide variety of forms. In France, where 64 percent of the public describes itself as worried about the globalization of trade,[46] these attitudes can be seen in the highly publicized exploits of Jose Bove, an anti-globalization activist who learned his tactics while a foreign student at the University of California at Berkeley (yet another example of cultural cross-fertilization) and who gained notoriety by driving a tractor into a McDonald's restaurant in the provincial town of Millau. However, the presence of more than 1,000 of these fast-food restaurants in the country suggests that French consumers in large numbers find their own reasons to patronize the franchise.

Other components of European cultural response to modernity are conditioned by a distrust of modern science and technology. In Britain and France, as a result of deadly medical fiascos in the 1980s and 1990s, a degree of cynicism and suspicion has developed against experts in modern science and technology. In the French case, the reaction stems from the government's deliberate delay in licensing an American test for the HIV/AIDS virus in donated blood in order to await a French-made product. As a consequence, hundreds of people who received transfusions during this period became infected with the deadly virus. In Britain, public distrust reflects the "mad cow" disease experience when public health officials wrongly assured the public that there was no danger in eating beef from diseased animals. The backlash can be found in the refusal of many British parents to have their infants inoculated for measles, mumps, and rubella, not because of scientific evidence but due to the speculation of a single doctor that the vaccine might cause autism.[47]

Anxiety of this kind is reflected in European references to the "precautionary principle," the idea that even in the absence of scientific evidence, regulators should be suspicious of or even ban products or technologies that might pose a potential risk. The concept was loosely referenced in the European Union's 1997 Amsterdam Treaty, and in the year 2000 the European Commission widened the concept beyond the realm of environmental policy to areas of consumer protection and public health. The approach has been evident in European consumer suspicion of genetically modified (GM) crops. Evidence of harm from products available to the public or to the natural environment has never been documented. Nonetheless in 1998, without any scientific confirmation, the European Union imposed an open-ended moratorium on the approval of new GM crops for use or import into the EU. This moratorium was eventually challenged by the United States in the World Trade Organization, and as a result partially lifted in 2004, but replaced with a new stipulation that all products with ingredients more than 0.9 percent genetically modified must be labeled "GM" and traced through the market with an audit trail of documentation.[48]

While much of the reaction against globalization identifies it with the United States, the phenomenon also has had notable effects on popular culture and attitudes within America itself. Paul Cantor, in his book *Gilligan Unbound: Pop Culture in the Age of Globalization*,[49] explores four television series over the course of four decades (*Gilligan's Island*, *Star Trek*, *The Simpsons*, and *The X-Files*) to demonstrate how globalization, together with the impact of mass media, has undermined traditional domestic attitudes concerning power, authority, and the role of the state.[50] Cantor argues that the traditional importance of the state and other institutions has been superseded in the consciousness of most people (as represented, e.g., in *The Simpsons*) by a focus on the family, neighbors, and the marketplace.

Whether these trends are really so dominant is at the least debatable. For a time, they reflected the effects of a post–Cold War decade and the seeming absence of an external threat. Coupled with the impact of the information revolution and an extraordinary period of economic growth and lavish consumer spending, this allowed Americans and the media to focus on ephemeral stories about celebrities, life-style, crime, and the sexual peccadilloes of prominent personalities. Thus, the sordid Clinton scandals on cable television (all Monica, all the time), the O. J. Simpson trial, Princess Di, the life-styles of dot-com billionaires, and celebrity gossip were among the most prominent cultural symbols of the 1990s. However, these distractions, together with the waning public confidence in government, were the product of an era in which the role of the state at home and abroad seemed less essential.

In the aftermath of the September 11 terror attacks and of wars in Afghanistan and Iraq, these trends appear less dominant. The unprecedented nature and scope of the assault on the U.S. homeland, the mass murder of 3,000 Americans, the continuing threat from terrorism and weapons of mass destruction, and the effect on the U.S. economy impacted the lives of ordinary Americans and may well have had transformative effects.

The cultural impact of 9/11 can be gauged in many ways, large and small. One was by the outpouring of unabashed patriotic sentiment in response to the destruction of the World Trade Center and the bravery of passengers who fought with their hijackers on the doomed American Airlines flight 93. Other measures can be found in increased volunteerism, the unself-conscious display of the flag, and changes in public opinion. For example, confidence in national institutions, including the presidency and Congress, surged to levels not seen in decades, and trust in government rose – temporarily – to the highest levels since the mid-1960s. Over a period of several years, these numbers declined, but the percentage of those expressing a great deal of confidence in government remained slightly higher than in the quarter-century prior to 9/11.[51]

The influence of globalization on American culture and the United States more broadly has had contradictory effects. Until September 11, 2001, globalization, along with the end of the Cold War, the information revolution, and an economic boom, fostered the kind of shifts described above by Cantor. But especially since that time, Americans have discovered that key components of globalization (technology, openness, cell phones, the Internet, financial flows, modern air travel) can also be used to murderous effect against modern society.

In large areas of the developing world and especially in Muslim countries, reactions to globalization and to America's role take very different and more intense forms. Here, the intrusion of modern Western values and the crisis of traditional societies combine to foster a sometimes intense backlash. Often, the forces of both attraction and repulsion are simultaneously present. Thus, a kind of cultural schizophrenia is evident in the television viewing habits of Middle Eastern youths, who experience these contradictory sentiments in watching the portrayal of American society and the artifacts of its consumer culture.[52] As an example of such contrasting material and emotional dimensions, on September 11, patrons at a trendy Beirut coffee house applauded the televised pictures of the World Trade Center's destruction, while dressed in American-style clothing and gathered in an establishment that would have fit an upscale American neighborhood.[53]

Major conflicts that stem from radically different visions of society and identity are frequently played out in the cultural realm. Though a great deal of comment has been devoted to these reactions as stemming from problems of poverty, environmental degradation, or in response to American policies, the root causes lie elsewhere.

The most intense loathing of the United States is expressed by proponents of militant Islam. The words of Osama bin Laden are chilling in their unabashed hatred, as expressed, for example, in his February 1998 *fatwa*, or edict, proclaiming, "The killing of Americans and their civilian and military allies is a religious duty for each and every Muslim to be carried out in whichever country they are found."[54] But, as Fouad Ajami has observed, what really motivates bin Laden and his followers is rage over their inability to overthrow the existing Arab ruling order, which they redirect at America. Ajami captures both the paradoxical attraction and repulsion toward the United States and the bitterness of Arabs at their own broken societies and corrupt and authoritarian regimes:

Nothing grows in the middle between an authoritarian political order and populations given to perennial flings with dictators, abandoned to their most malignant hatreds. Something is amiss in an Arab world that besieges American embassies for visas and at the same time celebrates America's calamities.[55]

This phenomenon embodies both a historical and a modern component. There is frustration at the loss of grandeur by a Muslim Arab civilization that once far outpaced Europe in its achievements but has in recent centuries fallen into anger and despair. Evidence of this can be found in a bin Laden video aired in October 2001, which revels in the destruction of the World Trade Center, calls upon Muslims to wage war against America, and invokes the memory of past Arab indignities:

What America is tasting now is something insignificant compared to what we have tasted for scores of years. Our nation [the Islamic world] has been tasting this humiliation and this degradation for more than 80 years.[56]

The reference to "80 years" would be obscure for most Western audiences but readily understood in the Arab world. The year 1921 marked the collapse of the Ottoman Empire and foreshadowed the ultimate demise of the Caliphate – Muslim civil and religious rule by the successors of Muhammad, which had lasted, at least symbolically, for nearly 1,300 years. Documents found at sites in Afghanistan abandoned by al-Qaeda fighters contained even more explicit reference to the Caliphate, as in the words of one of the recovered texts:

[The Caliphate] is the only and best solution to the predicaments and problems from which Muslims suffer today and indubitable cure to the turbulence and internal struggles that plague them. It will remedy the economic underdevelopment which bequeathed upon us a political dependence on an atheist East and infidel West.[57]

What is revealing about this reference to the Caliphate is not only its irrelevance to the "predicaments and problems from which Muslims suffer today," but also the notion that reestablishment of the Caliphate could somehow solve contemporary problems of economic development. While bin Laden's October 2001 video lamented the carving up of the Middle East into a series of separate states that have largely failed to cope with the challenges of modernity, it ignores the fact that the United States had little to do with the Ottoman breakup and the subsequent drawing of borders. That legacy is shared by France and Britain, as the prevailing colonial powers of the day. Moreover, the events took place a quarter-century before the United States became a superpower in the aftermath of World War II, and long before the creation of the state of Israel in 1948. But bin Laden's focus nonetheless on America is evidence of how this rage has been redirected at the United States as the most powerful symbol of Western values and modern economic, military, and cultural influence.[58]

The hostility is driven far less by poverty than by issues of identity, and its proponents are mostly from the university-educated professional and middle classes who comprise an embittered counter-elite within their own societies. Martin Kramer observes how this is embodied by militant Islam:

[It is] the vehicle of counter-elites, people who, by virtue of education and/or income, are potential members of the elite, but who for some reason or another get excluded. Their education may lack some crucial prestige-conferring element; the sources of their wealth may be a bit tainted. Or they may just come from the wrong background. So while they are educated and wealthy, they have a grievance: their ambition is blocked, they cannot translate their socio-economic assets into political clout. Islamism is particularly useful to these people, in part because by its careful manipulation, it is possible to recruit a following among the poor, who make valuable foot-soldiers.[59]

This is not an entirely new development. Some two decades ago an Egyptian study found that jailed Islamists in that country were mostly of middle-class origin and had often been educated in engineering or science. Indeed, fifteen of the nineteen September 11 hijackers came from Saudi Arabia, one of the Muslim world's wealthiest countries. Moreover, of the two top leaders of al-Qaeda, Osama bin Laden and Ayman al-Zawahiri, one is the son of a Saudi billionaire, the other a wealthy Egyptian doctor. Militant Islam's ability to attract such competent, well-motivated, and ambitious people resembles that of fascism and Marxism-Leninism in their day.[60]

These traits of Islamic extremists are apparent not only in their own countries, but also among some Islamic and Arab émigrés in Europe. For example, Mohamed Atta, the Saudi who piloted the hijacked airliner that slammed into the North Tower of the World Trade Center and is believed to have been the ringleader of the hijackers, had lived with several of the terrorists in Germany and appeared to become increasingly alienated by his inability to find a place and purpose in that society despite his graduate education in urban planning. As Fouad Ajami has eloquently observed, "The modern world unsettled Atta....The magnetic power of the American imperium had fallen across his country. He arrived here with a presumption and a claim. We had intruded into his world; he would shatter the peace of ours. The glamorized world couldn't be fully had; it might as well be humbled and taken down."[61]

The Madrid terrorist bombing of March 11, 2004, provides graphic evidence that this impulse is not just directed at the United States. The operational chief of the attack that took the lives of 191 commuters was an immigrant from Tunisia who had first sought to adapt to the society of modern Spain and then withdrew into an increasingly isolated and fanatical environment. Sarhane Ben Abdelmajid Fakhet had moved to Madrid eight years earlier to study economics at the Autonomous University of Madrid. He then worked as a real estate agent and lived in a middle-class Spanish neighborhood. With time, however, he pulled back into a narrow world of Islamist extremism. Several weeks after the attack, Abdelmajid died when he and four other men blew themselves up as Spanish police raided their apartment.[62]

In its most delusional expressions, this kind of reaction takes the form of conspiracy theories directed at the United States, the West, or Israel. As evidence, a Gallup survey of public opinion in nine Muslim countries found only 18 percent of respondents believing that Arabs carried out the September 11 attacks.[63] Arab and Muslim media disseminated stories claiming a Jewish or Israeli conspiracy behind the attack on the World Trade Center, and even three years later, long after bin Laden and al-Qaeda had made clear their responsibility for 9/11, claims that the hand of America or Israel lay behind the 9/11 attacks could still be found in Arab and Iranian government-controlled media and in statements by officials, prominent professors, and religious leaders.[64] In addition, leading Saudi, Egyptian, and Syrian papers have continued to carry crude anti-Semitic stories, including the old Czarist forgery, "The Protocols of the Elders of Zion," the ancient libel that Jews use the blood of non-Jewish children in food prepared for Purim or Passover, and claims that the Holocaust is a "Zionist lie."[65]

Though especially virulent, these are by no means the only instances of scapegoating amid the disruptions of globalization and modernity. In India, for example, a leading political party, the Hindu nationalist BJP, prioritizes not the alleviation of poverty but rebuilding of a historic temple in the town of Ayodhya – on the site of a recently demolished mosque and despite deadly confrontations with the local Muslim population.

VI. GLOBALIZATION, CULTURE, AND CONFLICT

In an increasingly globalized world, culture has emerged as a central arena of conflict. Other issues on the globalization agenda, especially economic ones such as trade, aid, and investment, are more readily subject to negotiation and compromise, but culture in its various forms serves as a primary carrier of globalization and modern values. Cultural issues are so fraught precisely because of their impact on both individual and national identity, and because culture has become a signifier for other more deep-seated and intractable issues, the problems it poses are harder to resolve.

The idea that modernization can be disruptive to traditional societies and that this can cause revolutionary turmoil is not new. In the mid-19th century, Alexis de Tocqueville concluded that rage and political upheaval stemmed not from poverty and deprivation or from the exercise of power itself but from more symbolic causes including rising expectations, feelings of humiliation, and reactions against a ruler considered "illegitimate . . . and oppressive."[66] A century later, a leading American social scientist, Seymour Martin Lipset, identified relative deprivation as a source of upheaval and found that disruptions caused by economic and social modernization could radicalize sections of the middle and professional classes and cause them to be attracted to extremist movements.[67]

The animus directed against the United States is by no means uniform. And as noted above, expressions of it in Europe tend to be more modest and symbolic because globalization there (and in other regions where modern values prevail) does not dictate a profound cultural clash with pre-modern values. Moreover, in the post-9/11 era, Europe will continue to require close links with America because of shared economic interests and as insurance in a dangerous world.

Elsewhere, although American policies and practices can be a source of resentment, and primacy can readily translate into bruised feelings about the exercise of American power, the predominant sources of anti-Americanism are deep-seated and structural and are only secondarily due to specific policies. This was especially evident in the aftermath of September 11, and a statement by sixty leading American scholars made a telling point when it observed the way in which bin Laden and the attackers directed their hatred against the United States itself rather than make any specific policy demands:

. . . the killing was done for its own sake. The leader of Al Qaeda described the "blessed strikes" of September 11 as blows against America, "the head of world infidelity." Clearly, then, our attackers despise not just our government, but our overall society, our entire way of living. Fundamentally, their grievance concerns not only what our leaders do, but also who we are.[68]

The Anglo-Indian author, Salman Rushdie, himself a target of a *fatwa* calling for his death as punishment for supposed blasphemy, captures this phenomenon when he writes that even if a Middle East peace settlement between Israelis and Palestinians were achieved, anti-Americanism would be likely to continue unabated.[69] This animosity toward America is driven by several mechanisms: the desire of authoritarian regimes to deflect criticism away from their own corrupt rule, the agendas of virulently anti-modernist movements that paradoxically can now utilize television and the Internet to disseminate their views, and widespread frustration and alienation. Yet Islamic radicalism is by no means dominant, and it remains contested within these societies, not least (as Afghanistan under Taliban rule demonstrated) because its anti-rational, theocratic, and misogynist values do not provide a viable option for successfully confronting the tasks of modernization. Moreover, hostility to the United States is not universal, and America's successful exercise of power may sometimes actually discourage opposition.[70]

In parts of the Muslim world, modernist views have surfaced to contest the radical Islamist vision. In at least some cases, journalists, intellectuals, and government leaders condemned the 9/11 attacks, spoke out against extremism and the search for scapegoats, and challenged the notion that returning to practices of the distant past can solve practical problems of society and economy. Thus, as a former Libyan Prime Minister has observed, "Perhaps most of the things we complain of ... stem from our own flaws."[71] Similarly, following the July 2004 release of the 9/11 Commission Report, the former dean of the Faculty of Islamic Law at the University of Qatar wrote an article calling on Arabs to recant their conspiracy theories about the September 11 attacks and to apologize for spreading theses ideas:

Why won't we take the opportunity of the appearance of the 9-11 Commission's report to ponder why destructive violence and a culture of destruction have taken root in our society? Why won't we take this opportunity to reconsider our educational system, our curricula, including the religious, media, and cultural discourse that causes our youth to live in a constant tension with the world?[72]

Ultimately, the root causes of fanaticism and cultural backlash lie not within the United States and the West but inside the foreign societies themselves. Culture is both a mode of self and group expression and a source of upheaval and contestation. There is less a "clash of civilizations" than a clash *within* civilizations. Outsiders can take steps to encourage moderate elements within these societies, but much more depends on developments inside the countries concerned. The outcome of this competition may ultimately shape whether globalization itself continues or instead is violently overturned, much as the guns of August 1914 touched off a world war and reversed a century's trend of increasing openness, integration, and interdependence.

5 Iraq and the Middle East: Dilemmas of U.S. Power

Cry "Havoc" and let slip the dogs of war.

– Shakespeare, *Julius Caesar*, Act III

But what we know now would not necessarily have changed the calculus for preemption. Could the United States wait until weapons were actually produced by a country with the largest army in the region, the second-largest potential oil income, a record of having used these weapons against its own population and neighbors, and – according to the Sept. 11 commission – intelligence contact with al-Qaeda?

– Henry Kissinger[1]

Nothing short of a military intervention could have exerted any political pressure on the region. It's the only solution, the only lesser among many evils.

– Hisham Kassem, head of the Egyptian Organization for Human Rights[2]

The Middle East has thrust itself onto the American agenda in a spectacular way. In the past, the subject had intruded during periods of crisis or war, but never with the same level of urgency. Arab-Israeli wars, the oil shocks of the 1970s, the Iranian hostage crisis in 1979–80, terrorist attacks against the U.S. embassy and Marine barracks in Beirut in 1983, and the U.S.-led Operation Desert Storm to liberate Kuwait from Iraqi occupation in 1991 all captured public attention for a time, then these concerns receded as the events passed.

Now, however, debates of the highest order about grand strategy, foreign policy, and America's proper role in world affairs are inextricably bound up with policies toward a broad region extending from North Africa to Pakistan and from Afghanistan to the southern end of the Persian Gulf. As for Iraq, not since Vietnam has a foreign policy crisis attracted such impassioned argument.

This debate focuses broadly on America's role in Iraq, as well as on the war on terror and the wider Middle East. The impetus for it stems not only from acrimonious disagreements prior to the war in Iraq, but also from the failure to find stockpiles of weapons of mass destruction and in reaction to instability and insurgency in postwar Iraq. Particularly within the Middle East, there is the allegation that the war in Iraq, as well as the intervention to overthrow the Taliban regime in Afghanistan, show that America is at war with the Muslim world. Some European and Muslim critics claim that the decision to use force against Iraq was driven by Bush policymakers' desire to make

126

the region safe for Israel. They also allege that terrorism, instability, and anti-Americanism are a product of pro-Israel policies that have failed to address the plight of the Palestinians and that have alienated people throughout the region. An extreme variant of this belief purports to explain U.S. policy as the product of a sinister cabal.

Especially – but not exclusively – among foreign audiences, ideas about U.S. Middle East policy sometimes became entangled with conspiracy theories and such views are rarely susceptible to rational discourse or any kind of evidence. But beyond incantations of no-blood-for-oil, the ranting against an "axis of oil and Jews" that rules the world,[3] or claims that the Iraq crisis was manufactured by Israel and a cabal of its American supporters,[4] a more rational set of arguments in opposition to the use of force merits attention.

Serious critics of U.S. policy make several core arguments. First, they depict Iraq as an unnecessary war. They assert that Saddam Hussein was neither reckless nor irrational and that any threat from Iraq could have been contained, just as we were successful in containing the Soviets during the Cold War. They add that even if Saddam obtained nuclear weapons, he would have been deterred from using them by the ability of the United States to retaliate with overwhelming force.

Critics also add a second argument, that war in Iraq resulted in disproportionate opportunity costs and a distraction from the war on terror. The money, lives, and political capital spent there would have been far better directed elsewhere, especially in Afghanistan, in efforts to secure loose nuclear materials in the former Soviet Union, and in making America more secure at home.

A third major criticism focuses on the negative costs of the war. The use of force without specific authorization by the U.N. Security Council is described as ill-advised or even illegal and as setting an ominous precedent. In contrast to the international expressions of solidarity with America in the aftermath of 9/11, the United States now faces widespread criticism and condemnation in many parts of the world. Moreover, Iraq threatens to become a quagmire in which the United States expends blood and treasure without the likelihood of success while the ongoing insurgency emboldens terrorists there and elsewhere.

This chapter responds to those arguments. In it, I first provide historical context and set out the case for the Iraq War. I then turn to an analysis of the war's aftermath and trade-offs in the use of force, the wider implications of that conflict, and consequences for the region as well as for the United States itself.

BACKGROUND: AMERICA AND THE MIDDLE EAST

Arguments about Iraq are fundamentally about U.S. grand strategy, and an assessment of them needs to begin with some recent historical background. America's involvement in the Middle East has greatly intensified since 9/11, but its importance to the stability of the region is long-standing. The American commitment in the Gulf has been evident from at least 1943, when President Franklin Roosevelt declared the defense of Saudi Arabia a vital interest of the United States, and from early 1945, when he and Saudi King Ibn Saud met aboard a U.S. warship to personify the two countries' special relationship. In the following decades, the American presence became increasingly important as the influence of the former colonial powers, Britain and France, ebbed.

During the past half-century, the United States has intervened when it saw its national interests or regional stability at stake. In 1956 the Eisenhower administration pressured Britain and France to withdraw from the Suez Canal and Israel from the Sinai after their military campaign against Egypt's President Nasser. In the following years, American Presidents sent Marines to Lebanon in 1958 and again in 1982–83; embraced the Shah of Iran (who owed his throne to a 1953 coup engineered by the CIA) and supported him as a regional proxy in the 1970s; negotiated disengagement agreements after the October 1973 Arab-Israeli War; established close political, military, and economic relationships with the Egypt of Sadat and Mubarak;

brokered the historic 1979 peace treaty between Israel and Egypt; armed the *mujahadeen* fighting against the Soviets in Afghanistan from 1980 to 1988; and intervened to protect Persian Gulf shipping in 1986–88 during the latter years of the Iran-Iraq War.

In 1991, the United States led a broad international coalition against Iraq's occupation of Kuwait and inflicted a stunning defeat on Saddam's forces. At the end of that year, the collapse of the Soviet Union, which had been the principal arms supplier and geopolitical backer of radical Arab regimes, left America as the unchallenged external power in the region. The administration of the elder George Bush also broke new ground by organizing direct Arab-Israeli talks in the October 1991 Madrid Conference.[5] These began a process that eventually led to the Oslo Agreements signed by the leaders of Israel and the Palestinians at the Clinton White House in September 1993. During the remainder of the decade, the United States established or expanded military bases in Saudi Arabia and a number of Gulf states, led in enforcing U.N. sanctions and inspections against Iraq, and maintained economic aid to moderate regimes in Egypt and Jordan.

Throughout the Middle East, no other external power possessed anything close to America's capacity to deter local threats, to counter the proliferation of weapons of mass destruction, to promote the Arab-Israeli peace process, and to protect stable supplies of oil from a region with almost two-thirds of the world's proven petroleum reserves. Yet this also made the United States a target for local actors who saw it as the guarantor for policies and regimes they detested. This tension has been aggravated by the failure of many of these societies to cope with modernization and by public frustration at corrupt and authoritarian rulers.

Not surprisingly, the U.S. role brought it into direct confrontation with Saddam Hussein's Iraq. This experience deserves special attention not only because of its intrinsic importance, but because it exemplifies many of the requirements and dilemmas of America's position in the region and in the wider war on terror.

IRAQ: A NECESSARY WAR?

Major combat operations against Saddam Hussein's regime began on March 19, 2003, and in little more than three weeks, coalition forces prevailed in occupying Baghdad and then in eliminating organized resistance by main force units of the Iraqi army and Republican Guard.[6] In that sense, the initial military campaign unfolded more quickly, more successfully, and with far fewer casualties to allied forces – and to Iraqis – than had been widely feared prior to the war.

Problems of insecurity and insurgency in postwar Iraq, however, proved to be vastly more difficult and costly than American policymakers had anticipated. In addition, the absence of the widely expected quantities of WMD led critics to insist that America should never have gone to war and that the war had taken place at the expense of the wider effort against al-Qaeda terrorism. In turn, revelations of the abuse of Iraqi prisoners at the notorious Abu Ghraib prison proved intensely embarrassing, and broadly disseminated photos of the mistreatment – though trivial compared with Saddam's long reign of terror – dealt a damaging blow to America's human rights reputation.

These are serious matters, but both the intelligence failures and Iraq's dangerous postwar instability do not mean the United States necessarily erred by invading Iraq. Certainly, the use of force against Iraq is bound to be debated for years to come. The resort to war invariably carries great risks, and it is not surprising that the case for it was widely challenged in advance as well as in the war's aftermath. Most important, however, these problems have to be weighed against the broader danger evident from Saddam Hussein's history, capability, and intent, and the strategic threat he posed to a vital region, to America's allies, and to U.S. national security.

Arguments in opposition to the use of force variously maintained that Iraq could have been contained, that inspections would have been more successful if expanded or made coercive, that any action should have been contingent on authorization by the U.N. Security Council, and that even if Saddam ultimately did acquire nuclear weapons, he could have been deterred. Many critics offered dire warnings about the risks of war, including Iraq's likely use of WMD, massive civilian casualties, protracted urban warfare, destruction of oil facilities, uprisings by the Arab "street" against American-supported regimes throughout the region, and chaos in a post-Saddam Iraq. In the event, many of these things never happened; however, instability and insurgency have become serious problems, especially among the 20 percent of the population who are Sunni.

The proposed alternatives to war included, for example, "coercive inspections" (advocated by a respected group of authors in a report of the Carnegie Endowment for International Peace),[7] "vigilant containment" (urged by prominent international relations scholars),[8] "disarmament through peaceful means" (French President Jacques Chirac),[9] insistence that the issue must be decided by "the international community as a whole" (UN Secretary-General Kofi Annan),[10] and an effort to change the subject by concentrating on the Israeli-Palestinian issue and the war on terrorism "before we turn on Iraq."[11]

Two leading academic realists, John Mearsheimer and Stephen Walt, made the case for containment. They asserted that Saddam was not a reckless expansionist and that during the past thirty years Iraq had started "only [sic]" two wars.[12] They maintained that the Iraqi leader's decision to attack Iran in 1980 was not without reason and that he did so for essentially defensive purposes. They described Saddam's August 1990 invasion of Kuwait as "an attempt to deal with Iraq's continued vulnerability." And they rationalized his failure to withdraw from Kuwait in early January 1991 at a time when, with an unprecedented U.N. Security Resolution, the American-led coalition had assembled an overwhelming force in preparation for war, by asserting that Saddam had good reason to hold out because of his belief that the United States could not sustain for very long the casualties Iraqi forces would inflict on them.

Opponents of the use of force also insisted that even if Saddam had WMD, he was no less susceptible to pressure than previous adversaries. A belief in Saddam's ultimate strategic rationality was fundamental to this assumption. In the words of Shibley Telhami, Saddam's regime was "ruthless" but not "suicidal."[13] A group of authors under the auspices of the Carnegie Endowment emphasized that Saddam did not pose an immediate threat, and the foundation's president, Jessica Tuchman Mathews, wrote, "The idea is to disarm Iraq, and that can be done by truly muscular inspections backed by a multinational military force."[14] Pushing these ideas even further, the head of the Endowment's nonproliferation project and a coauthor insisted that the members of the Security Council could "compel" Iraq's answers to the remaining nuclear program questions and "establish a permanent monitoring system to keep Saddam under house arrest [sic] for the rest of his life."[15]

A more practical set of arguments was offered by a group of thirty-three prominent international relations professors who signed an ad appearing in the New York Times.[16] They asserted that although war is sometimes necessary, it was not called for against Iraq. They insisted that Saddam Hussein could be contained, that war would involve great risks because of Saddam's biological and chemical weapons, that Iraq had not been collaborating with al-Qaeda, and that war with Iraq would be a distraction from the fight against terrorism. In support of these propositions, the principal authors of the ad subsequently argued that Saddam never used weapons of mass destruction against an adversary who could retaliate in kind, and they insisted that Saddam had been "neither mindlessly aggressive nor particularly reckless."[17]

All these views, however, gave insufficient weight to the history of eroding inspections and sanctions, the long-term nuclear peril, Saddam Hussein's character, the meaning of 9/11, and Iraq's relationship to terrorism. A dozen years of experience with U.N. sanctions and weapons inspections ought to have dispelled the notion that more and better inspections could succeed. In 1991, following Iraq's ouster from Kuwait and the end of the Gulf War, the Security Council had passed Resolution 687, under Chapter VII of the U.N. Charter, which made it binding on all member states. This resolution required Iraq to relinquish all weapons of mass destruction, abandon its programs for biological, chemical, and nuclear weapons, as well as missiles with ranges beyond 150 kilometers, and cooperate with U.N. inspectors in their identification and elimination of these weapons. Sanctions that had been imposed following the August 1990 invasion were to be kept in place until the disarmament was completed.

But as accounts by the successive heads of the U.N. Special Commission for the Disarmament of Iraq (UNSCOM), Rolf Ekeus of Sweden and Richard Butler of Australia, made clear, Saddam's record was one of cheat and retreat. Initially, the Iraqis did make available large stocks of chemical warheads – many of them dangerously unstable – for destruction. But Iraq dragged its feet and a pattern emerged whereby the inspectors would find nothing, Iraq would claim that it had complied, and its advocates in the Security Council, especially France and Russia, would seek to ease or lift sanctions. Periodically, evidence would emerge of previously unknown programs. The Iraqis would then offer grudging acknowledgment, rewrite their submissions, and reassert that they were now in full compliance.[18]

With time, the inspections regime and the sanctions weakened. The inspection teams themselves were penetrated by Iraqi intelligence, and their members relentlessly monitored and spied on. Saddam acted to encourage division within the coalition, and Iraq launched a massive propaganda campaign replete with inflated claims about Iraqi women and children victimized by shortages of food and medicine. Meanwhile, Saddam enlarged the holes in the sanctions and gained access to additional revenues by illegally exporting oil via Turkey and Syria as well as along the coastal waters of Iran, by dangling lucrative contracts in front of the French, Russians, and Chinese, by employing numerous illicit means to purchase materials for his weapons programs, and by getting other countries (Russia and France among them) to violate a ban on airline travel. In addition, Iraq's bribery and manipulation of the U.N. oil-for-food program along with its covert oil exports yielded roughly $10 billion in illegal oil revenues.

Periodic rejoinders by UNSCOM officials and American diplomats that sanctions did allow ample supplies of food, medicine, and other critical items, especially after the U.N.'s 1996 adoption of a supervised oil-for-food program, fell on deaf ears. The fact that suffering by Iraqi civilians was caused by Saddam's deliberate policies and his diversion of resources to pay for his palaces, his military, and the loyalty of his Ba'ath Party cronies was drowned out by Iraqi propaganda and censorship and self-censorship on reporting from Iraq. As a case in point, a month after the fall of Baghdad, the chief news executive of CNN publicly acknowledged that his network had deliberately refrained from reporting horrifying stories about Saddam and his regime ("events that were not reported but that nonetheless still haunt me") because to do so would have jeopardized the local staff and possibly CNN's ability to broadcast from Iraq.[19]

The more that international pressures weakened, the more Saddam obstructed the work of the inspections teams. Ultimately, in 1998, with their work impossible to carry out, the UNSCOM inspectors were withdrawn. The Clinton administration, supported by Britain, launched four days of air strikes in Operation Desert Fox, but these did not compel changes in Saddam's behavior. After tortuous negotiations, a new and different inspection regime, the U.N. Monitoring, Verification and Inspection Commission (UNMOVIC), was created with significantly weaker authority and under a new chief, Hans Blix, acceptable to the Iraqis after they had rejected his UNSCOM predecessors. Blix himself had been head of the International Atomic Energy Agency during the time that body certified Iraq as in full compliance with the requirements of the Non-Proliferation Treaty, and had taken umbrage at accusations that Baghdad was pursuing a nuclear proliferation program under the nose of IAEA officials. Blix's denials persisted until the moment in 1991 that an UNSCOM team discovered one of Iraq's massive nuclear sites.

Only after it became obvious that the Bush administration was preparing to use force did elaborate diplomatic efforts produce action within the U.N. Security Council. The unanimously approved Resolution 1441 of November 8, 2002, finally brought the UNMOVIC inspectors to Iraq after a four-year period in which there had been no inspections at all. This resolution, the *seventeenth* in the UNSC's long history of demands that Iraq comply with its disarmament obligations, contained unambiguous language stating that Iraq had been in "material breach" of previous resolutions, that it was being offered a "final opportunity" to comply with its disarmament obligations under relevant resolutions of the council, that it must deliver within thirty days a "full, and complete declaration of all aspects of its programs," that "false statements or omissions in the declarations submitted by Iraq . . . and failure by Iraq at any time to comply with, and cooperate fully in the implementation of, this resolution shall constitute a further material breach of Iraq's obligations," and that Iraq would "face serious consequences as a result of its continued violations of its obligations."

Thirty days later and despite the explicit wording of the resolution, Iraq delivered a 12,000-page report that claimed its WMD programs no longer existed. In response, on January 27, 2003, Hans Blix reported to the Security Council that "Iraq appears not to have come to a genuine acceptance, not even today, of the disarmament which was demanded of it." In doing so, he named specific materials as unaccounted for, including 6,500 chemical bombs, stocks of VX nerve agents and of anthrax, 3,000 tons of precursor chemicals, 360 tons of bulk agents for chemical weapons and thousands of munitions for delivering such agents. Later, Blix observed that it was only after the end of May 2003 (i.e., after the war) that he concluded that the unaccounted-for weapons did not exist.[20]

Passage of Resolution 1441 was a consequence of the dispatch of troops to the Gulf by the United States and United Kingdom and their realistic threat of force, but an impetus of that kind could not be sustained indefinitely. Under this intensified pressure, Saddam eased the obstructions that had prevented UNMOVIC from beginning its inspections, but past experience made it likely that Iraqi cooperation would quickly diminish once the immediate pressure let up. Indeed, Saddam himself had been remarkably explicit about his calculations. In November 2002, in a rare interview, he told an Egyptian weekly,

Al Usbou, "Time is working for us. . . . We have to buy some time, and
the American-British coalition will disintegrate because of internal
reasons and . . . the pressure of public opinion in the American and
British street."[21]

Often overlooked in the controversy over the status of Saddam's
nuclear program, the intelligence failure on WMD, and the issue of
how long it would have taken Iraq to produce its own highly enriched
uranium or plutonium was the fact – established in 1991 by UNSCOM –
that Saddam already possessed a workable implosion design for a
nuclear weapon. While it would have taken years for Iraq to produce
the fissile material to make such a bomb (German intelligence in 2001
had estimated as little as three years, others, including the CIA, said
before the end of the decade), it was believed the timetable could drop
to as little as one year if the Iraqis succeeded in buying or stealing
plutonium or highly enriched uranium from, for example, the former
Soviet Union, Pakistan, or North Korea. And it is well to bear in mind
that the amount required for a single fission weapon is small, no more
than the size of a grapefruit. Meanwhile, during the years that sanctions were in place, Saddam had forgone as much as $180 billion in
oil revenue rather than comply with his disarmament obligations, and
up to the moment that the coalition launched its invasion of Iraq, the
intelligence agencies of the United States, Britain, Germany, France,
Russia, and Israel continued to believe that Saddam maintained a large
WMD program, despite claims to the contrary by the Iraqi regime.

In insisting that even if Saddam acquired nuclear weapons, he could
be successfully deterred, critics of the use of force pointed to past experience with the Soviet Union. However, that history was far from reassuring. During the Cold War, stability had required careful judgment
on both sides, as well as the deployment of a large American force in
Europe. But for Saddam, a nuclear device was the ultimate weapon. He
believed that possession of nuclear arms would allow him to dominate
his neighbors while dissuading the United States from intervening as
it did in Kuwait. Indeed, following his 1991 defeat, he lamented that
he had invaded too soon. He may not have been correct in believing

he could deter the United States, but he appeared to believe it. More-over, for America, there was a major difference between the Soviet Union and Saddam Hussein's Iraq. That is, the United States had the option of disarming Iraq. By contrast, to preempt or to destroy the Soviet arsenal in its earliest stages would have resulted in mass deaths and destruction as well as the possible conquest of Western Europe by Stalin. In later years, an effort to disarm the USSR would have meant mutual destruction.

Arguments against the use of force consistently underestimated the long-term threat posed by Saddam Hussein. In September 1980, twenty months after the Iranian Revolution and the ascent to power of the Ayatollah Khomeini, Saddam invaded Iran. That war lasted eight years, caused more than one million casualties, nearly resulted in Iraq's defeat, and left the country deeply in debt. Saddam followed, in 1988, with his notorious Al Anfal campaign against the Kurds of Northern Iraq, leveling villages, using poison gas (as he had done against Iran), and murdering as many as 180,000 people. In August 1990, Saddam invaded Kuwait in his determination to seize that country's oil, terri-tory, and financial reserves. This too became a debacle when, despite his belief to the contrary, the United States assembled a coalition of more than forty countries, backed by a U.N. Security Council Reso-lution authorizing use of force. The Iraqi leader refused to withdraw from Kuwait and instead saw his army decimated. He escaped being ousted from power only because the elder President Bush made the decision to halt the ground war after just 100 hours and because the victorious allied forces allowed the Iraqi military to use their heli-copters and armor to slaughter the Kurds and Shiites who rebelled in the months following the war.

Saddam constituted a serious strategic threat to the region. He had begun wars against Iran and Kuwait, launched missiles against these countries as well as Israel, Saudi Arabia, and Bahrain, used chemical weapons, and maintained a reign of terror at home during which he had murdered at least 400,000 Iraqis.[22] The historical record showed the Iraqi leader to be a gambler and a reckless expansionist.

He repeatedly disregarded the advice even of his own inner circle when it conflicted with his preconceptions, and his military actions brought great harm to his neighbors and his own country. For example, in deciding to attack Iran, Saddam relied primarily on the self-serving views of former Iranian military officers and launched the attack without any real military planning. From early 1984 onward, Iraq used chemical weapons in every major battle, and Saddam launched air and missile attacks against Iranian cities despite the fact that until early 1988 it was easier for Iran to hit Baghdad and Basra than it was for Iraqi missiles to reach Iran's major cities.[23]

Recklessness was also apparent in his disparaging of contradictory advice. A senior (and pro-Iraqi) Russian diplomat, Yevgeny Primakov, described meeting with the Iraqi leader in an effort to persuade him to withdraw from Kuwait, but concluded, "I realized that it was possible Saddam did not have complete information. He gave priority to positive reports . . . and as for bad news, the bearer could pay a high price."[24] This is more than a figure of speech. Leading Arab diplomats noted Saddam's propensity to discourage the kind of information he did not want to hear, and in one grisly example, after Saddam had his own Health Minister detained, the man's dismembered body was sent to his wife the next day. Authoritative accounts of Saddam as a gambler can be found in the work of Amatzia Baram, a leading expert on modern Iraq,[25] and psychologist Jerrold Post's work provides a compelling assessment of Saddam as a "malignant narcissist," with an extreme sense of grandiosity, sadistic cruelty, suspiciousness to the point of paranoia, and an utter lack of remorse. Those traits did not preclude shrewd calculations, but the overall pattern provided strong evidence that traditional assumptions about deterrence and containment could not be relied on.

Judgments about Saddam's Iraq also had to be considered in the context of a fundamentally changed threat environment in the post-9/11 world. The simultaneous attacks on the World Trade Center and the Pentagon had undermined the rationale for a policy of containment. The willingness of the nineteen hijackers to commit suicide in carrying out their attack, as well as the absence of certain knowledge about the source of the anthrax letters that followed, cast doubt on two central precepts of deterrence: an enemy's desire for self-preservation and knowledge of the adversary's identity.

The dangers of terrorism and WMD also changed the calculus of preemption and ideas about the imminence of threat. Individual and collective self-defense of the kind codified, for example, in Article 51 of the U.N. Charter derives from the world of Pearl Harbor. Even the widely accepted though not universally agreed-on concept of anticipatory self-defense, in which a country may resort to force when it finds that it is about to be attacked, stems from a very different era. But in an environment where an attack with chemical or biological weapons, or potentially with a concealed nuclear weapon, could kill unprecedented numbers of civilians and wreak havoc in the wider society, foreign policy decision makers have far more reason to take decisive action without waiting for absolute certainty that an attack is about to be unleashed.

The absence of WMD stockpiles represented a serious failure for the major intelligence agencies and had damaging political repercussions, though this does not mean that the WMD issue was baseless. Saddam, after all, not only had possessed WMD, but had used them and confirmed the existence of his programs to the UNSCOM inspectors in 1991. In 2003 following the war, the Iraq Survey Group (ISG) established by the coalition discovered a program to develop long-range missiles. David Kay, who headed the ISG, reported that his team had discovered "dozens of WMD related program activities and significant amounts of equipment that Iraq concealed from the U.N. during the inspections that began in late 2002." Iraqi scientists and senior government figures also told the ISG that Saddam remained firmly committed to acquiring nuclear weapons.[26] And Kay concluded that "Iraq was in clear violation of the terms of Resolution 1441."[27]

Subsequently, Charles A. Duelfer, Kay's successor, told Congress that Iraq possessed dual-use facilities that could have quickly produced biological and chemical weapons. And the final ISG report concluded that while Iraq had not begun a large-scale program for WMD production, Saddam's regime had the clear intent to produce biological, chemical, and nuclear weapons.[28] Consistent with these conclusions, the former head of Saddam's nuclear centrifuge program, Mahdi Obeidi, stated that the Iraqi nuclear program "could have been reinstated at the snap of Saddam Hussein's fingers."[29]

Critics were skeptical about the links between Saddam and terrorism and insisted that using force against Iraq was a distraction in the war on terror. But prior to the war, there had seemed to be reliable indications of these ties. In October 2002, CIA Director George Tenet testified to Congress that the agency had "solid reporting of senior level contacts between Iraq and al-Qaeda going back a decade," that there was evidence of al-Qaeda members in Iraq, including some in Baghdad, and that there was "credible reporting" that Iraq provided training to al-Qaeda members in poisons, gases, and bomb-making.[30] A year after the war, on a more definitive basis, the official 9/11 Commission did confirm that contacts between al-Qaeda and Iraq had taken place, but concluded that these did not constitute "a collaborative operational relationship."[31]

Differences of ideology did not necessarily prevent cooperation between the secular Saddam and the radical Islamist Osama bin Laden. Indeed, notwithstanding bin Laden's description of Iraq's Ba'ath Party leaders as "infidels," he insisted that "it does no harm in these circumstances that the interests of Muslims and socialists crisscross in the fighting against Crusaders."[32] In any case, beyond al-Qaeda there was a history of links between Iraq and terrorist groups. Baghdad had long provided a haven for terrorists, including Abdul Rahman Yassin (who helped make the bomb used in the 1993 attack on the World Trade Center), Abu Abbas (mastermind for the hijacking of the *Achille Lauro* cruise ship in 1985), and the notorious Abu Nidal,[33] the author of terror attacks in some twenty countries throughout Europe and the Middle East and who, perhaps having known too much, was found in November 2002 to have "committed suicide." And yet another example of Iraqi involvement in terrorism – and of Saddam's recklessness – was the attempt to assassinate President George H. W. Bush on his trip to Kuwait in April 1993.

Overall, three decades of Saddam Hussein's conduct demonstrated rash behavior, an obsession with obtaining WMD, including nuclear weapons, and a pattern of discouraging or minimizing accurate information when this conflicted with his preferences. The prospects for containment and deterrence thus were not encouraging. The weight of the evidence suggested that Saddam constituted a dangerous and long-term strategic threat and that it was preferable to act before that threat materialized.

TRADE-OFFS IN THE USE OF FORCE

Policy choices inevitably involve trade-offs, and the negative effects of the use of force in Iraq have been apparent. In Washington, these included budget and military manpower policies that were not as effectively developed for a wartime situation as they might have been. In the Iraq theater, the difficulties included seriously inadequate postwar planning, the chaos that marked the early days and months after the liberation of Baghdad, and flawed operation of the Coalition Provisional Authority that ran Iraq until the transfer of sovereignty at the end of May 2004. These shortcomings, together with the effects of the insurgency, fed a climate of deep suspicion and distrust within Iraq as well as in the wider region and beyond.[34] Though the United States and coalition countries did work diligently to restore essential services, including water, electricity, and sanitation, to levels often equal to or better than those of prewar Iraq, these facilities became targets for the insurgents and the coalition received little credit for the work. The killing of Saddam's much-hated sons, Uday and Qusay, as well as the capture of Saddam himself in December 2003 were welcomed, but had only modest impact on Iraqi public attitudes.

Military occupations are invariably problematic, for both the occupier and those who are occupied, and in Iraq the difficulties were multiplied. The cultural and linguistic chasm between Americans and Iraqis was a source of tension, and the Iraqi population that had endured three decades in what a leading exile had aptly termed the "Republic of Fear"[35] was highly susceptible to rumors and conspiracy theories about alleged transgressions by the occupation authorities. Save for the Kurdish areas (where, thanks to the no-fly zones, the United States and Britain were seen as guarantors of security), the longer the military presence, the more attenuated any gratitude for liberation and the more fraught the relationship between Iraqis and Americans became.

With the restoration of sovereignty to Iraqis, democratization and nation-building pose daunting tasks. Beyond the inherent difficulties of developing a political system encompassing Shiites and Kurds with their long and bitter historical memories of suffering under Sunni domination, there is the problem of national identity for a country whose borders were arbitrarily drawn by British and French diplomats as they divided up the Ottoman Empire more than eight decades ago. Not only is there little positive Iraqi institutional experience on which to draw in crafting a political system, but there is the harsh memory of a regional political environment where the watchword can well be described as "rule or die."[36] In addition, the countries bordering Iraq, especially Syria, Iran, and Saudi Arabia, have ample reasons for not wanting to encourage the establishment of a democratic political system in their midst.

There also are contradictory historical precedents. On the one hand, the American occupation of defeated countries after World War II might suggest models for successful political and social transformations in countries once ruled by brutal and aggressive regimes. But the cultural, geographic, religious, and historical difference between Iraq now and the defeated Germany and Japan of 1945 are enormous and the time available for effecting a transformation far more truncated.[37] Moreover, as Ian Buruma and Avishai Margalit[38] have noted, in citing the case of Napoleon's invasion of Prussia two centuries ago, universalistic values including the rule of law and religious toleration can be defiantly rejected in a nationalistic and nativist reaction against an occupying power.

Yet the human, material, and political costs of the war have to be weighed against the likely consequences of not acting. Those opposed to the use of force implicitly assumed that the Iraqi situation would revert to a more or less benign *status quo ante*. But past experience, as well as the insights of complexity theory, suggest that this kind of presumption was unwarranted.[39] War involved risks, but so did inaction in the face of Saddam's non-compliance and false WMD declarations of December 2002. Saddam had long since expressed his belief in the lack of U.S. staying power and his contempt for the U.N.[40] International failure to enforce the "serious consequences" stipulated in Security Council Resolution 1441 would have emboldened the Iraqi leader. Nor should it be forgotten that had Saddam remained in power, the continued operation of the U.S.-British no-fly zones and the American military presence in Saudi Arabia would have remained subjects of intensifying resentment. Were the sanctions to have collapsed, which was likely given the erosion of support for them, Saddam would have gained access to an unimpeded flow of oil export revenues and been free to resume his weapons programs. Thus there was the prospect of a more dangerous and unrestrained Saddam and ultimately the specter of a wider war when Iraq's actions became impossible to appease or ignore.

Perhaps most seriously of all, on the part of those opposed to the use of force, there was a failure of imagination: a stark unwillingness to conceive of what weapons of mass destruction in the hands of monstrous figures such as a Saddam Hussein or an Osama bin Laden could ultimately do. Given the balance of risk, it was preferable to act decisively rather than wait in the uncertain hope that no major threat would emerge or could be deterred if it did. Thus, in the words of British Prime Minister Tony Blair, a year after the fall of Baghdad:

It is possible...that Saddam would change his ambitions; possible he would develop the WMD but never use it; possible that terrorists would never get their hands on WMD, whether from Iraq or elsewhere. We cannot be certain....But do we want to take the risk?...[M]y judgment then and now is that the risk of this new global terrorism and its interaction with states or organizations or individuals proliferating WMD is one I simply am not prepared to run.... This is not a time to err on the side of caution.[41]

JUDGING AMERICA'S ROLE

The Chinese Communist leader Zhou Enlai, when asked what he thought about the French Revolution of 1789, is said to have replied, "It is too soon to say." A definitive judgment on the American-led ouster of Saddam Hussein's regime should not require such an extended time horizon, but a final verdict is not likely anytime soon. The judgment also depends on the criteria applied,[42] and for that there are at least three separate lenses through which to view Iraq: WMD and terrorism, the future of Iraq and the Middle East, and consequences for American leadership.

First, viewed through the prism of WMD and terrorism, there are reasons to render a positive verdict. Saddam's Iraq is no longer a long-term strategic threat to the region nor to America's allies or interests. Iraq's WMD programs are gone, with the weapons apparently having been removed at Saddam's order as an interim measure and the programs, scientists, and facilities mostly dispersed or destroyed in the war or its aftermath. Even in the worst circumstances, it will be a long time before any successor regime has the capacity and the will to resume a serious WMD effort.

The American-led ouster of Saddam, along with the defeat of the Taliban regime in Afghanistan, has also had a palpable effect on regional proliferation efforts. As a case in point, the Libyan regime of Muammar Qaddafi acted to dismantle its WMD facilities and programs and to open them to U.S., British, and IAEA inspection. Some have claimed that Qaddafi's decision was a result not of Afghanistan and Iraq but of five years of talks with Britain and the United States.[43] However, Qaddafi himself is reported to have told Italian Prime Minister Silvio Berlusconi in September 2003, "I will do whatever the Americans want, because I saw what happened in Iraq, and I was afraid."[44]

Moreover, the sequence of events and the timing of the Libyan decision seem a good deal more than coincidental. Added to this, there are the actions by Pakistan to halt the extensive role of its own scientists and firms in nuclear weapons proliferation. Nuclear proliferation in Iran does, however, remain a very serious potential risk.

In the terror war more broadly, al-Qaeda lost not only its critical operational base in Afghanistan, but also the haven provided to a number of its key operatives by Iraq. Much of the al-Qaeda leadership has been killed or captured, and the remaining figures, though still very dangerous, may be more preoccupied with avoiding capture or attack than with carrying out large-scale operations of their own. On the other hand, the insurgency in Iraq has acted as a magnet for terrorists throughout the region. In addition, the fragmenting of al-Qaeda and related groups represents a serious peril of its own. Local groups operating in loose relationship to al-Qaeda seek to carry out their own terror attacks, as evidently was the case with the Madrid train bombings of March 11, 2004, which killed 191 Spanish commuters.

Second, the implications for Iraq and the region remain to be determined. On the negative side, were Iraq to slip into chaos or civil war, with the coalition dissolving and the United States ultimately abandoning its costly efforts to shape the transition, the regional impact would be very harmful. It would embolden both secular and Islamist rejectionists and make even more distant the prospect of benign transitions in the region, whether toward political liberalization or toward the kind of economic and social transformation called for by Arab reformers themselves. An unstable Iraq could strengthen the most nihilistic and retrograde forces in the region and become a source of extremist mobilization throughout the Arab Middle East.

Opposition from neighboring countries also poses a problem. Syria had supported Saddam's regime until the very end and appears to have sheltered some of its leaders and provided a haven for terrorist militants seeking to enter Iraq. Iran, while welcoming the fall of Ba'athist rule in Baghdad, has undertaken a major covert intervention in Iraq with money and militants, to oppose the kind of change sought by the

United States and moderate Iraqis and to encourage the establishment of a hardline Shiite clerical regime.

In the long run, liberalization and democratization may well be the keys to fundamental change in the region and the ultimate answer to terrorism. Advocates have included not only the Bush administration, but also terrorism experts from the Clinton White House;[45] however, the accomplishment of such change in Iraq and elsewhere continues to face daunting obstacles.

Public opinion studies conducted in Iraq by Arab organizations have shown that a solid majority of the population welcomed the ouster of Saddam and, though worried about personal security and critical of the occupation, was at least cautiously optimistic about the future. Despite a history of repression and violence and the absence of norms of toleration, the balance of ethnic forces within Iraq could conceivably underpin some form of political pluralism. Both the Kurds (some 20 percent of the population) and Shiites (more than 60 percent) would bitterly oppose any effort to reassert Ba'athist Sunni dominance. In turn, a theocratic Shiite state would be resisted not only by Kurds and Sunnis, but also by important Shiite religious leaders who do not want to replicate the Iranian model and by portions of the Shiite population as well. These divisions could lead the Iraqis to create a political system designed to prevent the acquisition of undiluted political power by any one of these communities or by a single individual.

In this light, the successful holding of Iraq's first free elections in January 2005 represented a considerable achievement. The turnout of 8.5 million Iraqi voters, 58 percent of the eligible population and much higher as a percentage of Shiites and Kurds, provided solid evidence that most Iraqis did not either favor a return to Ba'athist rule or support the radical Islamists. The turnout was also noteworthy because it took place in the face of intimidation and death threats against those taking part in the election process. Only in the predominantly Sunni areas did this intimidation succeed. Osama bin Laden had declared, "Anyone who participates in these elections...has committed apostasy against Allah." In turn, Abu Musab al-Zarqawi, the commander of al-Qaeda in Iraq and leader of the jihadist insurgency, had stated that democracy is heresy.[46] As a counterweight and a sign that advocacy for the electoral process and democratization could not be dismissed as an American contrivance, the most senior Shiite cleric in Iran, the Grand Ayatollah Ali al-Sistani, called on his followers to vote and declared that those who would boycott the election were "infidels."[47]

Beyond Iraq, the regimes in Saudi Arabia and Pakistan that had once sought to deflect or even encourage radical Islamism have shifted to more active opposition to the Islamists and increased cooperation with the United States in the war against al-Qaeda and similar movements. The change in policy stems from a realization that the regimes themselves have become targets of these forces.

Less publicized was the fact that many Arab governments quietly collaborated in the war against Saddam. Egypt permitted military overflights and secure naval transport through the Suez Canal, while most of the Gulf states, Jordan, and Saudi Arabia allowed use of critical facilities and bases in the region.[48] And at the time, even Iran was acquiescent, to the extent of indicating that any downed coalition pilots would be returned safely.

Third and finally, there are the broader consequences for American primacy and leadership. Initially, it was expected that a successful campaign to liberate Iraq would cause much of the foreign skepticism to dissipate. However, continuing insurgency in Iraq and the failure to find quantities of WMD stimulated wide distrust of America's action and motives. The WMD controversy also hinders American credibility in the event that an imminent threat emerges in the future, for example, in Iran or North Korea, and to which an immediate response might be required. No matter how compelling the case, there will be those who will refuse to credit the intelligence evidence and the plausibility of Washington's assessment.

Despite acrimonious international debate and political struggles within the U.N. Security Council, the American-led war on terror has elicited extensive cooperation in intelligence, counter-terrorism, information-sharing, and combating money-laundering. For example,

French intelligence and counter-terror cooperation provides a marked contrast to the public opposition voiced by French political leaders. This is a product not only of 9/11, but also because many countries now find themselves targets of Islamist terrorism and – with exceptions – recognize that they cannot avoid the danger by sidestepping the war on terror. As a case in point, shortly after the Madrid bombing, the then European Commission President, Romano Prodi, flatly dismissed a bin Laden offer of a truce if the Europeans would withdraw troops from Muslim countries. In Prodi's words, "How could you possibly react to this statement? There is no possibility of a deal under a terrorist threat."[49]

THE LESSONS OF IRAQ

The Iraq experience can best be understood in terms of the three key premises that underlie this book: a perilous threat environment post-9/11, the inherent limitations of international institutions in facing the most lethal dangers, and – as a consequence – the necessity for the United States to be prepared for self-reliance, preemption, and even prevention when necessary.

First, the harsh realities of dealing with Iraq created imperatives for a more risk acceptant strategic posture, in that the ultimate dangers of inaction seemed to outweigh those of acting. Saddam counted on being free sooner or later to fully resume oil sales and to rebuild his weapons, and the nature of his regime, his record of aggression, and his capability and intent posed a strategic threat. In the aftermath of 9/11 and as murderously evident in the March 11, 2004, Madrid attack, it is preferable to act decisively in advance of lethal dangers rather than count on deterring them or retaliating following a mass casualty attack. In short, 9/11 has altered the balance of risk.

Second, the limits of international institutions were also palpable. Neither the U.N. nor any other international body possessed the will or capability to deal decisively with Iraq. With Resolution 1441, the Security Council had unanimously pronounced Iraq in "material breach" of its obligations and had threatened serious consequences. Renewed inspections under UNMOVIC found that Saddam was not providing the cooperation mandated by the resolution, and even opponents of the use of force, including France and Russia, assumed that Saddam retained substantial quantities of WMD. Yet there is little reason to believe that the Security Council would have been willing or able to support real enforcement, rather than continuing with the status quo. This was not only a matter of political objections by France, Germany, and Russia, but also because these countries sought to entangle the United States in a Gulliver-style web of restraints. Indeed, in a remarkable example of contrived delay and wishful thinking, French Ambassador Dominique de Villepin urged that Iraq pass "legislation" forbidding itself to manufacture prohibited weapons.[50] But further delays would have meant leaving U.S. troops in Saudi Arabia indefinitely – a continuing source of friction and a red flag to bin Laden and the Islamists. And had Saddam's regime remained in place, "vigilant containment" would have required a tighter stranglehold on Iraq and hence more propaganda about starving infants. In addition, maintaining the U.S. and British enforcement of the no-fly zones meant risking the loss of allied aircraft and pilots as well as collateral damage to Iraqi civilians from air attacks against Saddam's military installations.

The U.N.'s own institutions and procedures also proved wanting. For example, from 1996 to 2003, the massive U.N. oil-for-food program became the object of widespread corruption, with Saddam successfully pocketing $4.4 billion in cash, as well as an additional $5.1 billion in illegal revenue from oil smuggled outside the U.N. program.[51] France and Russia had benefited from the oil-for-food arrangements as a lucrative source of contracts – some $3.7 billion in the case of France and $7.3 billion in business for Russia[52] – and both countries were unwilling to support efforts to deal with abuses in the program.

Another institutional vulnerability became tragically apparent when the U.N. did establish a presence in post-Saddam Iraq. In this case, the unwillingness of its officials to take realistic security precautions had lethal consequences when in August 2003 its Baghdad headquarters was hit by a massive suicide truck bomb. The blast not only killed twenty-three people, including one of the U.N.'s best and most accomplished officials, Sergio Vieira de Mello (who might well have become the next Secretary-General), but it caused immediate withdrawal of the U.N. mission.

Third, there was a powerful motivation for the United States to take the initiative in leading a coalition of countries willing to support the use of force. Not surprisingly, the American-led course of action evoked strident criticism. This was inevitable in view of the lack of an unambiguous *casus belli*. As a counterfactual example of this problem, it is possible to imagine a similarly negative international response had the U.S. launched a war against the Taliban regime of Afghanistan before rather than after September 11, 2001.

There are earlier historical cases that illustrate the problem of taking action amid uncertainty and in anticipation of a profound strategic threat rather than waiting. For example, historians examining the events of the 1930s have asked whether, instead of appeasement, an allied military action against Hitler in response to one or another of his transgressions during the mid- to late 1930s would have evoked widespread complaint that he was merely a misunderstood nationalist. In the years after he came to power in 1933, each of the steps Hitler took, including breaking of international agreements, territorial claims, or outright aggression, could be rationalized by those opposed to action as somehow due to German grievances or – as the actions became more blatant – not in themselves sufficient to warrant a major war. Thus if France, Britain, and Russia had taken military action at the time of Hitler's reoccupation of the Rhineland, or his abandonment of the military limitations imposed on Germany after World War I, or his demands on Czechoslovakia in 1938, they would have faced criticism for launching an unnecessary war.

The use of force brings not only great risks but also opportunities. If, despite the costs and dangers, the U.S.-led coalition effort ultimately results in the creation of a sovereign, stable, and democratically inclined (or at least pluralistic) Iraq, this will have a significant positive influence in the wider Arab world and will be a serious blow to Arab and Muslim rejectionist forces. In this regard, it is worth bearing in mind the words of Hisham Kassem, head of the Egyptian Organization for Human Rights, who despite the war and chaos in Iraq, still finds the American intervention a lesser evil:

When you look at the intervention itself, you look at the people who will die as a result. Well, a great many more would have died from sanctions and from Saddam than from any intervention. All those arguments about how you can't bring democracy in on the wings of a B-52 are garbage. The only thing that can bring about a change here is American foreign policy. . . . There was no way we could have done this on our own. We were going nowhere.[53]

In the context of the contemporary Middle East, these are iconoclastic and courageous views. However, they reflect a keener sense of regional history than much more widely heard complaints in the Arab world and Europe, as well as among some American observers whose views may owe more to political partisanship and wishful thinking than to an appreciation of the Middle East's brutal realities.

POSTSCRIPT: WHAT ABOUT ISRAEL?

There remains the question of linkage to the Israeli-Palestinian conflict. In advance of the Iraq War, as well as with regard to the war on terrorism, some critics demanded prior American action to impose a peace settlement in the long and bitter Israeli-Palestinian conflict, insisting that the road to Baghdad led through Jerusalem. (Indeed, this issue was even raised at the time of the American-led war against the Taliban and al-Qaeda in Afghanistan.) Others made the reverse case, in anticipation that the defeat of Saddam (who had been donating up to $25,000 to the families of every Palestinian suicide bomber) would deal a heavy blow to rejectionists and jihadists throughout the region.

In the Arab and Muslim worlds, it is often alleged that the United States is biased in favor of Israel. America is accused of taking action against Iraq while ignoring Israel's nuclear program and the plight of the Palestinians. Moreover, the widespread dissemination of images and allegations via the Internet and satellite television stations, especially Al-Jazeera, serves to inflame public opinion and stimulate anti-Americanism. But to what extent is there a relationship between the Israeli-Palestinian conflict and Iraq?

There can be no doubt that the United States has played an indispensable role in dealing with the Arab-Israeli conflict and that it is the only effective broker or mediator between the two sides. American diplomats and Presidents helped to negotiate cease-fire and disengagement agreements in the successive wars, hosted the Camp David talks of 1977 that led to peace between Israel and Egypt, provided economic aid to the former belligerents, and stationed troops in the Sinai to monitor compliance. Under President Clinton, the United States provided the venue for the signing of the Israeli-Palestinian Oslo Agreement in 1993, acted as indispensable intermediary during the rest of the decade, and led negotiations in the year 2000 that came close to ending the conflict.

Following the collapse of those efforts and the coming to office of the Bush administration in January 2001, there was widespread criticism of the United States for its ostensible inaction. However, the administration repeatedly sought to halt the violence and renew the peace talks through a series of measures, including the Mitchell and Tenet Plans. In June 2002, President Bush took a groundbreaking step by calling for the establishment of an independent Palestinian state within three years, but conditioned this on the Palestinians achieving new leadership not compromised by corruption and terror. In 2003, together with the U.N., E.U., and Russia, a group known as the "Quartet," his administration co-sponsored a new "road map" for peace.

Despite a lesser degree of diplomatic engagement than had been the case in earlier years, there was a fundamental coherence to Bush policies, including the insistence that no progress could be made with Arafat, that Israel had the right to fight terrorism, that Arab neighbors needed to play a constructive role, and that Europeans should use their influence and financial incentives to discourage corruption and authoritarianism. In the meantime the United States would stand ready to facilitate peace once the necessary local conditions began to emerge.

With the death of Arafat, followed by elections in Gaza and the West Bank in January 2005, progress toward deescalating the conflict and establishing a viable peace process seemed to reemerge. The Israel government of Prime Minister Sharon and the Palestinian Authority under President Mahmoud Abbas agreed on a cease-fire and direct negotiations. Egypt and Jordan joined in this effort and returned their ambassadors to Tel Aviv, and Washington made clear its strong support for Israel's disengagement from Gaza and for steps to strengthen the new and relatively pragmatic Palestine leader. Daunting obstacles remained, including ensuring a lasting halt to terrorism, improving the living conditions of Palestinians, and the prospect of difficult final status issues (borders, right of return, settlements, Jerusalem, security). However, after the January 2006 elections gave control of the legislature to Hamas, the peace process again ground to a halt.

Again and again during the past half-century it has been painfully clear that only the United States has the ability to serve as an effective interlocutor between Israel and its Arab adversaries. This is a direct result of not just America's power, but especially its long-standing ties with Israel. Other world actors lack sufficient weight, are seen by Israel as tilting toward their adversaries, or – in the case of the U.N. – so dominated by the weight of the Arab and non-aligned voting blocs in the General Assembly as to be biased against the Jewish state. Any resolution of the Israeli-Palestinian conflict is inconceivable without Washington's leadership. All the same, peace requires that each of the belligerents be prepared for a lasting peace. In assessing the failure of the peace talks that took place in the year 2000, Dennis Ross, America's leading negotiator under three Presidents, later observed that although there was some blame on all sides, the tragic failure had stemmed primarily from Yasir Arafat's ultimate unwillingness to end the conflict.[54]

Although America's role makes it the target of intense criticism within the Arab world, the problems plaguing the region occur largely independent of the Arab-Israeli conflict. The political, economic, and social difficulties of the Middle East would only secondarily be affected by a Palestinian solution. And some of the worst problems would be totally unaffected, for example, ethnic cleansing and murder in the Darfur region of Western Sudan, misrule by the mullahs in Iran, the treatment of women in Saudi Arabia, or the Islamists' obsession with overturning existing regimes and imposing puritanical Muslim rule throughout the region. Insofar as Iraq is concerned, the Israeli-Palestine conflict was irrelevant to Saddam's invasions of Iran (1980) and Kuwait (1990), his regional ambitions, weapons programs, and defiance of the U.N., his use of chemical weapons against Iranians and Kurds, his era of brutal Ba'athist rule, and his murder of at least 400,000 Iraqis.

Indeed, after Saddam's defeat, many Iraqis expressed intense resentment at the silence or even complicity of Arab countries during the long years of his tyranny. A number of Arab voices have been raised in criticism of the way in which the Palestinian issue has been used as a diversion from the real problems of the Arab world. For example, a leading Egyptian intellectual, Abel Monem Said, director of the Al-Ahram Center for Political and Strategic Studies in Cairo, has stated, "Making reform and human rights contingent upon resolving the Palestinian problem confirms what the American neo-cons are saying, that the political regimes harming human rights are using the Palestinian problem in order to divert glances from their own behavior."[55]

For their part, the most important jihadist movements arose for reasons having little to do with Israel. The ideological godfather of modern Islamist holy war, Sayid Qutb, whose ideas later influenced al-Qaeda, spent the years 1948–51 in the United States. There he developed a deep rage against what he saw as American decadence, and he did so well before America and Israel had established their close military, political, and economic relationship. Al-Qaeda itself grew out of the Afghan *mujahadeen* of the late 1980s, which had waged a bitter guerrilla war against the Soviet occupation. Israel was irrelevant to that struggle, and when Osama bin Laden did make the Jewish state a target, he added it opportunistically to an already crowded list, including the American presence in Saudi Arabia and the Gulf, the Russians in Chechnya, India in Kashmir, and the oppression of Muslims in the Balkans. Bin Laden viewed Israel as secondary to America, which he described as the "head of the snake."

In sum, the weakness of the argument connecting the Israeli-Palestinian conflict with Iraq is doubly clear: It sheds light neither on Iraq and wider problems in the region nor on the Palestinian issue itself. First, Saddam's murderous tyranny and the strategic threat that he and his Ba'athist regime posed had nothing to do with the Palestinian problem. And post-Saddam, the Israeli-Palestinian issue is only tangential to the insurgency in Iraq and either of limited importance or largely irrelevant in relation to terrorism, jihadism, instability, authoritarianism, and economic and social stagnation in neighboring countries.

Second, demands for U.S. action to solve the Palestinian problem were pointless while Arafat presided and terrorism continued unabated. The demise of the one and the defeat and abandonment of the other were preconditions for any peace process to resume. Indeed, the road map itself stipulated a definitive halt to terrorism as a necessary precondition. A negotiated settlement requires that the parties be prepared to enter into an agreement to end the conflict, and no amount of pressure would have made a difference until that opportunity emerged. Even then, however, a two-state solution would not mollify the most extreme elements in the region, who are committed to the outright destruction of Israel – something that even Israel's most severe critics in Europe and the United States claim to reject.

6 Asia's American Pacifier

☆ ☆ ☆

The country that would defend Japan at the time of crisis is Japan's only ally, the U.S.

– Japanese Defense Minister Shigeru Ishiba[1]

We are surrounded by big powers – Russia, Japan and China – so the United States must continue to stay for stability and peace in East Asia.

– North Korean leader, Kim Jong Il[2]

Kill! Kill! Kill!

– Chinese spectators shouting at the winning Japanese soccer team after the Asian Cup finals in Beijing[3]

☆☆☆

Parallels between America's role in East Asia and its involvements in Europe might seem far-fetched. Asia's geography and history are enormously different, there is no regional organization in any way comparable to the European Union, the area is not a zone of peace, conflict among its leading states remains a potential risk, and there is nothing remotely resembling NATO as a formal multilateral alliance binding the United States to the region's security and the regional states to one another. Yet, as in Europe, the United States plays a unique stabilizing role in Asia that no other country or organization is capable of playing. Far from being a source of tension or instability, this presence tends to reduce competition among regional powers and to deter armed conflict. Disengagement, as urged by some critics of American primacy, would probably lead to more dangerous competition or power-balancing among the principal countries of Asia as well as to a more unstable security environment and the spread of nuclear weapons. As a consequence, even China acquiesces in America's regional role despite the fact that it is the one country with the long-term potential to emerge as a true major power competitor.

THE UNITED STATES AS AN ASIAN POWER

Since the end of World War II, America has been extensively engaged in Asia. Unlike the pattern in Europe, however, where membership

Table 6.1. *U.S. Military Deployments in Asia*[a]

Location	Army	Air Force	Navy	Marines	Total
Singapore		39	50		89
Japan	1,750	14,700	9,250	17,850	43,550
South Korea	25,000	8,900	420	180	34,500
Guam		2,100	2,300		4,400
Australia		59		31	90
Diego Garcia		901	370		1,271
Thailand		30	10	29	69
Total					83,969

[a] Forces assigned to U.S. Pacific Command (USPACOM). In addition, USPACOM includes the Pacific Fleet, with 140,400 personnel, and forces stationed in Alaska (Army 9,100, Air Force 9,550) and Hawaii (Army 21,300, Air Force 4,600, Navy 7,500, Marines 5,600).

Source: Table based on data from International Institute for Strategic Studies, *The Military Balance: 2004–2005* (London: Oxford University Press, October 2004), p. 31.

in NATO not only commits the United States to the security of all its participants but collectively binds the member states to each other, most of America's Asian commitments take the form of bilateral agreements or informal understandings. This results in what has been termed a "hub and spoke" system in which countries have established important links to the United States, but – apart from loose economic and consultative groupings – they are not formally bound to each other for their security.

Among America's formal bilateral military ties, the most important are with Japan and South Korea. The United States maintains military bases and tens of thousands of troops in both countries. Together with deployments elsewhere in the region, this brings the total East Asian figure to some 84,000 (see Table 6.1). However, the American security role extends far beyond the presence of troops and bases, and it incorporates elements that are political, diplomatic, economic, and even psychological.

For example, in the case of China and Taiwan, an American policy of strategic ambiguity serves to reduce the immediate risk of open conflict. The concept dates from the early 1970s and the Nixon-Kissinger rapprochement with the People's Republic of China (PRC). While it implies that the United States would help to defend Taiwan, the conditions under which it would do so are left unspecified in order to avoid needless antagonism of China, while discouraging Taiwan from actions that might provoke the PRC. And it lessens the temptation for China to invade the island by making clear to the Taiwanese that a move to formal, de jure, independence could negate the implied U.S. security guarantee.

Elsewhere in Asia, the United States finds itself actively involved in important political or security relationships with countries including, among others, the Philippines, Indonesia, Australia, Vietnam, India, and Pakistan. Beyond military and security commitments, the United States takes part in the Asia-Pacific Economic Cooperation Council (APEC), an inter-governmental group of twenty-one member countries from the Americas and Asia that serves as a forum for discussing economic co-operation, trade, and investment and that relies on consensus and non-binding commitments. The United States also participates in the ASEAN Regional Forum (ARF), established for security dialogue among twenty-three countries of the Asia-Pacific region.

Trade and investment relationships with South Korea, Taiwan, and other East Asian counties have expanded rapidly and with Japan and China have reached extraordinary levels. The latter two countries have become the third and fourth largest trading partners of the United States (Canada and Mexico are first and second), and the flood of imports from Asia's two largest economies is reflected in enormous U.S. trade deficits. In 2004, these totaled $147 billion with China and almost $68 billion with Japan.[4] The numbers would seem to suggest a mounting financial problem for the United States, but there are key economic trade-offs. The vast flow of cheap imports from China exerts a strong downward pressure on domestic inflation and provides a competitive stimulus for American businesses. In addition, to stem an increase in the value of their own currencies against the dollar, which would cut into the competitiveness of their exports, Asian countries have purchased huge sums of U.S. dollars on world currency markets and invested these in American equities, real estate, and especially in American treasury securities. Japan maintains a large portion of its financial reserves in U.S. currency; China has acted in a similar fashion; and Asian central banks together hold some $2 trillion in foreign exchange reserves, mainly in U.S. treasury bills and bonds.[5]

Japanese and Chinese policies, along with America's overall size and preponderance, make it easier for the United States to sustain large trade and budget deficits without having to adopt the adjustment measures that countries with such imbalances would normally be required to implement. As a result, the American economy can continue to benefit from historically low interest rates, expansionary fiscal and monetary policies that promote economic growth, and low prices for imported cars, electronics, clothing, and other consumer goods. Yet the huge deficits do create a serious vulnerability as well. A major reversal of policy by China, Japan, and other East Asian countries could trigger a run on the dollar and require painful changes in the domestic economy. However, precisely because they hold such large dollar-denominated balances, these countries do have an incentive not to take precipitous action that would sharply reduce the value of the assets they hold.

Overall, the scale and importance of America's involvement in Asia and especially its security commitments bear comparison with the part it plays in Europe and the Middle East. The characterization of this role as described by Joseph Nye a decade ago remains apt: "Our forward deployed forces in Asia ensure broad regional stability, help deter aggression against our allies, and contribute to the tremendous political and economic advances made by nations of the region."[6] Yet, just as there are important parallels with America's engagement elsewhere, so too there are disputes about this role and demands for radical alterations of it. In essence, the domestic critiques of America's Asian policy are of two kinds.

On the one hand, there are calls for a reduced presence in Asia as part of an overall transformation in American grand strategy. From this perspective, the end of the Cold War removed a shared threat that had caused countries in Europe, the Middle East, and Asia to ally with the United States. Now, however, with the demise of the Soviet Union long since past, the continued commitment of the United States to major regional alliances is often described by critics as anachronistic or at the least a politically and economically costly effort to postpone the inevitable weakening or breakup of existing security arrangements. According to many critics, especially those within the realist tradition, the United States would do well to follow a more discriminating approach of selective engagement,[7] proceed with a more complete disengagement,[8] or move toward a strategy of "offshore balancing."[9] Others see America's preponderance and unipolar role as fleeting and urge adjustments in foreign relationships in order to take this into account.[10] And a prominent China expert sharply criticizes the United States for maintaining what he calls a "global empire" and urges the withdrawal of ground troops from South Korea and military bases from East Asia.[11]

Among some experts on Asia, critiques of the U.S. role are more nuanced and tend to focus on policy changes toward individual countries. For example, in reaction to South Korea's "sunshine policy" of attempted rapprochement with North Korea and shifts in public opinion as a younger generation less sympathetic to the United States comes to the fore, some domestic observers have called for American disengagement from the Korean peninsula.[12] Others see changes in Japan and Korea as well as surging economic strength throughout the region and especially in China as sorely testing the ability of the United States to deal with increasingly independent and successful regional powers.[13]

The flaw of such criticisms, however, is two-fold. First, potential conflicts in the region threaten America's own vital interests, and thus the United States has compelling reasons of its own to remain engaged. Second, most of the important countries in Asia do not seek America's departure from the region, and were this to happen, they would be likely to balance against one another in ways that sharply increase the risk of conflicts and that would adversely affect U.S. interests and allies.[14]

ASIA'S AMERICAN PACIFIER

The countries of Asia are emerging for the first time in modern history as a regional cluster of strong, relatively prosperous and independent states. But will the 21st century see them increasingly engaged in the type of strategic rivalry previously experienced in Europe?[15] In this light, the American presence in Asia significantly mitigates the security dilemmas that would otherwise exist. With its military deployments and a major political and diplomatic presence, the United States provides both deterrence and reassurance. In key respects, and despite obvious differences of geography and history, this resembles America's presence in Europe over the past six decades. There, Europe's "American pacifier"[16] resolved the insecurities that Western Europe's major states had long had vis-à-vis one another. With the United States bound to Europe's security through its deployment of troops and leadership of NATO, and with Germany, France, Italy, Britain, and others securely embedded within the alliance, each of the European powers no longer had to prepare for or seek alliances to ensure their security, especially against a future resurgent Germany whose power had destabilized the continent after 1871 and caused two devastating world wars. In short, the American role largely eliminated the security dilemma for the countries of Western Europe.

In Asia, even more than in Europe, no international organization or institution can offer the kind of reassurance the United States provides nor have a comparable impact in reducing competition among regional powers. Despite the successes of Asian regional bodies in playing larger economic and political roles, no one realistically looks to APEC, ARF, or any other regional actor to cope with major security threats.[17] Moreover, potential conflicts in Asia are at least as dangerous as those in the Middle East and far more so than in Europe. They include the China-Taiwan issue, North Korea's nuclear program and the threat its huge conventional forces pose to South Korea, the nuclear rivalry between India and Pakistan and their conflict over the disputed territory of Kashmir, instability in Pakistan, terrorism within countries such as the Philippines and Indonesia, increasing strains in the relationship between Japan and China, and a series of flashpoints involving China and its other neighbors. It is thus important to consider the major Asian cases individually.

Korea

On the Korean peninsula, in one of the world's most dangerous and most heavily armed regions, the American military commitment has deterred North Korea from seeking to invade the South. Paradoxically, even while they engage in their most important mutual contacts in half a century, the leaders of the two Koreas have called for the United States to remain on the peninsula. In the words of the North Korean leader, Kim Jong Il, as quoted by former South Korean President Kim Dae Jung, "We are surrounded by big powers – Russia, Japan and China – so the United States must continue to stay for stability and peace in East Asia."[18]

At the same time, there are risks that the United States could be drawn into a major military conflict in Korea. Though Pyongyang has at times been willing to negotiate with the United States, its strategy has habitually combined bargaining, deception, and blackmail. Notably, in the case of the October 1994 Agreed Framework, the North agreed to freeze its existing nuclear facilities, and Washington undertook to assist it in obtaining two new proliferation-resistant light water reactors for producing electrical power (mainly financed by South Korea and Japan) and in the interim to provide heavy fuel oil for free. However, within months of signing the agreement – and some seven years before President Bush labeled the regime as part of the "axis of evil" – North Korea began violating its terms by secretly constructing plants for the production of highly enriched uranium. In October 2002, the North privately admitted to U.S. diplomats the existence of this program, and in 2003 it forced the removal of outside inspectors, renounced its signature on the Nuclear Non-Proliferation Treaty, unsealed 8,000 fuel rods and proclaimed that it would reprocess the nuclear material in them, and announced that it possessed nuclear weapons. For more than a decade, North Korea thus has seemed determined both to negotiate for major concessions from the United States and others in the form of aid and security guarantees *and* to continue with its nuclear weapons program.[19]

America faces dangerous choices in dealing with North Korea, but it does not do so in isolation. Because of shared concerns over the North's behavior and the dangers a nuclear North Korea would pose, four strong regional neighbors – China, South Korea, Japan, and Russia – have been inclined to cooperate with the United States in six-party negotiations with Pyongyang. The relationships among these countries and with Washington have been complicated and often difficult, and China has sometimes been unhelpful, but all of them would face adverse security consequences from an unrestrained North Korean nuclear program. Based on past experience it is widely assumed that North Korean weapons and technology would be sold abroad and that a perilous regional nuclear arms race would erupt, with Japan and possibly South Korea going nuclear to deter Pyongyang,[20] China reacting by increasing its own nuclear weapons deployment, India expanding its arsenal in response to China, Pakistan seeking to keep up with India, Iran accelerating its nuclear ambitions, and other countries such as Taiwan attempting to acquire nuclear weapons as well.[21]

The South Korean case also provides evidence of why countries in the region continue to favor the American presence. In December 2002, South Korea elected a new president, Roh Moo-hyun, representing a new generation of democratic, affluent, and educated voters with little or no memory of the Korean War half a century ago. Roh came to office having pledged to deemphasize the long-standing relationship with the United States and to seek closer ties with North Korea. Anti–United States demonstrations in February 2003 seemed to suggest a shift in public sentiment as well. But Roh and his supporters ultimately found themselves closing ranks with America. North Korea's intransigence and its nuclear program provided strong motivation, as did Washington's mid-2003 unveiling of plans for realignment and rebalancing of its forces in Korea and East Asia. In February 2004, in an act that symbolized its solidarity with the United States, the South Korean government agreed to dispatch 3,000 troops to Northern Iraq, and the National Assembly approved the measure by a three-to-one margin.[22] A few months later, in June 2004, when Washington announced that one-third of the 37,000 American troops stationed in Korea would be withdrawn and the remainder repositioned to bases less vulnerable to a sudden North Korean attack across the demilitarized zone, the South Korean President, political leaders, and media responded with concern. Anxious about any sign of a weakened U.S. presence, the Seoul government gained Washington's agreement that the drawdown would take place gradually and would not be completed until 2008.

Reactions to this change in American deployment showed how much the U.S. presence is still desired. The realignment plan provided for a smaller and less intrusive "footprint" and one more appropriate to a democratic South Korean society that had chafed at a conspicuous foreign presence and a large base in the very heart of Seoul. The changes also modernized the foundation for a sustained American regional role by shifting to more flexible force structures with emphasis on high-tech weaponry and long-range precision strikes.

Japan

For Japan, long-standing security commitments by the United States reduce the incentive to acquire its own means of balancing against threats from China and North Korea. The post-9/11 era has actually seen Japan tighten its security relationship with the United States rather than edge away from it. For example, the Japanese defense minister has proclaimed, "The country that would defend Japan at the time of crisis is Japan's only ally, the U.S."[23] In addition, Japanese defense policy guidelines adopted in December 2004 have reaffirmed the security tie with the United States and described the alliance as indispensable.[24] This increased closeness contradicts the predictions of observers who anticipated that the end of the Cold War and the disappearance of the Soviet threat would result in Japan distancing itself from the United States. Instead, Tokyo's reaction is a product of anxiety over both China's growing military power and assertiveness[25] and the dangers posed by North Korea, as evident not only in Pyongyang's nuclear program, but also its August 1998 launch of an intermediate-range ballistic missile over Japanese territory. Additionally, Japan has gradually enhanced its own military capability and moved to spend $1.2 billion per year for a period of five years in order to purchase anti-ballistic missile systems from the United States.[26] In a practical demonstration of its determination to remain close to the United States, the Japanese government supported the Bush administration's use of force in Iraq and in early 2004 took the unprecedented step of sending military personnel to Iraq as part of the coalition effort to stabilize that country.

An American withdrawal from East Asia could very well result in a Japanese decision to build a more robust conventional military capacity and to acquire nuclear weapons – a contingency that Chinese leaders implicitly acknowledge and that has muted their calls for U.S. disengagement. The potential for a Japanese decision to go nuclear is not just theoretical. The country operates a fast-breeder nuclear reactor as part of its civilian nuclear program for producing electricity. Japanese authorities describe the fast breeder program as merely a component of their comprehensive nuclear fuel cycle, but there is another implication. The fast-breeder reactor itself is costly and difficult to maintain and is of dubious economic value.[27] However, the plutonium the reactor produces is not only available as fuel for nuclear reactors, but also has the potential to be used in the manufacture of nuclear weapons. Moreover, there is an additional source of fissile material in the stockpiles of plutonium that have been reprocessed in Britain and France from Japan's used civilian nuclear reactor fuel and then returned to Japan.

China

America's relationship with China is especially complex. From the beginning of rapprochement in the early 1970s and until the late 1980s, the PRC and the United States found themselves in a de facto alliance against the Soviet Union. With the end of the Cold War, and especially in the mid- to late 1990s, China's stance began to change. On the one hand, it welcomed investment, found the United States to be its largest single export market, and sought American support for membership in the World Trade Organization. On the other hand, China's military leaders and strategists increasingly treated the United States as a potential regional adversary while strengthening the PRC's military capacity, and Chinese leaders referred to America's alliances in Asia as "mechanisms of the Cold War." Nuclear proliferation also became a source of tension in the relationship. Since the 1970s, and despite assurances to the contrary, Chinese firms have remained a covert source of nuclear and missile technology for would-be prolif-erators. At different times, the latter have included Pakistan, North Korea, Iran, and possibly others. In addition, intellectual piracy, copy-right protection, and human rights have been perennial areas of dis-pute.

The single most dangerous issue remains that of Taiwan. Though both Washington and Beijing have been careful in avoiding direct con-frontation, there have been occasions in which the scale of risk was clearly evident. For example, as China first began to deploy intercon-tinental ballistic missiles capable of striking the American mainland, a leading Chinese military officer warned in October 1995, "In the end you care more about Los Angeles than you do about Taipei."[28] The statement was uttered near the end of a long argument over Chinese military maneuvers and in a deterrent context. Nonetheless, it car-ried ominous overtones, and in the following year, Beijing's threats to Taiwan and its testing of missiles near Taiwan's two main ports led the Clinton administration to signal American resolve by sending an aircraft carrier task force group through the Taiwan Straits.

Another controversy erupted during the U.S.-led NATO air war aimed at halting Serbia's ethnic cleansing in Kosovo. When in May 1999 an erroneously targeted bomb struck the Chinese embassy in Belgrade, the Chinese media adopted a stridently nationalistic and conspiratorial tone, and students erupted in protest outside the U.S.

Embassy in Beijing. With a PRC leadership transition and the coming to office of the Bush administration, the tension continued. In April 2001, a serious incident took place when a Chinese fighter plane collided with an American surveillance aircraft off the coast of China. The Chinese fighter crashed and the U.S. plane made an emergency landing on China's Hainan Island. After tense days of negotiation, the crew was released and Beijing moved to defuse the crisis. Just three weeks later, President Bush replied to a television interviewer that while he opposed formal independence for Taiwan and believed the issue could be resolved peacefully, in the event of a Chinese attack on Taiwan, the United States had "an obligation to defend the Taiwanese" and to provide "whatever it takes" to help Taiwan defend itself.[29]

These disputes and the heightened rhetoric suggested the emergence of China as a revisionist power and rising regional challenger to the United States. With a population of 1.3 billion people, booming economy, increasingly dominant role in Asia, growing military capacity, and rising self-confidence, China is the one country in the world with the ultimate potential to challenge America's unipolar status, either by itself or in alliance with other countries. However, the PRC has not moved to open antagonism nor has it sought regional allies in a wider effort to do so. The reasons for this are both strategic and economic. A breakdown of relations would seriously damage China's economy, and in any case the PRC remains far behind the United States in military power.

Among its neighbors, the PRC's assertiveness, especially in territorial or border claims, could be counterproductive by motivating them to strengthen their links with the United States. In addition, there is a substantial list of unresolved issues. It includes islands and waters that are nearer to Indonesia and the Philippines than to the Chinese mainland, as well as Beijing's claims to the uninhabited Senkaku/Diaoyutai islands in the East China Sea near Japan. In the past, the PRC also had border disputes that led to military clashes with India (1962), Russia (1969), and Vietnam (1979), though these border issues have more recently been resolved. The Russian border issue was settled in 1994, but with a thinly populated Eastern Siberia and Pacific coast, Moscow still views a dynamic and populous China with anxiety.

Other historical legacies also weigh on contemporary relationships between China and nearby countries. For example, an emerging Korean flirtation with China was disrupted by one such dispute. In recent years, China had became South Korea's largest trading partner, and relations between the Koreans and the United States seemed to grow more tenuous. South Korean students showed increased desire to study Chinese rather than English,[30] and an early 2004 survey of South Korean parliamentarians found 80 percent agreeing that China was their most important economic partner. However, in mid-2004 a controversy erupted over the boundaries of the ancient Koguryo kingdom that had ruled large portions of northeastern China and North Korea between the years 37 B.C. and A.D. 668. Scholars and governmental institutions in China and Korea sharply disagreed about the history and legacy of this ancient kingdom, and the issue quickly galvanized anti-Chinese sentiment throughout South Korea. Newspapers editorialized against Chinese hegemonic ambitions, and legislators' opinion toward China, which had been overwhelming favorable only months earlier, plunged to 6 percent in the midst of this diplomatic crisis.[31]

China's relationship with Japan has been even more vulnerable to rekindled nationalist rivalry. Despite the huge volume of trade and Japan's extensive role in aid, investment, and technology transfer, Beijing has taken steps that not only demonstrate China's growing power but heighten tension between the two countries. The stirring of nationalist sentiment may serve to enhance the regime's support among the Chinese public in an era when Maoist ideology has long since lost any legitimacy, but the foreign policy consequences have been largely counterproductive and have even been felt in Europe, where the lifting of an embargo on arms exports was at least temporarily put aside. The issues have included a confrontational Chinese "anti-secession" law directed at Taiwan, controversy over Japan's bid for a permanent seat on the United Nations Security Council, intensified competition for gas and oil reserves in disputed areas of the East

China Sea, and mass protests over Japanese schoolbooks that seem to downplay the record of Imperial Japan's aggression in East Asia. In April 2005, after Beijing permitted anti-Japanese demonstrations over the textbook issue and Japan's insufficient contrition for its wartime role, the protests quickly escalated, spreading to provincial cities and leading to attacks on Japan's embassy, consulates, and businesses. In response, Beijing reined in the demonstrations and sought to ease the tension with Tokyo.

Despite the muscle flexing directed at Taiwan and Japan, the newer and more highly educated "fourth generation" Chinese Communist Party leadership of Hu Jintao has tended to downplay great power confrontation with the United States in order to continue to pursue development and modernization. China has an enormous stake in American trade and investment, and a serious conflict would have drastic consequences at a time when the country continues to undergo a wrenching transformation of its economy and society. China's trade (exports plus imports) with the United States in 2004 amounted to $179 billion,[32] dwarfing the $20 billion in trade with Russia, and not surprisingly the Chinese have been reluctant to jeopardize their relationship with America. Beijing thus has its own practical reasons for not seeking to challenge the pivotal U.S. role in East Asia and for avoiding major disruptions in its external environment. While it is conceivable that an economically powerful China could ultimately emerge as a revisionist power and seek to challenge the U.S. position of unipolar primacy, it is also possible that China's economic development, social change, integration with the world economy, and own self-interest could facilitate both a liberalizing political transition and sustained cooperative relations with the United States.[33]

Paradoxically, improvement in U.S.-China ties has also been a consequence of the 9/11 terrorist attacks. The Bush administration welcomed Beijing's cooperation in the war on terror, and this enabled China to cooperate in ways that did not make it appear subservient to the superpower. China also found good reasons of its own for cooperation with the United States in facing the problem of North Korea. For its part, Washington supported China in its ongoing conflict with Uigur separatists in Sinjiang province, while downplaying other areas of disagreement, including human rights. Nonetheless, tensions remain evident in other areas, as, for, example, over Iran's nuclear program. China has courted Tehran as an important energy supplier and has opposed American efforts to bring the issue of Iran's nuclear program to the U.N. Security Council.

Vietnam

Also noteworthy is the degree of rapprochement between the United States and Vietnam. Given the bitter history of American intervention in Indochina and the persistence of a communist regime in Hanoi, Vietnam might have been expected to bandwagon with Beijing and others in opposition to the United States. However, the tense relationship between the two Asian neighbors has very deep historical roots. Vietnam revolted against Chinese domination in the year 40, and beginning in 967 had maintained its autonomy for most of the next thousand years, except for the century of French rule prior to 1954. Just four years after Hanoi's 1975 victory in its long war against the United States and South Vietnam, China and Vietnam clashed militarily when the PRC launched an offensive across their mountainous border. It is thus not surprising that Vietnam has chosen to balance against China by establishing an increasingly close relationship with the United States and has even signed a major free trade agreement with Washington.

India

The American regional commitment in Asia also provides reassurance to India vis-à-vis China, with which the memory of a brief but bitter border war in 1962 still lingers. In recent years, India's relations with the United States have improved significantly, and there is no sign of India seeking to join with others in balancing against American primacy. Moreover, as a consequence of 9/11, the United States has become increasingly engaged in South Asia, not only in the war against terrorism but in the effort to dampen conflict between India and Pakistan.

Leaders of India, along with those of Pakistan, have been remarkably explicit in expressing their desire for continuing American engagement in the region. India, which for half a century had emphasized its neutrality yet had done so in ways that typically brought it closer to the Soviet Union than to the United States and which had equipped its military with Soviet weapons, has in recent years clearly tilted toward Washington. As an Indian author has observed, "New Delhi has transacted more political business with Washington in the last four years than in the previous four decades."[34] Moreover, in the aftermath of 9/11 and the successful U.S. military campaign to oust the Taliban regime in Afghanistan, the Indian Foreign Minister observed, "I don't think America can give up its Central Asia presence now,"[35] and he expressed his preference that American forces remain in Pakistan indefinitely in order to stabilize that country. For his part, the Pakistani President, General Pervez Musharraf, made clear his view that U.S. air power should remain in Afghanistan as a coercive force and the key to peace there, adding that "the U.S. presence in the region must remain as long as it is needed."[36]

Indonesia

Here, too, relations have improved in the years since 9/11. Indonesia, with 238 million people, is the largest Muslim country in the world, and the United States has established a credible working relationship with the government of the democratically elected president, Susilo Bambang Yudhoyono, who took office in October 2004. Yudhoyono, a former general who twice received military training in America, is a cautious reformer, and while his relationship with Washington is much more at arm's length than is the case for Pakistan or even India, there has been an improvement in cooperation. The United States has supported Indonesia's efforts to deal with terrorist violence, and American military personnel provided substantial aid in the aftermath of the deadly December 2004 tsunami.

ASIA WITHOUT TEARS

Taken together, these Asian involvements are not without risk, especially vis-à-vis North Korea, China-Taiwan, and the uncertain future
of a nuclear-armed Pakistan. Nonetheless, the American engagement
provides both reassurance and deterrence and thus eases the security dilemmas of the key states there, including countries that are
America's allies but remain suspicious of each other. Given the history
of the region, an American withdrawal would be likely to trigger arms
races and the accelerated proliferation of nuclear weapons. It is thus
no exaggeration to describe the American presence as providing the
"oxygen" crucial for the region's stability and economic prosperity.[37]

The U.S. involvement in Asia benefits not only regional stability but
the national interest and security of the United States itself. And contrary to expectations of those who have called for disengagement or
who have argued that wars in Afghanistan and Iraq would jeopardize
relationships elsewhere, America now encounters a better situation in
Asia than at virtually any time since the end of the Cold War.[38]

Consider each of the major relationships in turn. South Korea has
reaffirmed its security partnership with the United States, even to the
extent of sending troops to Iraq. Japan's ties with America have become
increasingly close. In both its official rhetoric and in its actions, Tokyo
has actively embraced the alliance in a more overt manner than at any
time in the past quarter-century. Japan has increased the activities and
reach of its Self-Defense Forces to take part in peace-keeping operations and has sent troops to Iraq. In doing so it has broken taboos of
long-standing. Tensions between America and China are at their low-
est level in at least a decade, and although the Taiwan issue remains a
potential peril, both Beijing and Washington have sought to reduce the
risk of confrontation. China has joined the World Trade Organization,
opted for economic policies that – at least for the medium term – create
incentives for it not to disrupt its standing with the United States, and
quite clearly accepts or at least tolerates the American role as regional
pacifier. Vietnam and the United States have achieved a remarkable

degree of rapport, especially considering the traumatic experiences of the Vietnam War. India and the United States, after decades in which they were often at odds, are experiencing a close and cordial interaction. The gradual opening of India's economy, the surge in information technology including the outsourcing of services, the part played by a large and dynamic expatriate community in America, and the U.S. ability to act as an intermediary in the conflict over Kashmir have all contributed to this change. American diplomatic intervention was crucial in averting war between India and Pakistan in 2002, and leaders of both countries want the United States to maintain its regional engagement. In the case of Pakistan, despite the potential for very dangerous instability and revelations about that country's role in aiding the nuclear proliferation programs of North Korea, Iran, and Libya, the relationship between Washington and the government of President Musharraf is closer than with any of his recent predecessors. And finally, multilateral cooperation has been increasing through organizations, including the Asia-Pacific Economic Cooperation Council and the ASEAN Regional Forum.

History does not stand still, and a grand strategy that may be well suited to a given set of geopolitical realities can become outdated when those realities change. Dangerous regional flashpoints exist, and the longer term question of China's role as a rising power remains imponderable. However, the balance sheet on American primacy and grand strategy in Asia is positive. By contrast, the most commonly cited strategic alternatives, especially a reduced presence or outright withdrawal, would not only be less effective, but could precipitate more dangerous instability and conflict as well as a regional nuclear arms race. Based on past experience, were these to occur, the United States could very well find itself drawn into the fray under adverse circumstances. For the immediate future, America's role in Asia clearly satisfies the twin criteria of regional stability and national interest.

7 Why They Hate Us and Why They Love Us

☆ ☆ ☆

Let faraway America and its white buildings come crashing down.
– Louis Aragon, 1925[1]

The U.S. has rabies.
– Jean-Paul Sartre, 1953[2]

The U.S. is the greatest danger in the world today to peace.
– President Charles de Gaulle, 1965[3]

Yankee go home but take me with you.
– Jairam Ramesh, 1999[4]

You should know that seeking to kill Americans and Jews everywhere in the world is one of the greatest duties [for Muslims], and the good deed most preferred by Allah, the Exalted....
Osama bin Laden, 2003[5]

May the U.S. Marines finally come.
– *Sueddeutsche Zeitung* (Munich), calling for American intervention in Liberia, 2003[6]

☆☆☆

Foreign reactions to the United States are remarkably contradictory. In large parts of Europe there was a spontaneous outpouring of solidarity with the American people immediately after the 9/11 attacks, and in a widely quoted headline, the elite French newspaper *Le Monde*, normally the exemplar of condescension toward the United States, proclaimed, "We are all Americans now." However, within months, much of the European media and intellectual elites shifted toward fiercely critical attitudes, and opinion polls showed alarming increases in negative views of American policies and of the United States itself. Elsewhere, especially in Arab and Muslim countries and portions of the developing world, pervasive hostility has been widely evident. Yet many of the same people who denounce the United States and demonstrate against the Great Satan find that the lure of an American education or the employment opportunity provided by a green card exerts an immense attraction. They also watch American movies, eat at American-style restaurants, and seek an American-style future for their children. This ambivalence is summed up in the words, "Yankee go home, but take me with you."

A striking example of these contradictions can be found in the case of one of the most influential clerics of Sunni Islam. As tellingly described by Johns Hopkins professor Fouad Ajami, the Qatar-based Sheik Yusuf al-Qaradawi has denounced the United States for "acting like a god on earth" and compared its conquest of Baghdad to the actions of Mongols who in the year 1258 sacked the city and slaughtered its inhabitants. Yet the Sheik, whose views are spread widely via television and a Web site, has sent his daughter to the University of Texas for a graduate degree in biology, his son for a doctorate at the University of Central Florida, and another son for an MBA degree at the American University of Cairo.[7]

Such contrasts are not confined to the Middle East nor are they entirely new. Even among those who expressed strong initial sympathy after 9/11, there has been a rising chorus of criticism, at least among journalists, authors, and opinion leaders, and reactions such as these have left many Americans bewildered and even angered. What accounts for this spectacle of attraction and backlash? Why, despite American efforts to promote democracy and the market economy, to open borders to trade and human interchange, to achieve a remarkably open domestic society that attracts people from every region, race, and religion, and despite periodic military interventions to halt the oppression or slaughter of innocent people in Somalia, Kuwait, Northern Iraq, Bosnia, Kosovo, Afghanistan, and Iraq – all of these, incidentally, Muslim populations – have reactions to America been so polarized and – on September 11 – so deadly? In short, why do they hate us and why do they love us?

To answer this question, I first weigh a number of commonly cited but often flawed explanations for anti-Americanism and then elaborate on the impact that globalization, American primacy, and problems of identity in foreign societies have in shaping these attitudes. I next examine the phenomenon of anti-Americanism in two of its all too common and ugly manifestations: the conspiracy myth and the connection with explicit anti-Semitism. I analyze the way in which this hostility unfolds within different societies and then examine what, if any responsibility the United States itself has for this phenomenon. I conclude by asking whether we are indeed witnessing the emergence of a concerted balancing among key foreign countries in an anti-American coalition to oppose U.S. power and to what extent this represents a real threat to the United States.

EXPLANATIONS OF FOREIGN HOSTILITY

In seeking to understand foreign hostility, critics of the United States at home and abroad have frequently pointed to poverty as the root cause, to U.S. antipathy toward Islam, to support for Israel, to unilateralism, or to indifference to world problems. Yet while seemingly plausible, none of these commonly cited explanations withstands careful scrutiny.

Poverty

Virulent opposition to the United States, including terrorism, does not correlate with poverty. The most thorough study of this subject, by Alan B. Krueger and Jitka Maleckova, concludes that "there is little direct connection between poverty, education and participation in or direct support for terrorism."[8] The authors find that terrorism can be more accurately understood instead as a response to political conditions and long-standing feelings of indignity and frustration. Elsewhere, it has been widely noted that the September 11 hijackers mostly came from middle-class or professional families in Egypt or Saudi Arabia and had gone for advanced education to Europe, where they became progressively more alienated and radicalized.[9] As for the top leadership of al-Qaeda, Osama bin Laden is the son of a billionaire Saudi businessman and his second-in-command, Dr. Ayman al-Zawahiri, who heads the Egyptian "Islamic Jihad" and is al-Qaeda's ideological leader, was born into the Egyptian upper class and trained as a surgeon. A 1988 survey of the literature on terrorism concluded that social background and educational level did not seem to be closely correlated with terrorism, and a subsequent Library of Congress report prepared for the CIA in September 1999 found that terrorists have more than average education.[10] Similar conclusions have been reached about various forms of extremism, including ethnic violence in post–Cold War Germany and suicide terrorism against Israel, as well as in earlier studies of Japanese, German, Irish, Italian, and Turkish terrorists.[11]

Alleged U.S. Antipathy toward Islam

Though this has been repeatedly claimed, especially in Arab and Islamic criticisms of America, the reality is quite different. Both the Clinton and Bush administrations were at pains to differentiate between the mainstream of Islam (which President Bush repeatedly cited as a "religion of peace") and the threat presented by radical Islamists. Remarkably, most of the post–Cold War American military interventions abroad have been to save Muslim populations from starvation, ethnic cleansing, civil war, invasion, and oppression – as large numbers of Kuwaitis, Somalis, Kurds, Bosnians, Kosovars, Iraqi Shiites, and the people of Afghanistan, especially women, can attest. Moreover, the absorptive character of the United States has made it far better than any of the countries of Europe or Asia in accommodating and integrating Muslim immigrants.

American Support of Israel

Prior to September 11, the most deadly terrorist attacks or attempted attacks on American targets took place not during periods of acute Arab-Israeli violence but when the peace process was in full flower. For example, in January 1995, when Israel had turned over control of Gaza and most of the West Bank, including almost all of the local population, to the Palestinian Authority and when optimism about resolution of the conflict was at its peak, al-Qaeda planned to blow up as many as twelve American wide-bodied aircraft over the Pacific in a plot that was interrupted by a chance event in the Philippines.[12] Other attacks, including those against the American embassies in Kenya and Tanzania, also took place while expectations still ran high for a settlement of the conflict. In addition, for half a century, the United States has been the indispensable catalyst and intermediary for almost every one of the negotiations and agreements reached between Israel and its Arab adversaries.

Unilateralism and Indifference to World Problems

The complaint that the United States does not give enough emphasis to multilateral cooperation and that it is too inclined to act unilaterally is widely expressed in Europe and by other moderate critics of the United States. Yet it contains a contradiction stemming from the weakness of most international bodies and their frequent inability to act decisively in the face of urgent and deadly problems. This is evident especially in cases of civil war and ethnic cleansing, where American administrations receive blame both for acting and for failing to act. In the case of the Clinton presidency, vacillation over Bosnia (until mid-1995) and deliberate indifference to genocide in Rwanda brought criticism for lack of leadership. By contrast, the American-led NATO air war to halt ethnic cleansing in Kosovo was criticized for the absence of U.N. Security Council authorization. The proliferation of weapons of mass destruction creates similar dilemmas; however, in the post-9/11 world, the Bush Doctrine has committed the United States to a risk-acceptant strategy of acting to avert threats and doing so with or without the collaboration of other countries. In any case, no foreseeable change in U.S. policies on these issues would be likely to have much impact on al-Qaeda and related terrorist groups nor diminish their lethal hostility toward the United States.

In contrast to the commonly cited explanations above, which place the blame largely on America for sins of omission or commission, the primary causes of antipathy to the U.S. are instead to be found in three major features of the post–Cold War world: globalization, American primacy, and problems of social identity.[13]

Globalization

This feature opens a window to the outside world for those living in traditional or closed societies, and people quickly begin to yearn for the material attractions of modern consumer society. Yet especially in large parts of the developing world, those whose lives have been disrupted by the changes wrought by globalization or who develop an intense loathing of what the modern world represents have frequently focused their rancor on the United States as the embodiment of everything they dislike.

American Primacy

This evokes not only admiration and respect, but also envy and resentment. These reactions become all the more intense because of the unique world role the United States plays. No other country possesses a comparable preponderance across so many dimensions of contemporary life. The very prominence and power of the United States invariably give rise to both admiration and alienation. Though foreign criticism of the United States has been common in reactions to the Bush Doctrine as well as in controversies over the use of force in Iraq and the war on terror, it should not be forgotten that reactions to American power were evident earlier during the (more multilateral) years of the Clinton administration. For example, criticisms of American *"hyperpuissance"* (hyperpower) by the then Foreign Minister of France, Hubert Vedrine, were widely publicized and much discussed in the late 1990s.

Identity

In large areas of the developing world and especially among Arab and some Muslim countries, tensions over individual and national identity have become aggravated by the failure of many societies to cope with modernization and by frustration at corrupt and authoritarian rulers. Blocked from access to power and unable to oppose these regimes effectively, educated professional and middle-class dissidents may turn to Islamic radicalism and transfer their rage to the United States as the foremost symbol of materialism and Western values. These sources of attraction and repulsion are deep-seated, and hostility directed against the United States is shaped less by what the United States actually does than by what it represents. This helps to explain why America has received so little credit for its military interventions to protect or save Muslims. A sense of perceived humiliation serves to intensify this sentiment. Celebration and relief at the downfall of the lethal Ba'athist regime in Iraq and the capture of Saddam Hussein were tempered by an awareness that the Iraqis themselves, let alone the Arab world, had been incapable of such actions. In the words of the leading Palestinian newspaper, *Al-Quds*, "The saddest and most disgraceful thing in all things concerning Saddam Hussein and his regime is that toppling the regime and arresting its head was carried out by the occupation forces. Had this operation been carried out by the Iraqis, it would not have caused such a flurry of emotions. Thus, every [incident] of resistance in Iraq will constitute a natural response to the desecration of Iraqi sovereignty."[14]

In their world view the leaders of al-Qaeda and of the extremist Salafi brand of radical Islam see the West itself as the font of evil. The United States as the most powerful Western country thus becomes the greatest target. Al-Qaeda leaders have expressed deep resentments not only in regard to the demise of the Islamic Caliphate in 1924 (in which the collapse of the Ottoman Empire ended a temporal and spiritual authority that had existed in some form since the 7th century), but also encompassing the loss of Al-Andalus – that is, the Andalusia region of Spain that had been controlled by the Moors from the year 711 until 1492. As for more contemporary sources of confrontation, Osama bin Laden's "Declaration of War against the Americans," issued in 1996, describes the stationing of U.S. troops on the Arabian peninsula as the greatest aggression against Muslims since the death of the Prophet in 632.[15]

STYLES OF ANTI-AMERICANISM

One of the remarkable features of contemporary anti-Americanism is the extent to which it has become bound up with delusional and conspiratorial notions about the world.[16] The spread of HIV/AIDS in Africa, financial crises, and even the September 11 attack on the

Pentagon and World Trade Center have been variously attributed to the CIA and American leaders, and not infrequently to Israel and the Mossad.[17] Such views are notoriously widespread in the Arab world, and a Gallup poll carried out in nine Islamic countries found that 61 percent of those surveyed believed Muslims had nothing to do with the attacks of September 11, 2001.[18] Beliefs such as these are not confined to the Middle East. For example, in Germany, some 20 percent of the population embraces conspiracy theories about 9/11.[19] In France, a best-selling book, *9/11: The Big Lie*,[20] by one Thierry Meyssan, makes allegations as lunatic as anything circulating in the Middle East, asserting that the Bush administration actually orchestrated the attack on its own Pentagon with a truck bomb and that it was not really struck by an airplane. Instead, the author claims the explosion was contrived as a rationale for attacks on Afghanistan and Iraq.

In the Middle East especially, there have been virulent and demonic expressions of anti-American hatred. These can be found in the language of radical Islamist clerics, media commentators, and intellectuals and in everyday discourse. Opinion polls show large sectors of the population subscribing to wildly irrational beliefs, with intermingled elements of conspiracy theory, superhuman powers, devilish attributes, and even sexual paranoia. In the words, for example, of a thirty-year-old Iraqi mechanic, Omar Habib, living in the Sunni town of Fallujah where fighting between Saddam Hussein loyalists and American troops had occurred, "I hate the Americans. I know they are wearing glasses that allow them to see through women's clothes. Even if they are only looking for weapons, they see the women naked."[21]

In addition, America's extraordinary preponderance has caused some foreign observers to credit it with virtual omnipotence and omniscience. As a result, there is a tendency to assume that major world events occur only because they have been willed by the Washington superpower. In the Middle East and especially among intellectuals and the media, this attribution of all-encompassing power fosters a pervasive evasion of responsibility for the shortcomings of domestic societies and provides a means by which local resentments can be redirected against the Great Satan.

Outside the region, the exaggerated responsibility attributed to the United States frequently fails to take into account the preferences and actions of local and regional forces. Among European critics of American Middle East policy, there was a widely voiced claim that the United State had armed Saddam Hussein and was responsible for keeping him in power. In fact, Saddam had risen to power through the ranks of the Ba'ath Party as a ruthless thug and enforcer with close ties to key party leaders. Iraq's forces were equipped mainly with Soviet heavy weapons and with more advanced aircraft and missiles from France, while the American contribution consisted largely of battlefield intelligence supplied during the mid-1980s at a time when the Reagan administration feared Iraq might lose its war with Iran, thus allowing Khomeini's brand of Islamic radicalism and violent antipathy to the United States to sweep the Persian Gulf region.

By contrast, a more nuanced conspiracy theory has been widely disseminated within the United States. It purports to explain how the foreign policy of the world's most powerful country has been captured by a sinister and hitherto little-known cabal. According to this view, during George W. Bush's first term, a small band of neo-conservative (read, "Jewish") defense intellectuals, led by "mastermind" and Deputy Secretary of Defense Paul Wolfowitz,[22] took advantage of the 9/11 terrorist attack to put their ideas over on an ignorant, inexperienced, and "easily manipulated" President,[23] his "elderly figurehead" Defense Secretary,[24] and the "dutiful servant of power" who was our Secretary of State.[25] Thus empowered, this neo-conservative conspiracy, "a product of the influential Jewish American faction of the Trotskyist movement of the 30s and 40s"[26] and its own "fanatic" and "totalitarian morality"[27] fomented war with Iraq – not in the interest of the United States but in the service of Israel's Likud government.[28]

This sinister mythology is worthy of the Iraqi Information Minister, Muhammed Saeed al-Sahaf, who became notorious for telling Western journalists not to believe their own eyes as American tanks rolled into

view just across the Tigris River. Not surprisingly, extreme versions circulate in the Arab world. For example, a prominent Saudi professor
from King Faysal University, Dr. Umaya Jalahma, speaking at a pres-
tigious think-tank of the Arab League, claimed that the U.S. attack on
Iraq was actually timed to coincide with the Jewish holiday of Purim.[29]
But the neo-con conspiracy notion has been especially conspicuous in
writing by leftist authors in the pages of American and British journals such as *The Nation*, the *Washington Monthly*, the *London Review
of Books*, the *New Statesman*, and the *International Herald Tribune*,
as well as in the arguments of paleo-conservatives such as Patrick
Buchanan and his magazine, the *American Conservative*.

Arguments about the invasion of Iraq asserted, for example, that
"the war has put Jews in the showcase as never before. Its primary
intellectual architects – Paul Wolfowitz, Richard Perle, and Douglas
Feith – are all Jewish neo-conservatives. So, too, are many of its
prominent media cheerleaders, including William Kristol, Charles
Krauthammer and Marty Peretz. Joe Lieberman, the nation's most
conspicuous Jewish politician has been an avid booster." The same
author adds, "Then there's the 'Jews control the media' problem." And,
"What's more, many of these same Jews joined Rumsfeld and Cheney
in underselling the difficulty of the war, in what may have been a deliberate ruse designed to embroil America in a broad military conflagra-
tion that would help smite Israel's enemies."[30]

Other writers use language that is more overtly conspiratorial. In an
essay appearing in the *New Statesman* (London) and in Salon.com,[31]
after dismissing Robert Kagan as a "neoconservative propagandist,"
Michel Lind confided the "alarming" truth that "the foreign policy
of the world's only global power is being made by a small clique."
They are "neoconservative defense intellectuals," among whom he
cites Wolfowitz, Feith, Cheney's chief of Staff Lewis Libby, John Bolton
at the State Department, and Elliott Abrams on the National Security Council. Most of these, we are told, have their roots on the left
and are "products of the largely Jewish-American Trotskyist movement of the 1930s and 1940s which morphed into anti-communist

liberalism" and now into a kind of "militaristic and imperial right with no precedents in American culture or political history." Lind complained that in their "odd bursts of ideological enthusiasm for 'democracy,'" they "call their revolutionary ideology 'Wilsonianism,' ... but it is really Trotsky's theory of the permanent revolution mingled with the far-right Likud strain of Zionism." Along with the Kristol-led *Weekly Standard* and allies such as Vice President Cheney, these "neo-cons took advantage of Bush's ignorance and inexperience."[32] Lind's speculation that the President may not even be aware of what this cabal has foisted on him embodies the hallmarks of conspiratorial reasoning. In his words, "It is not clear that George W. fully understands the grand strategy that Wolfowitz and other aides are unfolding. He seems genuinely to believe that there was an imminent threat to the U.S. from Saddam Hussein's 'weapons of mass destruction,' something the leading neo-cons say in public but are far too intelligent to believe themselves."

These themes are echoed at the opposite end of the political spectrum, in the *American Conservative*, where the embattled remnants of an old isolationist and reactionary conservatism can be found. The magazine's editor, Patrick Buchanan, targets the neo-conservatives, alleging that they have hijacked the conservative movement and that they seek "to conscript American blood to make the world safe for Israel."[33]

European and Middle Eastern versions of the neo-con conspiracy theory are typically more virulent. But even in its less fevered forms, this narrative simply does not provide a coherent analysis of American foreign policy. Especially among the more extreme versions, there are conspicuous manifestations of anti-Semitism: claims that a small, all-powerful, but little-known group or "cabal" of Jewish masterminds is secretly manipulating policy, that they have dual loyalty to a foreign power, that this cabal combines ideological opposites (right-wingers with a Trotskyist legacy), thus echoing classic anti-Semitic tropes linking Jews to both international capitalism and international communism, that our official leaders are too ignorant, weak, or naïve to grasp what is happening, that the foreign policy on which our country is embarked runs counter to or is even subversive of American national interest, and that if readers paid close attention to what the author is saying, they would share the same sense of alarm.

A dispassionate dissection of the neo-con conspiracy arguments is not difficult to undertake. For one thing, the Bush administration has included relatively few Jews in senior policy positions and none among the principal foreign policy decision makers. Indeed, the President, Vice President Richard Cheney, Secretary of Defense Donald Rumsfeld, Condoleezza Rice (National Security Advisor and then Secretary of State), former Secretary of State Colin Powell, and Stephen Hadley (National Security Advisor in the second Bush term) all are Protestants. And Prime Minister Tony Blair, the most influential non-American, is also Protestant. But even identifying policymakers in this way carries the insidious implication that religious affiliation by itself is all-controlling. In reality, Americans of all persuasions exhibited deep differences about foreign policy and war with Iraq. Prior to the war, public opinion polls consistently showed Jews about as divided as the public at large or even slightly less in favor of the war, and Jewish intellectual and political figures could be found in both pro- and anti-war camps. For example, Nobel laureate Elie Wiesel, professor and author Eliot Cohen of the Johns Hopkins University, and Senator Joseph Lieberman supported the President, while opposition came in various forms from the radically anti-American Noam Chomsky, the moderate-left philosopher Michael Walzer, liberal Democratic Senator Carl Levin, and a bevy of leftist Berkeley and New York intellectuals (Rabbi Michael Lerner, the editor of *Tikkun* magazine; Norman Mailer; Eric Foner, professor of history at Columbia University; and many others).

More to the point, Cheney, Rumsfeld, Powell, and Rice were experienced and strong-willed foreign policymakers, and the conspiracy theory fails utterly to take into account their own assessments of American grand strategy in the aftermath of the September 11 terror attacks. The theory also wrongly presumes that Bush himself was an empty vessel, a latter-day equivalent of Czarina Alexandra, some-how fallen under the influence of Wolfowitz/Rasputin. Condescension toward Bush was a hallmark of liberal and leftist discourse after the bitterly disputed November 2000 presidential election, and during his early years in office there can be few readers of this book who had not heard conversations about the President that did not begin with off-hand dismissals of him as "stupid," a "cowboy," or worse.[34] An extreme version of this thinking and the demonization of Bush can be found in the musings of the late Edward Said, as quoted in *Al-Ahram Weekly*: "In fact, I and others are convinced that Bush will try to negate the 2004 elections: we're dealing with a putschist, conspiratorial, paranoid deviation that's very anti-democratic."[35] This kind of disparagement left critics ill-prepared to think analytically about the foreign policy imperatives facing the United States after 9/11.

Regardless of one's overall view of Bush policies, the Bush Doctrine, as expressed in the President's January 2002 State of the Union address ("The United States of America will not permit the world's most dangerous regimes to threaten us with the world's most destructive weapons"), and the National Security Strategy Document of September 20, 2002, set out an ambitious grand strategy in response to the combined perils of terrorism and weapons of mass destruction. Reactions to the doctrine were mixed. Some foreign policy analysts were critical, especially about the idea of preemption and the declared policy of preventing the rise of any hostile great power competitor,[36] while others provided a more positive assessment.[37] But the doctrine was certainly not concealed from the public, and the President and his foreign policy team spoke repeatedly about its elements and implications. And while Bush's major foreign policy speeches, for example, in February 2003 to the American Enterprise Institute and in November 2003 to the National Endowment for Democracy, in which he articulated a vision for a free and democratic Middle East, were sometimes criticized as excessively Wilsonian, their key themes echo those found in the widely circulated *Arab Development Report*, written by a group of Arab economists for the U.N. Development Program, which decried

Arab world deficits in regard to freedom, access to knowledge, and the role of women.

Partisanship aside, the President had shown himself to be decisive and able to weigh competing advice from his top officials before deciding how to act. In August 2002, for example, he sided with Secretary of State Powell over the advice of Rumsfeld, Wolfowitz, and Cheney in opting to seek a U.N. Security Council resolution on Iraq. Powell's own February 5, 2003, speech to the Security Council provided a dramatic presentation of the administration's case against Iraq, and well before the outbreak of the war, Powell made clear his view that the use of force had become unavoidable. Conspiracy theorists were also naïve in expressing anxieties that the Defense Department was frequently at odds with the State Department or National Security Council about policy. Political scientists and historians have long described policy-making as an "invitation to struggle," and Richard Neustadt's classic work, *Presidential Power*, characterized the ultimate resource of the presidency as the power to persuade. Franklin Roosevelt deliberately played off his advisers against one another, the Nixon presidency saw Henry Kissinger successfully undercut Secretary of State Rogers, and the Carter and Reagan presidencies were conspicuous for the struggles between their national security advisers and secretaries of state. In short, far from being anomalous, competing views among presidential foreign policy advisers are typical of most administrations.

Nor was Bush's support for Israel somehow a sign of manipulation. From the time of Harry Truman's decision to recognize the Jewish state in May 1948, through Kennedy's arms sales, the Nixon administration's support during the October 1973 War, and the close U.S.-Israeli relationships during the Reagan and Clinton presidencies, American policy has generally been much more supportive of Israel than of its Arab adversaries. American public opinion has consistency favored Israel over the Palestinians by wide margins, and on the eve of the Iraq war, a Gallup poll put this margin at more than four to one (58% versus 13%). Indeed, the strongest source of support for Israel comes from within Bush's own Republican base, especially among Christian conservatives, and in addition to his own inclinations, as a politically adroit President he has repeatedly shown the determination not to alienate his political base.

Ultimately, the neo-con conspiracy theory, whether in its sophisticated versions or in its more venomous articulations, misinterprets as a policy coup a reasoned shift in grand strategy that the Bush administration adopted in responding to an entirely new and ominous form of external threat. Whether that strategy and its component parts proves to be as enduring as the containment doctrine during the Cold War remains to be seen. But to characterize it in conspiratorial terms not only is a failure to weigh policy choices on their merits but represents a detour into the fever swamps of political delusion.

ANTI-AMERICANISM: POLLS, PRECEDENTS, AND POLITICS

Anti-Americanism is both a contentious and elusive subject. Its causes, content, and effects need to be understood not only in themselves but in relationship to fluctuating attitudes in previous eras. There are pitfalls in seeking to draw easy conclusions from current data, not least because public opinion can vary sharply in reaction to major events and because expressions of views about America can have very different underlying causes. In addition, the views of intellectual elites often differ from broader popular sentiment. Attitudes toward U.S. policies can appear to be less favorable than toward America itself, and the way in which questions are posed can readily shade the results. Moreover, generalizations can distort reality. For example, the widely expressed notion that "Europe" opposed the American-led war in Iraq in effect seizes on the strong opposition of French and German leaders and publics but overlooks the fact that the governments of four of the six largest European countries (Britain, Spain, Italy, and Poland) plus Japan initially supported the use of force and that fifteen of the nineteen NATO governments did so as well – even while public opinion was mostly more critical. On the other hand, opinion elsewhere and especially in the Islamic world has become increasingly hostile.

Attitudes toward America and Americans are very much subject to change and – as noted above – are often contradictory. Based on widely publicized polls and media reports, the United States would seem to be facing a wave of hostile foreign opinion. The largest and one of the most widely cited studies, the Pew Global Attitudes Project,[38] depicted global support for American ideals but mounting European criticism of U.S. foreign policy as well as intensifying hostility in the Muslim world. The Pew studies and other reports have attributed these attitudes to the policies of the Bush administration and its unilateralist foreign policy.[39] To be sure, compared with the immediate aftermath of 9/11 in which there was an outpouring of sympathy for the United States, foreign opinion did become steadily more critical during the months prior to the start of the Iraq War in March 2003.

The problem with focusing on such studies, however, lies in assumptions about the novelty of the attitudes they identify while failing to take into account past waves of anti-American sentiment, as expressed both in public opinion and among intellectual elites. It is also useful to take into account the volatility of opinion in reaction to new events. For example, the seemingly relentless climate of European anti-Americanism appeared to ease after the Bush reelection of November 2004, followed by the death of Arafat and the holding of free elections in Afghanistan, the Palestinian territories, and Iraq.

This does not mean that negative attitudes and their potential effects should be ignored, but it does require that the phenomenon be put in context. For example, during the 1950s, opinion polls in Europe indicated that between one-third and one-half of the population of Italy, France, and Britain wanted to remain neutral in the Cold War.[40] Numerous other examples abound: Vice President Richard Nixon was met with mobs of rock-throwing demonstrators in Latin America in the late 1950s; large crowds demonstrated against the United States during the Cuban Missile Crisis of October 1962; the Vietnam War was the subject of growing and sometimes violent protests during the late 1960s and early 1970s; the deployment of intermediate-range missiles in Western Europe in the early 1980s was met with massive demonstrations; and the 1991 U.S.-led military campaign (supported by a U.N. Security Council vote) to expel Iraqi forces from Kuwait was nonetheless the focus of large anti-war rallies.

National leaders and the media can shape opinion quite dramatically. For example, prior to the war in Iraq, French President Jacques Chirac took the lead in condemning the American-led effort, and most of the French media took a similar stance. By contrast, British Prime Minister Tony Blair's own convictions led him to a powerful moral condemnation of Saddam Hussein's regime and the strategic threat that it posed. By the time the war began, British opinion, once heavily anti-war, had shifted so that a plurality of the public then supported the American-led coalition effort. Elsewhere, in much of the Muslim Middle East and including American allies such as Egypt, Saudi Arabia, and Jordan, public opinion was shaped by a torrent of anti-American invective dispensed by newspapers, radio, and television and by many of the most influential clerics. Only a small minority of commentators spoke publicly against such views, and they did so at their own peril.

Criticism of the United States among foreign intellectuals has a long and tangled history. In the 1950s, the distinguished French historical sociologist, Raymond Aron, while himself sometimes disagreeing with American policies, lamented the views of his fellow intellectuals who were all too often "merciless toward the failings of the democracies but ready to tolerate the worst crimes as long as they are committed in the name of the proper doctrines."[41] Indeed, the origins of this hostility can be found as far back as late 18th- and early 19th-century France, in the condemnations by Jacobin and Napoleonic regimes of British and American society as materialistic, treacherous, and plutocratic.[42] A similar strand was evident in the complaints of aristocratic and reactionary critics, such as the French poet Arthur de Gobineau, who in 1840 said about bourgeois society, "Money has killed everything."[43]

In post–World War I Europe, reactionary and fascist thinkers linked Britain and the United States to the Jews – who were vilified in contradictory terms as both capitalists and Bolsheviks.[44] And writing in the 1930s, the French proto-fascist author and propagandist Charles Maurras depicted American society and the Jews as driven by the requirements of the market at the cost of higher human concerns, in a realm of rootless cosmopolitanism and amoral capitalism.[45]

In the world of the 21st century, anti-Americanism derives from a combination of sources. Especially among European intellectuals, critics, and commentators, but also in other parts of the world, the collapse of communism deprived the political left of a coherent doctrine. In its place, resentments against American power, primacy, and cultural dominance, combined with a greatly diminished ability to influence world events, provide a strong impetus and one that is driven by far more than reactions to specific American policies. Though the overall phenomenon can be found elsewhere, it takes its purist form in France, where as Ajami notes, "Envy of U.S. power and of the United States' universalism is the ruling passion of French intellectual life. It is not 'mostly Bush' that turned France against the U.S."[46]

These impulses are by no means unique to France, and they are common elsewhere among the "chattering classes." In Britain, for example, the sentiments of left-of-center journalists and intellectuals find frequent expression in the broadcasts of the BBC. The use of words such as "terrorism" was frowned on, and after the December 2003 capture of Saddam Hussein, BBC reporters were instructed not to describe him as the former dictator of Iraq, but as that country's former President. A critical assessment of BBC coverage of the Iraq war later observed:

[P]eople who work in its news and current-affairs departments mostly share a soft-left world-view: instinctive statism, cordial anti-capitalism, and bien-pensant liberal internationalism. Its reporters' prejudices, allied to the modern preference in broadcast news for context and commentary (that is, opinion) over facts, yielded a generally pessimistic account of British and American actions before, during and after the war.[47]

Similarly, an analysis of previous reporting on Iraq by five of the major French newspapers found that they had systematically underplayed the murderous brutality of the Ba'athist regime.[48] The pattern was far more evident among Arab newspapers and TV, but it also affected other Western journalists reporting from Iraq.

Ultimately, the frenzy of these resentments virtually defies caricature. Consider some of the more widely noted expressions by prominent European figures:

Unelected in 2000, the Washington regime of George W. Bush is now totalitarian, captured by a clique whose fanaticism and ambitions of "endless war" and "full spectrum dominance" are a matter of record. . . . Bush's State of the Union speech last night was reminiscent of that other great moment in 1938 when Hitler called his generals together and told them: "I must have war." He then had it. (John Pilger, the *Daily Mirror* (London))[49]

My anti-Americanism has become almost uncontrollable. It has possessed me, like a disease. It rises up in my throat like acid reflux, that fashionable American sickness. I now loathe the United States and what it has done to Iraq and the rest of the helpless world. (Margaret Drabble in *The Daily Telegraph* (London))[50]

Dear President Bush, I'm sure you'll be having a nice little tea party with your fellow war criminal, Tony Blair. Please wash the cucumber sandwiches down with a glass of blood, with my compliments. (Harold Pinter, playwright (London))[51]

[T]he leaders of . . . [the United States] are, quite simply, psychopaths. (François de Bernard in *Liberation* (Paris))[52]

I hate Americans and everything American. (Mikis Theodorakis, Greek composer)[53]

U.S. RESPONSIBILITY?

Anti-Americanism stems from deep and complex sources and cannot be understood simply in terms of the defects or virtues of U.S. foreign policy at any given moment. To be sure, policies and the way they are conducted do have an effect. Expressions of anti-Americanism have a history of more than two centuries, but the sentiment does wax and wane, and there is evidence that it has increased in reaction to American policies in Iraq and in reaction to the real or imagined actions of the Bush administration.

Here it is useful to differentiate between broad policies and the implementation of those policies. In response to the profound threat represented by the terrorist attacks of 9/11 and the potentially catastrophic danger of terrorism coupled with weapons of mass destruction, a grand strategy that responds to such threats and that does so in a world where international institutions do not provide a timely means of response makes sense. A U.S. strategy that protects American national interests but lacks the endorsement of the U.N. Security Council will inevitably draw criticism, as will the use of force even when it is essential. Yet policies have not always been carried out in a manner that optimizes foreign support. Some of this problem has to do with diplomatic skill, some with rhetoric, some with more subtle judgments about where to draw the line between seeking broader international backing without compromising security and effectiveness. Foreign policy decision-making, especially on the most urgent questions, inevitably involves decisions based on partial information and thus amid uncertainty. Nonetheless, while disparaging descriptions of "old" versus "new" Europe or casual reference to Germany in the same sentence with Libya and Cuba may be understandable reactions to the position taken by governments in Paris and Berlin, they are costly luxuries.

The Bush Doctrine, as noted in chapter 2, embodied not just primacy and preemption, but also multilateralism and the promotion of democracy. To some extent, the doctrine itself is more multilateral than the actual policies of the Bush administration. Indeed, the entire document, including its most benign features, was bound to incur criticism, although such critiques are often contradictory. For example, U.S. policies are bemoaned for both the self-interested exercise of raw power and for the idealistic aim of spreading democracy in the Middle East. Moreover, genuine policy trade-offs are inevitable. In the aftermath of 9/11, even a hypothetical Gore-Lieberman administration would have been likely to make overtures to the authoritarian regime in Uzbekistan in order to secure the uses of air bases essential for the conduct of the war in Afghanistan. And in view of the importance of good relations with Russia, China, and India, no government in Washington, would have accorded priority to the cause of self-determination for Chechens, Uiguhrs or Kashmiris.

More skillful diplomacy can be useful. For example, rather than flatly repudiating the Kyoto Treaty on global warming (an agreement that even some of its most ardent European backers may be unable to implement[54]), the Bush administration could instead have proclaimed that the aim of reducing CO_2 emissions was laudable even if the agreement as written posed intractable problems, but that the United States would look with favor on working with others to seek ways of protecting the common heritage of mankind on land, sea, and air. Such an approach might ultimately have produced acceptable agreements, but even if tangible results were not forthcoming, the international diplomatic and political costs would have been lessened. There are, after all, precedents to which not only the United States, but France, Britain, Russia, and China subscribe. For example, the Nuclear Non-Proliferation Treaty (NPT) contains language holding the signatories, including the five formal nuclear weapons states, to the ultimate objective of eliminating nuclear weapons altogether. None of the five has pursued this goal, yet all accept and even emphasize the NPT as part of the effort to combat nuclear proliferation.

Additional tools of foreign policy would also be of use in gaining wider support abroad while serving American interests and values. Some of these include programs that brought real advantages during the Cold War but were later deemphasized or abandoned altogether. American public diplomacy has suffered badly in recent years, and as a result the case for the United States and its policies and values has not been effectively presented abroad. The 1997 decision to dismantle the United States Information Agency (USIA) and fold its remaining functions into the State Department was taken as an economy measure and because the USIA was seen as a Cold War relic. Yet this bipartisan Clinton-era decision, based in part on the notion that the

USIA's programs, cultural exchanges, American Centers, and libraries were obsolete in the era of the information revolution with its satellite broadcasts, cable TV, the Internet, and the idea of a world global village, has proven to be a serious mistake.

Time and again, during the past half-century, the formative experience of visiting or studying in the United States and encountering American culture here or abroad has left its mark on foreign politicians, journalists, teachers, and businesspeople. To be sure, these consequences were not uniformly positive – as evident in the case of French President Jacques Chirac or that of Sayyid Qutb, the founding father of the Egyptian Muslim Brotherhood's most extreme wing and whose ideas later influenced al-Qaeda. Nonetheless, the long-term cumulative effects of public diplomacy programs were enormous, and their virtual demise has left an information vacuum. The perceptions of foreigners, especially those of a younger generation seeking knowledge about the United States, are increasingly shaped by the hostile or disparaging views provided by local actors or the diatribes of domestic American critics such as Michael Moore, whose books have become best-sellers in the German language and whose views go largely unrebutted. Similarly, foreign broadcasting both in English and in local languages, through the Voice of America, Radio Free Europe, Radio Liberty, and newer media directed at Iran and Iraq, has been stagnant or – in the case of the older operations aimed at Eastern Europe and the former Soviet Union – starved of resources.

DANGER OR DISTRACTION?

Does anti-Americanism signal a hostile world? Does it suggest that lesser powers are beginning to ally with one another in order to counterbalance American power? Those most alarmed by the evidence of anti-Americanism often argue that this is the case. They, along with a number of prominent international relations scholars in the realist tradition, warn of a growing mood of foreign hostility, the dangers it may pose to the United States, and the likelihood that American primacy will be short-lived. As evidence they cite adverse foreign public opinion, opposition in the United Nations Security Council where France led a bloc of countries in opposition to U.S. Iraq policy, and the expansion and deepening of the European Union as a counterweight to the United States.[55]

Yet in contrast to these arguments, there is considerable evidence that balancing is not really taking place.[56] Elsewhere, Gerard Alexander and Keir Lieber have shown that despite claims to the contrary, there is little sign of true balancing behavior.[57] Notwithstanding foreign and domestic rhetoric, the two key indicators of balancing – serious increases in foreign defense spending and the creation of new alliances – are not evident. Moreover, it is not at all clear that acrimonious criticism of the United States, especially by allies, is of an order of magnitude greater than during the periodic disputes that erupted during the past half-century.

As additional evidence that real counterbalancing has not been taking place, consider the following.

– The countries of the European Union have not sought to align themselves against the United States, because of both overwhelming American preponderance and their own long-term military weakness as well as the persistence of national sovereignty in obstructing the development of a true European common defense. Though France and Germany did oppose the Bush administration's Iraq policy, and European public opinion was generally hostile to the use of force, the majority of European governments expressed support.[58] And subsequent to the Bush reelection and then the holding of free elections in Iraq, the intensity of opposition visibly lessened.

– The American-led coalition war in Iraq to oust the regime of Saddam Hussein and the violent insurgency that has followed did not trigger an upheaval in the region nor lead to the collapse of friendly governments. To the contrary, countries such as Libya and Syria have acted to reduce confrontation.

- Far from disintegrating, as Kenneth Waltz, the foremost realist critic, had predicted,[59] the American-led NATO alliance has continued to flourish and expand because it provides a hedge against potential long-term security dangers in a world of nation-states. Its existence offers a security umbrella for the countries of Europe,[60] and its assumption of responsibility for peacekeeping in Afghanistan provides clear evidence of its ongoing importance.[61]
- Among major powers elsewhere, China, India, and Russia have not sought to join with each other or with France and Germany in balancing against the United States. Instead, each has taken steps to maintain viable and even close working relationships with Washington.
- Allied countries in other regions, including Japan, South Korea, and Australia, have maintained or enhanced cooperation with the United States, as have the Philippines, Indonesia, Thailand, and (more tenuously) Pakistan.

In sum, despite a very real climate of critical opinion abroad, assessments of actual counterbalancing appear quite overstated. Steven Peter Rosen has noted, "A surprising number of major states are not now engaging in the self-help that Waltz says is at the heart of interstate relations, but are relying instead on the United States for their security."[62] Note that one explanation may be that while Waltz's well-known description of the organizing principle of the international system as anarchical is widely accepted by other realist authors and even a number of more practical neo-liberals, there are elements of the current international system that, because of American primacy, are actually hierarchical. Authors such as Rosen and John Owen have made this point, and Owen has explained the absence of counterbalancing against the United States by Europe and Japan by observing that the extent to which a state counterbalances against American is a function of how liberal that state is, because liberal states treat each other benignly. Insight into why this is the case can be found in the remark of a leading member of the governing German Social Democratic Party. In his words, "There are a lot of people who don't like the American policeman, but they are happy there is one."[63]

While American policies do matter, it is nonetheless a mistake to assume that these are chiefly responsible for triggering hostility. The United States needs to be actively engaged abroad, both in its own national interest and because its role remains indispensable for coping with common world problems. This role can be carried out to a greater or lesser extent in cooperation with others, and with more or less diplomatic skill. But even the best of circumstances and the most carefully crafted policies will not prevent others from blaming America for problems whose causes lie elsewhere.

In sum, in a world where the demand for "global governance" greatly exceeds the supply, and in which the U.S. role remains central to the management of security threats as well as to resolving problems of cooperation, both attraction and backlash are unavoidable. America can do more to win "hearts and minds," but the beginning of wisdom is to know that these contradictory reactions and an accompanying anti-Americanism are inevitable as long as the United States exists as a great power.

8 Postscript: The Future of the American Era

This book has presented a forthright argument about the dangers of the post-9/11 era, the fundamental limitations of international institutions, and the importance of American power and primacy in confronting the world's most lethal threats. In the time since this work was first published, events in the Middle East and elsewhere have continued to unfold in ways that impact American foreign policy and national security. The following pages provide a reassessment in light of more recent developments and examine whether the basic assumptions of this volume need to be reconsidered as a consequence of the insurgency in Iraq, Iran's nuclear program and intensifying regional challenges, the ambiguous results of elections in the Middle East, an increasingly assertive China, a dramatic surge in oil prices, and the domestic reaction to such events.

The chapter begins with a balance sheet of achievements and setbacks for American grand strategy and foreign policy. It then goes on to revisit the most prominently suggested alternative strategies and finds that these remain unlikely to provide better guidelines for the future. A reexamination finds that the threats facing America in the "Long War" against radical Islamist terrorism have not fundamentally changed, nor have the United Nations or other international institutions become more capable of coping with the most deadly perils. In addition, despite warnings by domestic policy critics, other countries have not banded together to counterbalance against the United States, and some, including much of Europe as well as India and Japan, have actually moved toward closer cooperation with Washington. The analysis then turns to a series of "What about?" questions concerning not only Iraq and Iran, but Israel and the Palestinians, Europe, and China. Any number of challenges will continue to face policymakers, and potential pitfalls exist both at home and abroad, but American primacy is likely to persist along with the key elements of the strategy that sustains it.

I. ACHIEVEMENTS AND SETBACKS

American involvement in World War II, beginning with the Japanese attack on Pearl Harbor on December 7, 1941, and ending with Japan's surrender on September 1, 1945, lasted slightly less than three years and nine months. By contrast, in the lengthening period since 9/11, the United States has already been engaged longer than in World War II and finds itself in a conflict with no end in sight. During the intervening years, foreign policy, grand strategy, and especially the Iraq War and its conduct have become the subject of intense and often partisan dispute. The debate ranges across fundamental issues: doctrines of preemptive and preventive war, the nature – or even existence – of lethal threats to national security, international legitimacy, "over-stretch" of the armed forces, and the credibility, performance, and competence of American foreign policymakers.

On the positive side of the ledger, American policy has caused or contributed to major accomplishments.[1] These include the defeat of Afghanistan's Taliban regime in a quick and stunning military campaign with few U.S. casualties, the emergence of a plausible and broad-based Afghan government under President Hamid Karzai, the denial of state support and sanctuary to al-Qaeda and other Jihadist groups in Afghanistan and Iraq, and the disruption and destruction of important parts of the al-Qaeda network. In Iraq, Saddam Hussein's tyrannical regime has been removed and with it the long-term strategic and regional threat that it had posed, and a real, though weak and embattled, Iraqi government based on free elections and a representative parliament has been formed. Developments elsewhere include the thwarting of Islamist ambitions to depose existing governments and – with the possible exception of Somalia – take control of any additional Middle Eastern state, the abandonment by Libya of its WMD programs, and exposure and dismantling of the A.Q. Kahn nuclear black market ring in Pakistan. On a wider geographic scale, anti-terrorism coordination with European and many Asian governments remains solid, political tensions with France and Germany have eased, relations with India and Japan have become increasingly close and cooperative, and the United States (to date) has not experienced a major post-9/11 terror attack on its territory.

Positive achievements must, of course, be weighed against negative events. These include an intensifying guerrilla war in Eastern and Southeastern Afghanistan where, despite the commitment of thousands of combat troops from the United States and from the European allies under a NATO mandate, the Taliban and al-Qaeda insurgency shows no sign of abating. In Iraq, a successful military campaign that in just three weeks resulted in the capture of Baghdad on April 9, 2003, and the collapse of Saddam's regime was followed by a "post-conflict" phase for which American and coalition forces were poorly prepared. The dangers for which preparations had been made – a humanitarian crisis, a flood of refugees, destruction of oil facilities – did not occur, but measures to provide immediate security and stabilization were dangerously inadequate or even altogether absent. In retrospect, troop levels were too low, Ba'athist forces were able to escape to the Sunni triangle where they went unchallenged during the first weeks of the occupation, the Coalition Provisional Authority was haphazardly organized and supported, there were long delays in handing over functions to Iraqis who could have taken charge of them, and only belatedly was sufficient attention given to rebuilding the Iraqi military and security services.[2] The administration's de-emphasis and even suspicion of nation-building thus contributed to a period of chaos and insecurity after the fall of Baghdad and was followed by a bloody conflict, which became a focal point for radical opposition to the

United States. Despite the fact that support for insurgency and jihadist terrorism is largely concentrated in the Sunni community, suicide terrorism, ethnic killings, militia violence, and governmental failure have become severe obstacles to stabilization.

Beyond Iraq, the proliferation peril from North Korea continues and Iran, along with its Hezbollah client in Lebanon, poses a potentially explosive problem. There are also long-term concerns about the stability of a nuclear Pakistan and the continuing threat from radical jihadist groups not only in the Middle East, but in Asia, Europe, Africa, and even the Western Hemisphere. In addition, despite an initially promising "Arab spring," the road to political liberalization and democratization in the Middle East faces daunting obstacles. Then there is the persistent climate of anti-Americanism in parts of Europe and much of the Middle East. Finally, there remains uncertainty as to whether the absence of a major terrorist attack against the United States since 9/11 will only be temporary.

II. ALTERNATIVE STRATEGIES

This balance sheet of progress and dangers provides a portent for the longer term. The global war against Islamist terrorism could well prove to be as protracted as the Cold War, and it will involve a struggle waged as much or more with political, economic, ideological, cultural, and covert means as in conventional battle. In the lengthening shadow of the Iraqi insurgency and the array of other tenacious policy problems, fundamental alternatives to prevailing American grand strategy have been increasingly asserted by domestic critics. The two that merit the most attention have been proposed by realists and by liberal internationalists.

Realists
Realist scholars and former policymakers contend that the use of force in Iraq was a serious mistake, that Saddam could have been contained and deterred even if he acquired nuclear weapons, and that

the same logic applies in dealing with the Iran of President Mahmoud Ahmadinejad. The Iraq issue has been considered in Chapters 1 and 5, but several additional points deserve mention. One is that insofar as threats emanate from terrorist groups rather than states, the relevance of Cold War containment precepts is likely to be limited. As John Lewis Gaddis has observed, containment required that the adversary share one's own sense of risk, that the threat be state-centric and that it be based on "the existence of identifiable regimes that could manage the running of risks short of war,"rather than movements seeking martyrdom.[3] In addition, Gaddis has noted that containment took place during an era when the United States did not possess the preponderance of power that it later possessed after the collapse of the Soviet Union. Hence America does not face the kind of constraints on its power that existed during the Cold War.

Limitations on the applicability of the Cold War containment model also apply to certain state-centric threats. The logic of containment and deterrence rests on the assumption that one's adversary is a value-maximizing rational actor. In the case of Saddam, there was already ample evidence that he was both reckless and a gambler, and that he brutally discouraged information and advice that differed from his own preferences. New corroboration of these traits has come to light in a U.S. Joint Forces Command (USJFCOM) study based on debriefings of Saddam's top generals and officials and from official documents captured in the 2003 Iraq war.[4] In the words of a senior Iraqi official, "Directly disagreeing with Saddam Hussein's ideas was unforgivable. It would be suicide."[5] Indeed, Saddam decided to invade Iran in 1980 without consulting any of his advisors and made the decision to invade Kuwait in 1990 after talking only with his son-in-law.[6] And he forbade his own intelligence apparatus from giving him analysis about America because he claimed a superior understanding of the Americans and their behavior.[7] Saddam so intimidated his generals that they dared not tell him the truth about the rapid pace of the American offensive in March–April 2003, and even as U.S. tanks entered Baghdad, Saddam believed his forces were prevailing and was still ordering the movement of Iraqi units that no longer existed.[8] Even months after the fall of Baghdad, senior Iraqi officers who had been captured by the coalition forces continued to believe it possible that Iraq still possessed a hidden WMD capability.[9]

Moreover, at the time the Bush administration took the decision to invade Iraq, there were other factors at work that undercut realist arguments against the use of force. One of these was that containment of Iraq was not in a state of stable equilibrium that could be maintained indefinitely. Instead, there was every reason to anticipate that the entire sanctions regime and international constraints upon Saddam would continue to unravel and that eventually the Iraqi president would be able to free himself of these restraints, resume the unhindered export of oil, regain the full use of oil revenues, rebuild his military forces and WMD programs, and renew his ambition to dominate the region. Both David Kay and Charles Duelfer, successive heads of the CIA's Iraq Survey Group after the 2003 war, concluded that Saddam planned to resume production of WMD and delivery systems once the UN sanctions ended.[10] Moreover, as the official 9/11 Commission concluded, Iraq did have a relationship with al-Qaeda, even though not an operational tie. Captured Iraqi documents indicate that beginning in 1998, Saddam's Fedayeen military units began training "Arab volunteers from Egypt, Palestine, Jordan, the Gulf, and Syria." Prior to summer 2002, most of these volunteers appeared to have returned home after completion of training.[11] And the USJFCOM study, partially declassified in February 2006, found that in the period leading up to the March 2003 U.S.-led invasion, the Iraqi president had preparations underway for ambitious foreign terrorist operations under the code name "Blessed July" to be undertaken by the Saddam Fedayeen,* presumably in July 2003:

The Saddam Fedayeen also took part in the regime's domestic terrorism operations and planned for attacks throughout Europe and the Middle

---

* The Saddam Fedayeen were a permanent state security force created in 1994.

East. In a document dated May 1999, Saddam's older son, Uday, ordered preparations for "special operations, assassinations, and bombings, for the centers and traitor symbols in London, Iran and the self-ruled areas [Kurdistan]." Preparations for "Blessed July," a regime-directed wave of "martyrdom" operations against targets in the West, were well under way at the time of the coalition invasion.[12]

Although dealing with the Islamic Republic of Iran under President Ahmadinejad poses its own severe challenges, here too Washington policymakers face a potential adversary whose conduct is hardly characteristic of a value-maximizing rational actor. The Iranian president's apocalyptic beliefs offer little cause for comfort. He has stated that Israel should be "wiped off the map,"[13] called into question the Holocaust and the events of 9/11, and views himself as in a position to hasten the arrival of the 12th Imam, which in millenarian terms is expected to follow the equivalent of Armageddon. In addition, Iran's supreme leader, Ayatollah Ali Khamenei, has told President Omar al-Bashir of Sudan that Iran is prepared to share nuclear technology with other countries.[14]

Liberal Internationalists

Advocates of multilateralism have been relentless critics of what they consider America's unilateralism (if not imperialism) and its failure to cooperate effectively with international institutions as well as to meet the requirements of international law and legitimacy.[†] The lengthening period of the war on terror, international criticism of the use of force in Iraq, the inability to find stockpiles of WMD there, and the human and material costs of the Iraq war have led many liberal internationalists to intensify their criticisms and urge a change of course in policy and strategy. Yet in doing so, they tend to overlook both the degree to which Washington has sought to work with other countries and organizations in the post-9/11 world and the extent to which previous

---

[†] The core liberal internationalist arguments and their weaknesses are addressed in Chapter 2.

administrations were prepared to act unilaterally when they deemed it necessary to do so.

In the case of the Bush administration, there was an early emphasis on forming "coalitions of the willing." The October 2002 National Security Strategy included a strong commitment to multilateralism, and the administration was at pains to attract as much support as possible for its decision to use force against Saddam. The administration also engaged in multiple forms of international collaboration and in doing so it engaged in six-party talks with North Korea; deferred to Germany, Britain, and France (the EU-3) in negotiations with Iran over its nuclear program and violations of the Nuclear Nonproliferation Treaty (NPT); ardently sought Security Council approval to sanction Iran; promoted the multilateral Proliferation Security Initiative aimed at strengthening the NPT; and with France co-sponsored UN Security Council Resolution 1559 calling for the withdrawal of Syrian forces from Lebanon and Resolution 1701 to achieve a ceasefire between Israel and Hezbollah and to establish a more effective UN force in Southern Lebanon. It also launched a major international initiative with a large increment in funding to fight AIDS, increased its support for economic development through the Millennium Challenge account, sought reform of the United Nations, established the Asia Pacific Partnership for Clean Development and Climate (with key regional powers including China, India, Japan, and Australia), agreed on a NATO role in Afghanistan, took part in the Doha round on world trade liberalization, and secured a UN mandate – UNSC Resolutions 1546 (2004) and 1637 (2005) – for the U.S.-led multinational force in Iraq.[15]

The multilateralist argument not only overstates the degree of unilateralism that has characterized American policy since 9/11, but it oversimplifies earlier history. The United States led the creation of key international and regional institutions after the end of World War II and accepted certain costs in doing so. Yet when circumstances demanded, successive presidents were prepared to take decisive action without the prerequisite of securing international agreement. Truman dispatched air and navy forces to Korea without awaiting the subsequent UN endorsement; Eisenhower sent troops to Lebanon in 1958; Kennedy was prepared to use force in the Cuban missile crisis of October 1962; and he, Johnson, and Nixon committed the U.S. military to a long guerilla war in Indochina. President Reagan used force in Grenada, as did his successor in Panama, and even at the end of the Cold War (as noted in Chapter 3), George H. W. Bush pushed through German unification over the reluctance of France and Britain.

During the Clinton administration, punitive air and cruise missile strikes were launched against the Libyan and Iraqi regimes. Indeed, in February 1998, Clinton warned against the likely consequences should the United States fail to act against Saddam: "What if he fails to comply and we fail to act, or we take some ambiguous third route. . . . [Saddam] will conclude the international community has lost its will. He will then conclude that he can go right on and do more to rebuild an arsenal of devastating destruction. . . . And some day, some way, I guarantee you, he'll use the arsenal."[16] And, though the 1999 intervention in Kosovo was carried out in agreement with the NATO countries, it lacked UN Security Council authorization at a time when Russia would have vetoed such a resolution.

Recent evidence about the incapacity of international institutions can hardly be reassuring either. For example, in the case of Iran, as a result of Russian and Chinese reluctance, based in part on commercial interests as well as Russian geopolitical resentments, the IAEA and the UN Security Council have been handicapped in their ability to take effective measures despite Iran's flagrant breach of the NPT and nearly two decades of covert nuclear development. As if to underscore the United Nations' own limitations, in April 2006, at the very time Iran was under intense scrutiny for its defiance of these institutions, it was nonetheless selected to serve as one of three countries to co-chair the UN Conference on Disarmament. This case is reminiscent of the UN Human Rights Commission's dreary history, in which notorious human rights violators were repeatedly elected to serve on the Commission and made a travesty of its operations.

The UN Security Council effort to halt the fighting after the July–August 2006 Israeli-Hezbollah war in Southern Lebanon and to stabilize the situation there by restoring Lebanese sovereignty, overseeing the withdrawal of Israeli troops, and monitoring the disarmament of Hezbollah took place against a record of more than a quarter century of failure to implement such resolutions. As long ago as 1978, UNSC Resolution 425 had called for the extension of Lebanese government authority to the south, and a similar Resolution (520) was passed in 1982, but UNIFIL proved ineffective – or worse – during the intervening years. More recently, in September 2004, Resolution 1559 had called for "disbanding and disarmament" of all Lebanese and non-Lebanese militias, the withdrawal of all foreign forces, including Iran's Revolutionary Guards, and the "extension of control of the government of Lebanon over all Lebanese territory."

In the face of these efforts, Syria and Iran continued to violate Lebanese sovereignty and to arm Hezbollah with an extensive arsenal of modern weapons including some 13,000 short-, medium- and long-range missiles. Not only was the Security Council resolution flaunted, but the UN's demarcation of the "blue line," Lebanon's southern border after Israel withdrew in 2000, was ignored by Hezbollah, whose actions subsequently triggered the 2006 war. Resolution 1701 (August 2006) reiterated the previous resolutions and called for a cease-fire, the extension of Lebanese government authority over all its territory, full respect for the blue line, the removal of all weapons and forces not those of the Lebanese government from the area south of the Litani river, and for this area not to be used for hostile operations (i.e., attacks against Israel). In addition, it authorized a considerably stronger UNIFIL mission with up to 15,000 troops. Nonetheless, it did not actually mandate UNIFIL to enforce the disarmament of Hezbollah, and absent an effective performance by the UN force and the Lebanese government, it would not be surprising if yet another war erupts in the immediate region.

Nor is the situation in Darfur a cause for optimism. There the United Nations' efforts to halt ethnic cleansing and killing have been modest at best, the forces dispatched by the African Union have been far too

small in number for the vast area of Western Sudan, and the government of Sudan has cynically obstructed international efforts. Even the
noncontroversial effort to feed more than six million people in Sudan
through the UN World Food Program (WFP) has had tenuous support. Thus in April 2006, the WFP reported that it would be forced to
cut food rations in half because it had received only $238 million, less
than a third of its annual appeal of $746 million for Sudan. Notably, the
United States was by far the largest donor, having given $188 million
for that program.[17]

More broadly with reference to America's own relationship to international institutions, it can be argued that the more ambitious liberal
internationalists are actually seeking something that goes well beyond
multilateralism as it has been practiced by the United States since
1945. Advocates in some cases are seeking policy outcomes that they
have been unable to attain within the American political process and
are appealing to forms of global governance and international law in
order to reverse these outcomes. Moreover, insisting that the use of
force must not be undertaken without UN Security Council authorization means ceding a veto power over American security to other
governments, including those such as China and Russia that conspicuously lack genuine democratic institutions of their own. Ironically,
as Stephen G. Brooks and William C. Wohlforth have noted, many
of those advocating greater global governance would readily embrace
"unilateral" U.S. actions that fit their policy preferences – as was evident in the Kosovo case.[18] And the appeal to international law in the
absence of formal treaty obligations seems to be, as Peter Berkowitz
has observed, an effort to circumvent not only American law, but the
constitution and majority will as expressed through representative
government.[19]

III. EXISTENTIAL THREATS AND THE "LONG WAR"

The "Long War" is a term coined by the Pentagon, whose February
2006 *Quadrennial Defense Review* begins with the words, "The United
States is a nation engaged in what will be a long war." The preface

continues with a succinct description of a protracted global war against terrorists who are seeking to use weapons of mass destruction against the United States and other free societies:

Since the attacks of September 11, 2001, our Nation has fought a global war against violent extremists who use terrorism as their weapon of choice, and who seek to destroy our free way of life. Our enemies seek weapons of mass destruction and, if they are successful, will likely attempt to use them in their conflict with free people everywhere. Currently, the struggle is centered in Iraq and Afghanistan, but we will need to be prepared and to arrange to successfully defend our Nation and its interests around the globe for years to come.[20]

Nothing that has occurred in the years since 9/11 serves to alter the fundamental reality of this long-term threat. Whether or not the 2002 National Security Strategy might have employed less controversial terminology about primacy and preemption, or the Bush administration's diplomacy might have been more nuanced, does not detract from this fact. Bin Laden, Zawahiri, and other radical Jihadist figures have reiterated their desire to acquire nuclear weapons and have continued to speak in apocalyptic terms about the destruction they hope to see inflicted upon the United States.

Emphasis on the lethality of this threat was also evident in the assessment by the bipartisan chairmen of the 9/11 Commission, former Democratic Congressman Lee Hamilton of Indiana and former New Jersey governor Republican Tom Kean. In an interview marking the conclusion of their efforts they warned that, in their view, there will be another attack and that the United States had not yet taken the necessary steps advocated by the Commission.[21] Moreover, a survey published in June 2005 by the Senate Foreign Relations Committee under the direction of its chairman, Senator Richard Lugar, found that non-proliferation and nuclear security experts assigned an average probability of 29% to the likelihood of a nuclear attack against a city or other target somewhere in the world during the next ten years, a 40% risk of a radiological attack, and a 70% estimate of the combined risk of some kind of WMD being used (nuclear, biological, chemical, radiological).[22] Thus it is appropriate that the March 2006 National Security Strategy (NSS) restates the logic of preemption:

If necessary, however, under long-standing principles of self defense, we do not rule out the use of force before attacks occur, even if uncertainty remains as to the time and place of the enemy's attack. When the consequences of an attack with WMD are potentially so devastating, we cannot afford to stand idly by as grave dangers materialize. This is the principle and logic of preemption. The place of preemption in our national security strategy remains the same.[23]

At the same time, the 2006 NSS offers an updating and restatement of ideas from the earlier document. It opens by reaffirming support for democracy:

It is the policy of the United States to seek and support democratic movements and institutions in every nation and culture, with the ultimate goal of ending tyranny in our world. In the world today, the fundamental character of regimes matters as much as the distribution of power among them. This is the best way to provide enduring security for the American people.[24]

Notably, by making the argument that the "character of regimes" is key to their international behavior this statement reflects a belief shared with liberal internationalists. This puts them at odds with realists who by and large tend to "black box" the state, in that they view a country's foreign conduct as largely determined by the international distribution of power rather than by the nature of its political system.

The 2006 NSS makes another key point that was also part of the 2002 document, but which is often overlooked by critics, in restating the importance of cooperation with allies:

To succeed in our own efforts, we need the support and concerted action of friends and allies. We must join with others to deny the terrorists what they need to survive: safe haven, financial support, and the support and protection that certain nation-states historically have given them.

Our strong preference and common practice is to address proliferation
concerns through international diplomacy, in concert with key allies and
regional partners.[25]

The sources of the radical Islamist threat remain deep-seated and (as
assessed in Chapter 4) are a product of the impact of globalization and
modernity upon societies that suffer from the severe deficits (identified
in the 2002 UN Arab Human Development Report) in political liberty,
knowledge and information, and the treatment of women. A sense of
resentment, humiliation, and deracination also can be found among
Muslims who have unsuccessfully sought to find their place in modern Europe and whose frustration and rage cause them to embrace
the apocalyptic nihilism of the Jihadists. As a leading French scholar
of radical Islamism wrote after the London underground bombings
of July 7, 2005, "The Western-based Islamic terrorists are a lost generation, unmoored from traditional societies and cultures, frustrated
by a Western society that does not meet their expectations. And their
vision of a global ummah[††] is both a mirror of and a revenge against
the globalization that has made them what they are."[26] Not only the
London bombers, but the 9/11 attackers and the Madrid bombers of
"3/11" (March 11, 2004) embody this phenomenon.

The ideology and resentment that fuels radical Islamist terrorism
is not likely to disappear any time soon, and it is wishful thinking to
suggest that those who express deadly and even apocalyptic threats
don't really mean what they say or that they can be mollified with
some well-timed concession to their demands. The historian Jeffrey
Herf has coined the term *reactionary modernism* to describe the ideas
propagated by Nazi ideologists who claimed that Germany could har-
ness modern technology while spurning the values of political modernity stemming from the Enlightenment and western liberalism, and
he points to parallels between contemporary radical Islamists and
the ideology of European fascism.[27] In turn, Paul Berman has shown

---

[††] The *ummah* is the global community of Muslim believers.

that Islamists share many of the European totalitarians' ideas including rejection of freedom of the individual, of liberal democracy, and of women's rights, and that they similarly propound virulent anti-Semitism, anti-Americanism, and fanatical conspiracy theories.[28] As Herf observes, "The result, in recent years, as it was in Europe's 1940s, is a legitimation of murder directed against defenseless civilians."[29]

IV. BEYOND IRAQ AND IRAN

For a period of several years, Iraq has become so much the focus of attention that arguments about strategy and foreign policy sometimes seem to be extrapolating from this singular case. More recently, Iran has moved closer to the center of attention as well, not only in relation to Iraq but because of the grave issues posed by its quest for nuclear weapons, by the fanatical beliefs of its president, and by its role in arming and funding Hezbollah. But Iraq and Iran do not by any means exhaust the list of key items on the foreign policy agenda, and three others deserve renewed attention here: Israel, Europe, and China.

What about Israel and the Palestinians?

A postscript to Chapter 4 sought to dispel simplistic notions linking the Israeli-Palestinian conflict with the war in Iraq. However, from the fever swamps of the far right and far left, from conspiracy theorists, and sometimes from less extreme observers, efforts continue to connect the wellsprings of Jihadist terrorism and the Iraqi insurgency to Israel. The more delusional interpretations have been widely disseminated in the Arab and Muslim worlds. They include the notorious Czarist forgery, *The Protocols of the Elders of Zion*, with televised dramatizations of that classic anti-Semitic screed and of the notorious blood libel. Despite the utter irrationality of this propaganda, it shows no signs of disappearing. While much of the material conveys lethal messages, urging the destruction of Israel, the killing of Jews wherever they are, and not infrequently the destruction of America and of its allies, the level of discourse can at times become quite farcical, as in a recent Iranian broadcast identifying the old and still popular "Tom and Jerry" cartoon series as a Jewish conspiracy.[30] In another example, the Syrian government daily *Al Thawra* published an article suggesting that Israel had created the avian flu virus in order to damage "genes carried only by Arabs."[31]

Views of this kind have been treated in previous chapters on globalization and culture and on anti-Americanism. However, with the continuing insurgency in Iraq, the ongoing war on terror, and the conflict in Lebanon precipitated by Hezbollah, the Israel-Palestine issue continues to be invoked as a root cause. For example, in the aftermath of the July 2005 London bombings, British Prime Minister Tony Blair cited the Palestinian problem as "the single most pressing challenge in the world today." Some journalists and a few prominent academic "realist" authors have linked terrorism and the Iraq war to America's support for Israel and at times have employed versions of a conspiracy theory, which depicts the decision to use force in Iraq as driven by a neo-conservative, pro-Israel, and significantly Jewish clique.[32] The latter argument has already been dissected in Chapter 7 and will not be repeated here. However, the selective and tendentious use of history by some recent proponents of this argument has resurfaced in heated foreign policy discourse and the shortcomings of that narrative deserve scrutiny.[33]

A key point here is that the al-Qaeda and the Jihadist movements derive from sources that had little to do with the Palestinian problem. Bin Laden's 1998 fatwa, for example, emphasized the American presence in Saudi Arabia and oppression of Iraq, and his October 2001 video invoked eighty years of Muslim "humiliation" and "degradation" at the hands of the West[34] – i.e., a period beginning long before the creation of Israel. Indeed, some of the most knowledgeable authorities on the subject, including Bernard Lewis and Fouad Ajami,[35] have pointed to four centuries of decline experienced by the Arab-Muslim world and the sense of humiliation this has engendered, and they and others cite the frustration of those who have become detached from one world and yet find themselves unable to be accepted in another.

Al-Qaeda itself was formed not in reaction to the Arab-Israeli wars of 1948, 1956, 1967, and 1973, but as a movement growing out of the war in Afghanistan against the Soviets and at a time when the Israeli-Palestinian peace process seemed to be proceeding toward an eventual conclusion. As Olivier Roy has observed, "Al Qaeda's fighters were global jihadists and their favored battlegrounds have been outside the Middle East: Afghanistan, Bosnia, Chechnya and Kashmir. For them, every conflict is simply part of the Western encroachment on the Muslim ummah."[36] To be sure, Osama bin Laden opportunistically added Israel to the list of adversaries to be fought, but the Jewish state remained of lesser priority than the United States, the "head of the snake."

The reasons for the Bush administration's fateful decision to launch Operation Iraqi Freedom against Saddam's Iraq regime in March 2003 were treated at length in Chapter 5, but the notion that they took this action at the behest of Israel or of the "Israel Lobby" reflects a remarkably blinkered concept of foreign policy making. These kinds of views are expressed in such phrases as, "[t]he War was motivated in good part by a desire to make Israel more secure"; and "Within the US, the main driving force behind the war was a small band of neo-conservatives, many with ties to Likud."[37]

In reality, Israeli leaders themselves were at first hesitant and did not move to support the use of force until the Bush administration signaled its own intentions. Whatever the judgment of history will ultimately be on the wisdom of the war in Iraq, there is no doubt that the principal decision makers – Donald Rumsfeld, Dick Cheney, Condoleezza Rice, Colin Powell, President George W. Bush, and British Prime Minister Tony Blair – chose to act based on their own calculations of strategy, foreign policy, and national interest. Nor is it the case that the long-standing American support for Israel has mainly been due to the allegedly relentless and often hidden hand of the Israel lobby.

An historic sense of identity and kinship has long been evident in the U.S.-Israeli relationship, and public opinion data show that Americans feel quite friendly toward Israel, ranking it third behind

Britain and Canada (and well ahead of Mexico, India, the United
Nations, Russia, France, China, Saudi Arabia, and others.)[38] Over-
all, when asked whether their sympathies are more with Israel or the
Palestinians, Americans have consistently expressed a preference for
Israel by margins of three or four to one. For example, a Pew Research
Center poll taken in mid-August 2006 found 52% of the public favor-
ing Israel compared with 13% for the Palestinians. At the same time a
Harris Poll found 75% identifying Israel as a close ally or friend.[39]

A stable and peaceful solution to the Israeli-Palestinian conflict
would be greatly welcome and would likely have a beneficial regional
effect, but many well-intentioned observers, especially in Europe, not
only overestimate the transformative impact of such an agreement,
but mistakenly assume that the key to a breakthrough merely requires
the United States to put pressure on Israel. That is a misreading of
modern history, in which Palestinian leaders rejected opportunities in
1947, 1967, 1979, and 2000 that would ultimately have given their people a state of their own, and it ignores the core objective of Hamas and
of some other important elements of the Palestinian leadership and
public that still insist on a Palestinian state not alongside Israel but
in place of it. Here, the words of the deputy head of Hamas's political
bureau convey a stark message: "One of Hamas's founding principles
is that it does not recognize Israel. The people voted for us based on
this platform. Therefore the question of recognizing Israel is definitely
not on the table unless it withdraws from all [sic] the Palestinian lands,
not only to the 1967 borders."[40] The Hamas Covenant itself contains
numerous statements of opposition to the existence of Israel and conspiracy theories linking Jews to the French and Bolshevik revolutions,
World Wars I and II, and even the creation of the United Nations:

The...land of Palestine is Waqf land given as endowment for all
generations of Muslims until the Day of Resurrection. One should
not...relinquish it or [even] a part of it. No Arab state, or [even] all of
the Arab states [together], have [the right] to do this.... (Article Eleven)

There is no solution to the Palestinian problem except by jihad. Initiatives,
proposals and international conferences are a waste of time and a farce.
(Article Thirteen)

The enemies have...taken control of the world media....With money they...were behind the French Revolution and the Communist Revolution....With money they have formed secret organizations, all over the world, in order to destroy societies and to serve the Zionists' interests....With money they were able to take control of the colonialist countries, and urged them to colonize many countries so that they could exploit their resources and spread moral corruption there. (Article Twenty-Two)

They were behind World War I, through which they achieved the destruction of the Islamic Caliphate...obtained the Balfour Declaration, and established the League of the United Nations [*sic*] so as to rule the world. They were behind World War II, through which they reaped enormous profits from commerce in war materials and paved the way for the establishment of their state. They suggested the formation of the United Nations and the Security Council to replace the League of the United Nations [*sic*] and to rule the world through this. Wherever there is war in the world, it is they who are pulling the strings behind the scenes. (Article Twenty-Two)

[T]he Zionist plan has no limits, and after Palestine they want to expand [their territory] from the Nile to the Euphrates. Their plan is expounded in The Protocols of the Elders of Zion. (Article Thirty-Two)[41]

Despite its desirability, a stable peace remains enormously difficult to achieve in the near future. Yet even if a peace agreement were achieved and the Israeli-Palestinian conflict somehow solved, much of the impetus for jihadism and the sources of threat faced by America and Europe and parts of Asia, as well as in much of the Muslim world, would remain.[42] Elsewhere, Josef Joffe has noted that even in a "world without Israel," rivalries among Arab and Muslim states, clashes between different religious tendencies (not only Sunni versus Shiite, but involving Wahabis, Copts, Alawites, and others), ideological rivalries, the lure of reactionary utopia versus modernity, and intrinsic problems of despotism, oppression of women, rule by mullahs, and obscurantism would remain or even intensify.[43]

What about Europe?

Despite earlier predictions of a geopolitical rupture, which would see an increasingly self-confident, unified, and expanding E.U. acting more and more as a coherent political entity, not only separate from the United States and often standing in opposition to it, Europe and America have moved closer together rather than farther apart. In the aftermath of the intense controversy about the Iraq war, and with the passage of time, the most divisive issues tended to fade, and a number of Washington's chief antagonists either left the political stage (as in the case of German Chancellor Gerhard Schroeder) or pulled back from their exposed position (as with France under the beleaguered Chirac government). The likelihood of a transatlantic divorce was typically overstated, not least because the leading countries of Europe were themselves initially divided over Iraq. Subsequently, polarization on that subject eased in the face of the post-Saddam realities and the realization that leaving Iraq in chaos would pose grave dangers not only to its neighbors, but to Europe as well.

Other factors also intruded, especially the May 2005 rejection by French and Dutch electorates of the E.U.'s constitutional treaty, which left the community of 25 member states with unwieldy machinery for decision making and a limited capacity for acting as a unified polity in world affairs. Despite truly historic achievements in regional integration and institution-building, the limits of political unity remain palpable. The member states of the E.U. continue to disagree on issues ranging from genetically modified organisms (GMOs) to corporate mergers across national boundaries, to extradition laws, immigration, and even a common European arrest warrant. And on a national basis, the major continental countries – France, Germany and Italy – have found themselves hampered by stubborn problems of unemployment, job creation, and lagging economic growth.

Most European countries do perceive the threat of terrorism as serious. They have maintained or intensified intelligence cooperation with the United States and have adopted stringent laws on the handling of terrorism suspects. Between 30 and 40 terrorist attacks have been prevented in Europe since 9/11, and even France, which had sought to put the greatest distance between itself and the United States on Iraq, Iran, and the Palestinian-Israeli conflict, has found there was no separate peace to be had.[44] For example, in September 2005, due in part to information provided by the United States, French authorities were able to arrest members of a terrorist cell that had been planning attacks against the Paris metro, airport, and the domestic intelligence agency (DST) headquarters. The terrorist group had links with the al-Qaeda in Iraq organization of Abu Musab al-Zarqawi (who was killed by U.S. forces in June 2006), and in recognition of such threats, France's former counterterrorism coordinator remarked – in words that could have come from the Bush administration – "We're not going to wait until the bomb goes off."[45] In all, according to a former assistant director of counterintelligence, French authorities have thwarted at least a dozen attacks in the past decade.[46] The contemporary reality of Europe's relationship with the United States was thus aptly summarized by German Foreign Minister Frank-Walter Steinmeier, a leading Social Democrat serving in the coalition government led by the Christian Democrat Chancellor, Angela Merkel. In Steinmeier's words, "German-American friendship and European integration must remain the two cornerstones of German foreign policy."[47]

What about China?

American engagement in Asia continues to underpin stability there and offers a good example of the kind of "public goods" that no other international actor is likely to provide.[48] Recent events have not changed the regional configuration treated in Chapter 6, and relations among China, Japan, and South Korea remain uneasy. For example, China and Korea canceled summit meetings with Japan's Prime Minister Junichiro Koizumi, and in crude reflection of this tension, the official newspaper of the Chinese Communist Party, *People's Daily*, compared Japan's leader to someone who eats "rat excrement" [*sic*].[49]

The sources of rivalry among these East Asian states vary and include conflicting island and seabed claims, Japanese textbooks' treatment of World War II, anxieties by China's neighbors at the PRC's remarkable economic growth and increasing military might, and Beijing's use of nationalism to sustain the legitimacy of its Communist

Party dictatorship. In addition, North Korea's development of missiles and nuclear weapons poses a continuing security concern, especially for Japan and South Korea. The Taiwan issue also remains a long-term potential flash point, and once again a senior Chinese military leader has threatened to use nuclear weapons against the United States if America were to intervene in a conflict over Taiwan. In the words of Major General Zhu Chenghu, "If the Americans draw their missile and position-guided ammunition on to the target zone on China's territory, I think we will have to respond with nuclear weapons."[50] For the immediate future, this is largely rhetoric, since China's own nuclear forces have developed at a slow pace and in the event of a conflict could readily be wiped out by a U.S. attack.[51]

Despite these rumblings, cooperation does take place, much of it in bilateral relationships between the United States and individual Asian powers. America's ties with Japan and India have become increasingly close and cooperative, and much the same can be said for U.S. relations with Indonesia, Vietnam, and the Philippines. China's long-term orientation toward the United States could involve either confrontation or collaboration,[52] but there is good reason to believe that PRC leaders are determined to focus on building their economy and national strength and to avoid conflict for at least the medium term.

Elsewhere there have been remarkably successful instances of multilateral cooperation. Thus, in the case of the devastating December 2004 Asian tsunami, the United States, in coordination with Japan, Australia, and India, was able to deploy extensive aid to Indonesia and other hard-hit countries within the first 48 hours.

Direct contact with U.S. humanitarian aid has had a positive impact on Muslim views of America. In Indonesia, 65% of the population had a more sympathetic view of the United States as a result of American humanitarian aid following the December 2004 tsunami. In Pakistan, between May and December 2005, 78% had a more positive view of America due to its humanitarian assistance for victims of the October 2005 earthquake, and the percentage of the population who believe terrorist attacks against civilians are never justified more than doubled to 73%.[53] And in India, favorable views of America increased to 71% in February 2006, compared with 54% three years earlier.[54]

V. PERSISTENT PRIMACY AND THE FUTURE OF THE AMERICAN ERA

Any number of authors have predicted the end of the American era. Before and increasingly since the Iraq war, many of them warned against the ostensibly self-defeating character of U.S. grand strategy and of its putative unilateral or aggressive behavior as bound to trigger the creation of an international coalition to counterbalance U.S. power.[55] Yet no such counterbalance has developed.[56] As Richard Betts, an advocate of more limited U.S. foreign engagement, has observed, objections to American primacy have been due more to style (or "impolite primacy") than to substance.[57] And, overall, despite the human and material costs of the Iraq war, Washington's mixed diplomatic record in dealing with allies and adversaries, continuing perils involving nuclear proliferation from North Korea and Iran, and the ongoing war against radical Islamist terrorism, the United States retains an impressive degree of primacy.

As described in Chapter 1, primacy encompasses not only military might, but power and leadership across a wide array of areas including economic strength, competitiveness, technology, education, and culture. And in virtually all these realms, America continues to rank highly. For example, the United States stands first in information technology,[58] places third (after New Zealand and Singapore) in offering the best conditions for companies,[59] ranks number two in overall competitiveness (after Finland),[60] and despite the costs of the Iraq war, it spends only 4.5% of GDP on defense, a figure well below average Cold War levels.

In higher education, the United States remains unmatched. It boasts 17 of the world's top 20 research universities and 35 of the top 50, and American institutions employ 70% of the world's Nobel prize winners.[61] In the commercial realm, despite sporadic calls for boycotts of American consumer products, especially in the Middle East and Europe, U.S. brands appear not to have suffered in comparison with their competitors in the same industries. Data for the sales of companies such as Coca-Cola and McDonald's for 2000–01 and 2003–04 showed that the American firms did at least as well as their European counterparts, and despite their conspicuousness as a cultural symbol, McDonald's restaurants in France have thrived, growing to more than 1000 locations.[62]

Pitfalls and Prospects

By virtue of its size, the breadth and depth of its power attributes, and the indispensable role it plays in world affairs, America possesses a unique degree of primacy. Yet pitfalls exist, and as recent events suggest, some combination of these could ultimately threaten the long-term continuation of this predominance and post-9/11 grand strategy. One especially significant yet often overlooked element concerns the maintenance of domestic support. Nearly a generation ago, a leading military historian, Michael Howard, called attention to the "forgotten dimensions of strategy." These included not only the capacity to deploy and support the largest and best-equipped forces but also the ability to maintain the social cohesion without which national power and strategy cannot be sustained.[63]

In this light, domestic public opinion and the maintenance of sufficient public consensus take on a crucial importance. One question is whether the American public will grow weary of a long, ongoing conflict with no end in sight, especially because of a focus on the painful loss of American lives in Iraq and Afghanistan, though the number killed remains far below the total lost in Vietnam and Korea, let alone the two World Wars. In addition, the rancorous partisan debates of recent years and deeply divided public views about the war in Iraq could limit America's ability to maintain broad international engagement and, when necessary, to employ armed force preemptively or preventively.

Perceptions of international "legitimacy" also can take on a life of their own in ways that affect domestic support. Though the term is much over-used in recent debates about grand strategy and Iraq, the cumulative effect of widespread international criticism – regardless of its merits – tends to feed back into domestic debates about policy and strategy and ultimately have a constraining effect. For example, the bitterness left by disputes about Iraq and failure to find significant quantities of WMD, despite the fact that not only American but virtually all the world's major intelligence services had assumed stockpiles to be present, is likely to exacerbate credibility problems in the event of a future showdown over Iran's nuclear program. No matter how blatant Teheran's violations of the NPT and IAEA standards, nor how cynical the public pronouncements of Iranian leaders, there will likely be a chorus of voices at home and abroad cautioning against the use of force and invoking comparisons with Iraq.

The domestic basis for American power and primacy includes not only public opinion and social cohesion, but governmental capability. The shortcomings of political and military leaders in planning for and implementing security and stability in post-Saddam Iraq have been widely described. The ineptitude of local, state, and federal authorities in responding to Hurricane Katrina of August 2005 provides another conspicuous example. In addition, there is the issue of whether the armed forces are large enough in numbers to cope with additional foreign threats. And there remains the question of the long-term fiscal basis for sustaining foreign and military commitments. By historical standards, though the current dollar amounts of more than $450 billion per year seem huge, the outlays are relatively modest when compared with defense spending as a percentage of GDP in previous eras. During the early years of the Cold War, American military spending at times amounted to double-digit percentages of GDP. In 1959, near the end of the Eisenhower era, the figure was 10%, and in the mid-1980s, during the Regan buildup, it was higher than 6%. But the underlying problem concerns the cumulative effect of large domestic budget deficits, which former Chairman of the Federal Reserve,

Alan Greenspan, described as ultimately "unsustainable."[64] The issue thus is not whether the United States can afford substantial levels of expenditure, but whether fiscal policies and problems of insufficiently funded entitlement programs such as Medicare, Medicaid, and Social Security may ultimately impose a tenacious constraint.

One other potentially critical limitation stems from America's growing dependence on imported oil. A generation ago, at the time of the 1973–74 energy crisis, the United States relied on imports for 35% of its total oil supply. Now, that dependence has swelled to 60%, and it leaves America vulnerable to the impact of events in the Middle East, where some two-thirds of the world's proven supplies of crude oil are located. In the highly integrated world oil system, events anywhere in the world involving supply or demand have an immediate global ripple effect. When the supply/demand balance is very tight, as was the case in 2006 with world oil demand at 85 million barrels per day (mbd) and little more than 1–1.5 mbd of spare production capacity, any incident of war, terrorism, political turmoil, or natural disaster can have disproportionate effects on oil price and availability. The largest net increase in oil demand in recent years has come from China, but growing American consumption and imports have been a significant factor.

The approximate tripling of oil prices between 2001 and 2006, to more than $70 per barrel did not have the kind of adverse economic impact that occurred with the oil shocks of 1973–74 and 1979–80 (the amount of oil required per dollar of GDP is now only half as much as in the earlier periods; adjusted for inflation, oil prices in 1981 would have been equivalent to $90 per barrel in 2006 terms). Nonetheless, a crisis affecting oil supply, especially in the Persian Gulf region, could have severe consequences. In geopolitical terms, the run-up in oil revenues strengthens the hands of oil-producing countries with regimes that are authoritarian and/or hostile to the United States (Iran, Venezuela), and it constricts American policy options, for example, in making an embargo on Iranian oil virtually impossible to use as a tool against Teheran's nuclear proliferation program.

And yet, with all these qualifications, American primacy is likely to continue. Regardless of debates about the Iraq war and the sins or virtues of the Bush administration, no real alternative to the American role exists, and the lethal perils that became apparent on 9/11 will not disappear anytime soon. Even during the acrimonious domestic political debates of recent years, very few of those who are likely to become foreign policy decision makers have called for radical disengagement or insisted that American use of force cannot be undertaken without first obtaining approval from the UN Security Council. Indeed, over the long term any American administration, whether Democratic or Republican, will need to adopt a national security strategy that largely incorporates key elements of what has become known as the Bush doctrine.[65] The chief difference will be that the next president, whether a Democrat or Republican, will call that doctrine by another name.

Notes

Introduction

1. The memos were sent in October–November 1993. See Richard Reeves, "Why Clinton Wishes He Were JFK," *Washington Monthly* 27, no. 9 (September 1995): 19. Clinton's initial inattention to foreign policy was evident in a long interview with Haynes Johnson, who had been preparing a book on the first year of his presidency. In the author's account, there was not a word on the subject, not even on the North American Free Trade Agreement (NAFTA). Stephen E. Ambrose, *Foreign Affairs* 73, no. 4 (July/August 1994): 168–69, reviewing Haynes Johnson, *Divided We Fall: Gambling with History in the Nineties* (New York: Norton, 1994).

2. In one opinion poll taken in the weeks prior to the war in Iraq, an extraordinary 89 percent of Americans said they were closely or somewhat closely following the subject, and only 2 percent were not doing so. Even the less familiar and more inscrutable situation in North Korea captured the attention of 67 percent of the public. Data from Gallup Poll Tuesday Briefing, Gallup.com, January 7, 2003.

3. According to the November 2004 election exit poll, a total of 34 percent of voters cited terrorism (19%) or Iraq (15%) as the issue mattering most in how they voted. The next most important subjects cited were moral values (22%) and the economy/jobs (20%). U.S. General Exit Poll, conducted by Edison/Mitofsky and reprinted in *Washington Post*, November 4, 2004. During the election campaign, an August 2004 poll found that 41 percent considered international issues to be the most important problems facing the country, compared with 26 percent who cited economic issues. Data from Pew Research Center, in Robin Wright, "How U.S. Fares in Iraq May Sway Swing Voters," *Washington Post*, August 19, 2004.

4. In a poll on the eve of President Bush's second term inauguration, 61 percent of the public cited the situation in Iraq and 52 percent the campaign

against terrorism as top priorities. The next highest issues were education (44%) and the economy (43%). *Washington Post*–ABC News Poll, *Washington Post*, January 18, 2005.

5. Structural realist authors make this argument and assert that U.S. primacy and power will necessarily stimulate counterbalancing by other countries. See, esp., Kenneth Waltz, "The Emerging Structure of International Politics," *International Security* 18, no. 2 (Fall 1993): 75–76; and "Structural Realism after the Cold War," *International Security* 25, no. 1 (Summer 2000): 5–41; also John Mearsheimer, "Back to the Future: Instability in Europe after the Cold War," *International Security* 15, no. 1 (Summer 1990): 5–56; and Christopher Layne, "The Unipolar Illusion: Why New Great Powers Will Rise," *International Security* 17, no. 4 (Spring 993): 5–51.

6. Colin Dueck makes a similar point in "New Perspectives on American Grand Strategy," *International Security* 28, no. 4 (Spring 2004): 197–216 at 212. Liberal internationalist approaches emphasize reliance on multilateralism, international institutions, and the promotion of liberal values. See, e.g., Joseph S. Nye, *Soft Power: The Means to Success in World Politics* (New York: Public Affairs, 2004); John Ikenberry, *After Victory: Institutions, Strategic Restraint and the Rebuilding of Order after Major Wars* (Princeton: Princeton University Press, 2001); Ikenberry, ed., *America Unrivaled: The Future of the Balance of Power* (Ithaca: Cornell University Press, 2002); Charles A. Kupchan, *The End of the American Era: U.S. Foreign Policy and the Geopolitics of the Twenty-first Century* (New York: Knopf, 2002); and Anne-Marie Slaughter, *A New World Order* (Princeton: Princeton University Press, 2004).

7. They include especially Jean Bethke Elshtain, *Just War against Terror: The Burden of American Power in a Violent World* (New York: Basic Books, 2003); John Lewis Gaddis, *Surprise, Security, and the American Experience* (Cambridge: Cambridge University Press, 2004); Walter Russell Mead, *Power, Terror, Peace, and War: America's Grand Strategy in a World at Risk* (New York: Knopf, 2004); Paul Berman, *Terror and Liberalism* (New York: Norton, 2003); Ian Buruma and Avishai Margalit, *Occidentalism: The West in the Eyes of Its Enemies* (New York: Penguin, 2004); and Eliot Cohen, "History and the Hyperpower," *Foreign Affairs* 83, no. 4 (July/August 2004): 49–63.

8. The discussion of these points is foreshadowed in my essay, "Rethinking America's Grand Strategy," *Chronicle of Higher Education* 50, issue 39, June 4, 2004.

9. John Lewis Gaddis makes a similar point and adds the 1814 case of the British attack on Washington in which the White House was burnt.

See, *Surprise, Security and the American Experience* (Cambridge: Harvard University Press, 2004).

10. The term was put forward by Michael Ignatieff, director of Harvard's Carr Center of Human Rights Policy, in *The Guardian* (London), October 1, 2001.

11. *The 9/11 Commission Report: Final Report of the National Commission on Terrorist Attacks upon the United States* (New York: W. W. Norton, 2004), p. 362.

12. A massive truck bomb destroyed the U.N.'s Baghdad headquarters on August 19, 2003, killing the head of the mission, Sergio Vieira de Mello, and resulting in the U.N.'s immediate withdrawal.

13. Stanley Hoffmann, "The United States and International Organizations," in Robert J. Lieber, ed., *Eagle Rules? Foreign Policy and American Primacy in the 21st Century* (New York: Prentice Hall and the Woodrow Wilson International Center for Scholars, 2002), p. 352.

14. For an elaboration of this argument, see Lieber, "Foreign Policy and American Primacy," in *Eagle Rules?*, pp. 1–15.

15. William Wohlforth makes this point in his assessment of American primacy. See "The Stability of a Unipolar World," *International Security* 24, no. 1 (Summer 1999): 5–41. Also see Stephen Brooks and William Wohlforth, "American Primacy in Perspective," *Foreign Affairs* 82, no. 4 (July/August 2002).

16. E.g., in John Kerry's words, "As president, I will not wait for a green light from abroad when our safety is at stake." Speech at UCLA Center for International Relations, *New York Times*, March 3, 2004. Kerry made similar statements in all three of the 2004 presidential debates with George W. Bush (September 30, October 8 and 13, 2004). For his part, Bush repeatedly made this point in his presidential speeches, in the National Security Strategy document of September 2002, and in the presidential debates.

17. See Gaddis, *Surprise, Security and the American Experience*, p. 94.

1. Caveat Empire

1. "The Eagle Has Landed," *Financial Times* (London), February 1, 2002.

2. Quoted in Neil MacFarquhar, "Can't Live With: Can't Live Without," *New York Times*, January 16, 2005.

3. Quoted in David Ignatius, "Beirut's Berlin Wall," *Washington Post*, February 23, 2005.

4. Portions of this chapter are adapted from Lieber, "Rethinking America's Grand Strategy," *Chronicle of Higher Education* 50, issue 39 (June 4, 2004): B6–B9.

5. Consider, e.g., Ivo H. Daalder and James M. Lindsay, *America Unbound: The Bush Revolution in Foreign Policy* (Washington, D.C.: Brookings Institution Press, 2003); and Charles A. Kupchan, *The End of the American Era: U.S. Foreign Policy and the Geopolitics of the Twenty-first Century* (New York: Knopf, 2002).

6. See, e.g., Anton W. DePorte's classic, *Europe between the Superpowers: The Enduring Balance* (New Haven: Yale University Press, 1986).

7. Stephen Sestanovich, "Not Much Kinder and Gentler," *New York Times*, February 3, 2005. Sestanovich emphasizes the importance of Condoleezza Rice's account in her book, co-authored with Philip Zelikow, *Germany Unified and Europe Transformed* (Cambridge, Mass.: Harvard University Press, 1995.)

8. Eliot Cohen emphasizes this point in "History and the Hyperpower," *Foreign Affairs* (July/August 2004). Also, Stephen Walt, a leading neo-realist author who was otherwise critical of the Bush administration, dissented from a report of the Council on Foreign Relations, which emphasized personality differences and philosophical disputes. He argued instead that "asymmetry of power – not philosophy – is the root cause of this dispute." Stephen M. Walt, "Additional View," in *Renewing the Atlantic Partnership*, Report of an Independent Task Force (New York: Council on Foreign Relations, 2004), p. 29.

9. "A Creaking Partnership," *The Economist* (London), June 5, 2004, p. 23.

10. See, esp., Keir A. Lieber and Gerard Alexander, "Waiting for Balancing: Why the World Isn't Pushing Back," *International Security* 30, no. 1 (Summer 2005). Also William C. Wohlforth, "The Stability of a Unipolar World," *International Security* 24, no. 1 (Summer 1999): 5–41; and Stephen Brooks and William Wohlforth, "American Primacy in Perspective," *Foreign Affairs* 82, no. 4 (July/August 2002).

11. Former French Foreign Minister, Hubert Vedrine, quoted in Craig R. Whitney, "NATO at 50," *New York Times*, February 15, 1999.

12. *Economist*, March 8, 2003.

13. "The Eagle Has Landed," *Financial Times* (London), February 1, 2002.

14. Data as cited in *The Economist* (London), November 23, 2002.

15. In 2004, the United States ranked second after Finland. Data from World Economic Forum, cited in *Economist*, October 16, 2004. Also see Michael Porter and Klaus Schwab, eds., *The Global Competitiveness Report 2004–2005* (New York: St. Martin's Press, 2005.)

16. *Economist*, June 29, 2002, "A Survey of America's World Role," p. 34.

17. See, e.g., C. Kupchan, *The End of the American Era*; "The End of the West," *Atlantic Monthly* 290, no. 4 (November 2002).

18. Measured in terms of purchasing power parity, Russia's GDP is estimated to be $1.28 trillion, compared with Italy at $1.55 trillion. Data for 2003 from *CIA World Factbook*, www.odci.gov, accessed April 17, 2005.

19. John J. Mearsheimer, "Guns Won't Win the Afghan War," *New York Times*, November 4, 2001.

20. U.S. Special Forces intervention in Afghanistan began on October 19, 2001. By the time the southern city of Kandahar fell on December 6, there were 316 special forces personnel in the country. See the detailed account in *Washington Post*, April 3, 2002.

21. CEP measures the average distance from the target in which half the munitions dropped are expected to hit.

22. Spec. Will Bromley, quoted in Daniel Williams, "Soldiers' Doubts Build as Duties Shift," *Washington Post*, May 25, 2004, p. A11.

23. Quoted in David Ignatius, "Beirut's Berlin Wall," *Washington Post*, February 23, 2005.

24. Quoted in Colonel Harry G. Summers, Jr., *On Strategy: A Critical Analysis of the Vietnam War* (New York: Dell, 1984), p. 21.

25. *The 9/11 Commission Report* (New York: Norton, 2004), pp. 362–63.

26. "The National Security Strategy of the United States of America," September 20, 2002, http://www.whitehouse.gov/nsc/nss.html, p. 28.

27. In a May 29, 1998, letter, Osama bin Laden called on his followers to acquire nuclear, biological, and chemical weapons. Cited in "Bin Laden Letter Orders U.S. Massacre," *The Guardian* (London), October 18, 2001.

28. On March 11, 2004, Islamist terrorists detonated ten explosive devices on Madrid commuter trains during the morning rush hour. The attack killed 191 people and injured 1,800.

29. Quoted in George Packer, "Comment: Invasion vs. Persuasion," *The New Yorker*, December 20 and 27, 2004, p. 41.

30. See, e.g., Noam Chomsky, *Hegemony or Survival: America's Quest for Global Dominance* (New York: Metropolitan Books/Henry Holt, 2003); Tariq Ali, *Bush in Babylon: The Recolonization of Iraq* (New York: Verso, 2003); Emmanuel Todd, *After the Empire: The Breakdown of the American Order* (New York: Columbia University Press, 2003); John Pilger, *The New Rulers of the World* (New York: Verso, 2002); and the books and movies of Michael Moore.

31. See chapter 7 for treatment of delusional and conspiratorial accounts.

32. E.g., Thierry Meyssan, *9/11: The Big Lie*, published in France as *11 Septembre 2001: L'effroyable imposture* (Paris: Editions Carnot, 2002).

33. The classic work of post–World War II realism is that of Hans Morgenthau, *Politics among Nations* (New York: Knopf, 1948). The most

important structural realist works are those of Kenneth Waltz, *Man, the State and War* (New York: Columbia University Press, 1959), and John Mearsheimer, *The Tragedy of Great Power Politics* (New York: W. W. Norton, 2001). For a thorough elaboration, including discussion of offensive and defensive realismand their variants, see Stephen M. Walt, "The Enduring Relevance of the Realist Tradition," in Ira Katznelson and Helen Milner, eds., *Political Science: The State of the Discipline III* (New York: W. W. Norton, 2002).

34. Kenneth Waltz, U.S. Congress, Senate, *Relations in a Multipolar World*, Hearings before the Committee on Foreign Relations, 102nd Congress, 1st Session, November 26, 28, and 30, 1990 (Washington, D.C.: Government Printing Office, 1991), p. 210, quoted in Gunther Hellman and Reinhard Wolf, "Neorealism, Neoliberal Institutionalism, and the Future of NATO," *Security Studies* 3, no. 1 (Autumn 1993): 17; also Waltz, "The Emerging Structure of International Politics," *International Security* 18, no. 2 (Fall 1993): 75–76, and "Structural Realism after the Cold War," *International Security* 25, no. 1 (Summer 2000): 19.

35. Benjamin Schwartz and Christopher Layne, "A New Grand Strategy," *Atlantic Monthly*, January 2002, pp. 36–42. Also, Christopher Layne, "The Unipolar Illusion: Why New Great Powers Will Rise," *International Security* 17, no. 4 (Spring 1993): 5–51.

36. Andrew J. Bacevich, *American Empire: The Realities and Consequences of U.S. Diplomacy* (Cambridge, Mass.: Harvard University Press, 2002.)

37. John Mearsheimer and Stephen Walt, "An Unnecessary War," *Foreign Policy*, January/February 2003. And see my letter and the authors' reply, "Iraq in a Box," *Foreign Policy*, no. 136 (May/June 2003): 4, 8–9. Also see an ad signed by a group of thirty-three prominent international relations professors, in *New York Times*, September 26, 2002.

38. E.g., Paul Kennedy, *The Rise and Fall of the Great Powers: Economic Change and Military Conflict from 1500 to 2000* (New York: Random, 1987); Jack Snyder, "Imperial Temptations," *National Interest* (Spring 2003): 29–40; and Stephen Walt, "The Ties That Fray," *National Interest* 54, no. 71 (Winter 1998/99).

39. Richard K. Betts, "The Soft Underbelly of American Primacy: Tactical Advantages of Terror," *Political Science Quarterly* 117, no. 1 (Spring 2002): 19–36 at 34.

40. Dimitri Simes, "Rethinking the Strategy," *National Interest*, no. 76 (Summer 2004): 11–14.

41. Some realists do – or probably should, based on the logic of their theory – tend to favor an ambitious American grand strategy because of a belief

that states inevitably seek to expand their power and that therefore a stance of assertiveness and forward engagement may serve to discourage or preclude such challenges. For the former (those who do), see Charles Krauthammer. "The Unipolar Moment Revisited," *National Interest*, no. 70 (Winter 2002/3): 5–17. For the latter (those who should, but don't), see Mearsheimer, *Tragedy of Great Power Politics*.

42. Wohlforth, "The Stability of a Unipolar World"; also Brooks and Wohlforth, "American Primacy in Perspective." John Mearsheimer notes that no country other than China has the potential to challenge the United States, though he cautions that the United States can get itself into serious trouble if it uses its formidable power foolishly – as he believes was the case in Iraq. Commencement Address, University of Chicago, June 11–12, 2004.

43. This issue is discussed in chapter 5.

44. E.g., Robert O. Keohane, *After Hegemony: Cooperation and Discord in the World Political Economy* (Princeton, N.J.: Princeton University Press, 1984).

45. E.g., Robert B. Reich, *Reason: Why Liberals Will Win the Battle for America* (New York: Knopf, 2004).

46. E.g., John Gerard Ruggie, ed., *Multilateralism Matters: The Theory and Praxis of an Institutional Form* (New York: Columbia University Press, 1993); and Anne-Marie Slaughter, *A New World Order* (Princeton, N.J.: Princeton University Press, 2004).

47. Prior to the Iraq War, this was the implication by a number of authors and prominent public figures who insisted that sanctions and enforcement must take place through the U.N. See, e.g., *Iraq: What Next?* (Washington, D.C.: Carnegie Endowment for International Peace, January 2003); Jacques Chirac, quoted in *Washington Post*, February 22, 2003; Kofi Annan, *Washington Post*, February 9, 2003; and Stanley Hoffmann, "The High and the Mighty," *American Prospect*, January 13, 2003.

48. E.g., Joseph S. Nye, who has written about the importance of soft power and initially supported the use of force by the United States in Iraq. See Kate Zernike, "Threats and Responses: Liberals for War; Some of Intellectual Left's Longtime Doves Taking on Role of Hawks," *New York Times*, March 14, 2003.

49. Jessica Tuchman Mathews, "Power Shift," *Foreign Affairs* 76, no. 1 (January/February 1997): 50–66, at 50. In a subsequent article, she argued, "Nation-states will not disappear, but new channels of interaction will so proliferate that governments' preeminence will wane." Mathews, "The Information Revolution," *Foreign Policy*, no. 119 (Summer 2000): 63–65, at 64.

50. E.g., John Gerard Ruggie, *Winning the Peace: America and World Order in the New Era* (New York: Columbia University Press, 1996).

51. John Ikenberry, *After Victory: Institutions, Strategic Restraint and the Rebuilding of Order after Major Wars* (Princeton, N.J.: Princeton University Press, 2001); Ikenberry, ed., *America Unrivaled: The Future of the Balance of Power* (Ithaca: Cornell University Press, 2002); and "The End of the Neoconservative Movement," *Survival* 46, no. 1 (Spring 2004): 7–22. See also the critique of Ikenberry by Randall L. Schweller, "The Problem of International Order Revisited," *International Security* 26, no. 1 (Summer 2001): 161–86.

52. Joseph S. Nye, *Soft Power: The Means to Success in World Politics* (New York: Public Affairs, 2004), p. x; also *Bound to Lead* (New York: Basic Books, 1990) and *The Paradox of American Power* (New York: Oxford University Press, 2002).

53. Moore's book, entitled *Stupid White Men*, sold 1.1 million copies in Germany, nearly double its U.S. sales, and at one point three of his books were simultaneously on the German top ten list. See Glenn Kessler, "Powell Takes Diplomacy into a German High School," *Washington Post*, April 2, 2004.

54. See the critique by Sebastian Mallaby, "NGOs: Fighting Poverty, Hurting the Poor," *Foreign Policy*, no. 144 (September/October 2004): 50–58.

55. A conspicuous example of corruption (discussed in chapter 5) can be found in the U.N.'s administration of the Iraqi oil-for-food program. As a result, large sums of money were siphoned off to favored individuals in various countries, and Saddam Hussein was able to divert some $10 billion that should otherwise have gone to purchase food, medicine, and essential supplies for the population of Iraq. See, e.g., Jim Hoagland, "U.N. Moment of Truth," *Washington* Post, April 13, 2004; and "Oil for Fraud," *The Economist* (London), April 22, 2004.

56. See, e.g., Daniel Patrick Moynihan, with Suzanne Weaver, *A Dangerous Place*: (Boston: Little, Brown, 1978). Also Anne Bayefsky, "One Small Step: Is the UN Finally Ready to Get Serious about Anti-Semitism?" speech delivered to the U.N. Conference on Confronting Anti-Semitism, New York, June 21, 2004, *Wall Street Journal*, June 21, 2004; and U.N. Wire, "U.N. Examines Its Role in Combating, Fostering Anti-Semitism," www.unwire.org/UNWire/20040622/449_25130.asp, accessed June 22, 2004.

57. Transcript of Blair's Speech to Congress, July 17, 2003, www.cnn.com/2003/us/07/17/blair.transcript.

2. New (and Old) Grand Strategy

1. John Lewis Gaddis, *Surprise, Security, and the American Experience* (Cambridge: Harvard University Press, 2004), pp. 21–22.
2. President Franklin Delano Roosevelt Fireside Chat to the Nation, September 11, 1941, in response to German submarine attack on the U.S. destroyer *Greer*. U.S. Maritime Service Veterans, President Roosevelt Speeches and Statements, www.usmm.org/fdr/rattlesnake.html, accessed April 22, 2005.
3. Henry A. Kissinger, *Newsweek*, November 8, 2004.
4. "Excerpts from the Report of the Sept. 11 Commission: 'A Unity of Purpose,'" *New York Times*, July 23, 2004.
5. Douglas Brinkley, "Analysis: Bush Administration's National Security Strategy," Talk of the Nation, National Public Radio, September 23, 2002, www.npr.org/programs/totn/transcripts/2002/sep/020923.conan.html, accessed April 22, 2005.
6. This discussion of Gaddis draws in part from my essay, "Rethinking America's Grand Strategy," *Chronicle of Higher Education* 50, issue 39, June 4, 2004.
7. Gaddis, *Surprise, Security, and the American Experience*, p. 64.
8. Ibid., pp. 76–77. He also notes the Clinton assumption that the progress of democracy and capitalism had become irreversible, so that all the United States needed to do was to engage with the rest of the world to enlarge the process. Gaddis takes the Bush Doctrine seriously, finding in it boldness and vision. However, he is critical of harsh rhetoric concerning the Kyoto Protocol on global warming, the International Criminal Court, and the Comprehensive Test Ban Treaty. He also notes wider fears of U.S. dominance galvanized by the rush to war in Iraq, stresses the importance of diplomatic finesse, and warns that hegemony can't be sustained without the consent of others. Ibid., 115–17.
9. This section incorporates portions of a previously published essay, Keir A. Lieber and Robert J. Lieber, "The Bush National Security Strategy," *U.S. Foreign Policy Agenda*: Electronic Journal of the U.S. Department of State, vol. 7, no. 4, December 2002, http://usinfo.state.gov/journals/itps/1202/ijpe/pj7−4lieber.htm, accessed April 22, 2005.
10. President George W. Bush, State of the Union Address, January 29, 2002, emphasis added.
11. *The National Security Strategy of the United States of America*, September 20, 2002, http://www.whitehouse.gov/nsc/nss.html, accessed April 22, 2005.

12. Al-Qaeda spokesman Suleiman Abu Gheith, part of a three-part article, "In the Shadow of the Lances," originally posted on an al-Qaeda Web site. Text, "Why We Fight America," translated by Middle East Media Research Institute, MEMRI, Special Dispatch Series, no. 388, June 12, 2002. See www.memri.org.

13. Security Council Resolution 1441 was passed by a unanimous 15-0 vote on November 8, 2002. The resolution, adopted under Chapter VII of the U.N. Charter, threats to the peace, which made it binding on all 191 U.N. member countries, cited Iraq's "material violation" of 16 previous UNSC Resolutions over the previous twelve years, established a timetable for compliance and inspections, and warned of "serious consequences as a result of [Iraq's] continued violations of its obligations."

14. Stephen Sestanovich, "Not Much Kinder and Gentler," *New York Times*, February 3, 2005.

15. Philip Zelikow and Condoleezza Rice, *Germany Unified and Europe Transformed: A Study in Statecraft* (Cambridge, Mass.: Harvard University Press, 1995).

16. Fred Hiatt, "Obstinate Orthodoxy," *Washington Post*, March 3, 2003.

17. *Remarks by President George W. Bush at the National Endowment for Democracy's 20th Anniversary Event*, Washington, D.C., November 6, 2003. Text available at www.whitehouse.gov.

18. George W. Bush, Presidential Inaugural Address, January 20, 2005.

19. Michael Walzer, "Lone Ranger," *New Republic* 218, no. 17 (April 27, 1998): 10–11. I deal with the anarchy problem and its implications in *No Common Power: Understanding International Relations*, 4th ed. (New York: Prentice-Hall, 2001), pp. 245–66.

20. Cited in Elaine Sciolino, "Bosnia Policy Shaped by U.S. Military Role," *New York Times*, July 29, 1996; and quoted in full in *Foreign Policy Alert*, no. 28, October 22, 1996, "Security in Central & Eastern Europe: The Clinton Record," American Foreign Policy Council, Washington, D.C., www.afpc.org/fpa/fpa28.htm, accessed April 22, 2005.

21. E.g., Kenneth Waltz, "The Emerging Structure of International Politics," *International Security* 18, no. 2 (Fall 1993): 75–76; and "Structural Realism after the Cold War," *International Security* 25, no. 1 (Summer 2000): 5–41; also John Mearsheimer, "Back to the Future: Instability in Europe after the Cold War," *International Security* (Summer 1990): 5–56.

22. Steven Peter Rosen, "An Empire If You Can Keep It," *National Interest*, no. 71 (Spring 2003): 61.

23. Niall Ferguson, "A World without Power," *Foreign Policy*, no. 143 (July/August 2004): 34.

24. Robert Jervis, "Understanding the Bush Doctrine," in Demetrios James Caraley, ed., *American Hegemony: Preventive War, Iraq, and Imposing Democracy* (New York: Academy of Political Science, 2004), p. 26. Paul Kennedy uses the term "imperial overstretch" in *The Rise and Fall of the Great Powers: Economic Change and Military Conflict from 1500 to 2000* (New York: Random, 1987). See also Robert Gilpin on the costs of hegemonic leadership, in *War and Change in World Politics* (New York: Cambridge University Press, 1981).

25. As of December 31, 2004, the number of active duty U.S. military personnel deployed in Operation Iraqi Freedom totaled 202,100. An additional 19,200 were deployed in Operation Enduring Freedom (Afghanistan). Data from Defense Manpower Data Center, Statistical Information Analysis Division, U.S. Department of Defense. See Active Duty Military Personnel by Regional Area and by Country, www.dior.whs.mil/MMID/military/MILTOP.htm, accessed April 22, 2005.

26. See Bruce Jentleson, "Who, Why, What and How: Debates over Post–Cold War Military Intervention," in Robert J. Lieber, ed., *Eagle Adrift: American Foreign Policy at the End of the Century* (New York: Longman, 1997), pp. 39–70; also Jentleson, "The Pretty Prudent Public: Post-Vietnam American Opinion on the Use of Military Force," *International Studies Quarterly* 36, no. 1 (March 1992): 49–73. Also Peter D. Feaver and Christopher Gelpi find public willingness to tolerate casualties is often greater than commonly assumed. See *Choosing Your Battles: American Civil-Military Relations and the Use of Force* (Princeton: Princeton University Press, 2003.)

27. Rosen, "An Empire If You Can Keep It," pp. 54–55.

28. Niall Ferguson, "The Euro's Big Chance," *Prospect Magazine* (London), June 2004. Available at www.prospect-magazine.co.uk.

29. Data from *The Economist*, December 4, 2004.

30. Robert L. Paarlberg argues that such restrictions threaten to undercut U.S. leadership in science and thus would impact on American military dominance as well. See "Knowledge as Power: Science, Military Dominance, and U.S. Security," *International Security* 29, no. 1 (Summer 2004).

31. As one observer has described this, "We come ashore only where it really counts. And where it counts today is that Islamic crescent stretching from North Africa to Afghanistan." Charles Krauthammer, "Democratic Realism: An American Foreign Policy for a Unipolar World," 2004 Irving Kristol Lecture (Washington, D.C.: American Enterprise Institute, 2004), pp. 18–19.

3. Europe

1. Interview, *Time* magazine, February 24, 2003.
2. Jean Baudrillard, "The Spirts of Terrorism," quoted in Alexander Stille, "French Philosophy and the Spirit of Terrorism," *Correspondence: An International Journal of Culture & Society* (New York: Council on Foreign Relations, no. 9, Spring 2002), p. 8.
3. The historian, Timothy Garton Ash, quoted in David Frum, "The Jeers Will Not Make Him Think Again," *Daily Telegraph* (London), November 23, 2004.
4. Quoted in *The Economist*, April 26, 2003.
5. Benjamin J. Cohen, " 'Return to Normalcy'? Global Economic Policy at the End of the Century," in *Eagle Adrift: American Foreign Policy at the End of the Century*, ed. Robert J. Lieber (New York: Longman, 1997), p. 74.
6. On the return to great power balancing, see, e.g., John Mearsheimer, "Back to the Future: Instability in Europe after the Cold War," *International Security* (Summer 1990): 5–56; Christopher Layne, "The Unipolar Illusion: Why New Great Powers Will Arise," *International Security* (Spring 1993): 5–51.
7. Kenneth Waltz, U.S. Congress, Senate, *Relations in a Multipolar World*, Hearings before the Committee on Foreign Relations, 102nd Congress, 1st Session, November 26, 28, and 30, 1990 (Washington, D.C.: Government Printing Office, 1991), p. 210, quoted in Gunther Hellman and Reinhard Wolf, "Neorealism, Neoliberal Institutionalism, and the Future of NATO," *Security Studies* 3, no. 1 (Autumn 1993): 17.
8. Robert Kagan, *Of Paradise and Power: America and Europe in the New World Order* (New York: Knopf, 2003), pp. 3–4. Emphasis added. Note Javier Solana's rejoinder that Mars found solace in the arms of Venus.
9. Charles Kupchan, "The Waning Days of the Atlantic Alliance," in Bertel Heurlin and Mikkel Vedby Rasmussen, eds., *Challenges and Capabilities: NATO in the 21st Century* (Copenhagen: Danish Institute for International Studies, 2003), p. 25. Kupchan elaborates on these themes in *The End of the American Era* (New York: Knopf, 2002) and "The End of the West," *Atlantic Monthly* 290, no. 4 (November 2002). Stephen M. Walt advocated American disengagement from European security commitments in "The Ties That Fray: Why Europe and America Are Drifting Apart," *National Interest*, no. 54 (Winter 1998/99): 3–11. My views are contrary to those of Kupchan and Walt. A pre-9/11 statement of some of the ideas in this chapter can be found in Robert J. Lieber, "No Trans-Atlantic Divorce in the Offing," *Orbis* 44, no. 4 (Fall 2000): 571–84; also Lieber, "The European

Union and the United States," working paper prepared for the American Consortium on EU Studies, August 2004.

10. The term is that of Josef Joffe, "Europe's American Pacifier," *Foreign Policy* (Spring 1984), and its applicability to Asia is considered in chapter 6.

11. Henry A. Kissinger, *The Troubled Partnership: A Re-Appraisal of the Atlantic Alliance* (New York: McGraw-Hill, 1965).

12. Mitterrand died in 1996. The passage is from a biography by Georges-Marc Benamou, *Le dernier Mitterrand* (Paris: Plon, 1997), quoted in Conrad Black, "Britain's Atlantic Option and America's Stake," *National Interest* (Spring 1999): 22.

13. Vedrine and Chirac, quoted in Charles Krauthammer, "Not for Moi, Thanks," *Washington Post*, November 26, 1999. Vedrine had used the word "hyperpuissance" to describe American power, though President Chirac later disavowed the term. Chirac's more restrained language can be found in an interview with Craig R. Whitney, "With a 'Don't Be Vexed' Air, Chirac Assesses U.S.," *New York Times*, December 17, 1999.

14. Polly Toynbee, "Special Report: European Integration," *The Guardian* (London), July 18, 2001.

15. For a pessimistic assessment of prospects for success in the battle for Afghanistan, written shortly before U.S. and Northern Alliance forces captured Kabul, see John Mearsheimer, "Guns Won't Win the Afghan War," *New York Times*, November 4, 2001.

16. *The National Security Strategy of the United States of America*, September 20, 2002, http://www.whitehouse.gov/nsc/nss.html.

17. Cited in R. C. Longworth, "Allies Are Worlds Apart," *Chicago Tribune*, July 29, 2002.

18. "Sondage Ifop," *Le Figaro* (Paris), April 2, 2002.

19. The letter is reprinted in "Europe and America Must Stand United," *The Times* (London), January 30, 2003.

20. *The Economist*, June 12, 2004.

21. Pew Research Center for the People and the Press, cited in "Sinking Views of the United States," *New York Times*, March 23, 2003.

22. "A Year after the Iraq War: Mistrust of America in Europe Ever Higher, Muslim Anger Persists" (Washington, D.C.: Pew Research Center for People and the Press, March 16, 2004), www.people-press.org.

23. According to a close associate of Henry Kissinger, Peter Rodman, neither he nor Kissinger have any recollection of the former Secretary of State having written or said this. Conversation with the author.

24. Michael Mandelbaum, "The Inadequacy of American Power," *Foreign Affairs* 85, no. 5 (September/October 2002): 66.

25. Jonathan Stevenson, "How Europe and America Defend Themselves," *Foreign Affairs* 82, no. 2 (March/April 2003): 75–90 at 77.

26. *New York Times*, August 6, 1981.

27. Elizabeth Becker, "U.S. Contests Europe's Ban on Some Food," *New York Times*, May 14, 2003, and "Bush Decries Europe's Biotech Policies," *Washington Post*, May 22, 2003.

28. On the controversy surrounding early steps toward what became the Cartagena Protocol, see Robert Paarlberg, "The Eagle and the Global Environment," in Robert J. Lieber, ed., *Eagle Rules? Foreign Policy and American Primacy in the 21st Century* (New York: Prentice-Hall and the Woodrow Wilson International Center for Scholars, 2002), pp. 333–40.

29. "Oxfam Brands EU Bloc as Most Protectionist," *Financial Times*, April 10, 2002.

30. Mark Sullivan, *Our Times*, 1900–1925 (New York: Scribner's Sons, 1935), a six-volume survey of national life, quoted in Robert J. Samuelson, "The American Edge," *Washington Post*, January 9, 2003.

31. Seymour Martin Lipset, "Still the Exceptional Nation?" *Wilson Quarterly* 24, no. 1 (Winter 2000): 31–45, at 45.

32. Walter Russell Mead, "The Case against Europe," *Atlantic Monthly* (April 2002): 26.

33. Inaugural address of President George W. Bush, January 20, 2005, www.whitehouse.gov.

34. "Condoleezza Rice Brings Morality to Realpolitik," *Daily Telegraph* (London), February 2, 2005, www.telegraph.co.uk.

35. E.g., Kagan, *Of Paradise and Power*; Brooks, "Among the Bourgeoiso-phobes," *Weekly Standard*, April 6, 2002; Mead, "The Case against Europe."

36. For elaboration, see Robert J. Lieber, *British Politics and European Unity: Parties, Elites and Pressure Groups* (Berkeley: University of California Press, 1970), pp. 16–27.

37. Immanuel Kant, *Critique of Judgment* (1790).

38. John J. Mearsheimer, *The Tragedy of Great Power Politics* (New York: W. W. Norton, 2001), p. 33.

39. Quoted in Dusko Doder and Louise Branson, *Milosevic: Portrait of a Tyrant* (New York: Free Press, 1999), p. 109.

40. *New York Times*, February 23, 2003.

41. "Lithuania: Officials Say Russia Stalling on Kaliningrad Transit Talks," Prague, Radio Free Europe, March 31, 2003, www.rferl.org/nca/features/2003/03/31032003155817.asp, accessed April 22, 2005. As a result of World War II, the Baltic port of Kaliningrad (formerly Koenigsberg and part of Germany) became Russian territory. However, it lies between Lithuania and Poland, and Russian access requires transit through Lithuania.

42. Robert Jervis makes a similar point in "The Compulsive Empire," *Foreign Policy*, no. 137 (July/August 2003): 83–87.

43. Data from "The European Defense Agency: Will It Make a Difference?" *Strategic Comments*, International Institute for Strategic Studies, vol. 10, issue 5, June 2004.

44. British Foreign Secretary, Robin Cook, Queen's speech debate, House of Commons, London, November 22, 1999 (New York: British Information Service), PressReleases@newyork.mail.fco.gov.uk.

45. John Tagliabue, "Airbus's Military Jet Gets a Boost," *International Herald Tribune*, May 28, 2003.

46. Meteor is being developed by a consortium of the French company Matra and British Aerospace, in a collaborative venture with Germany, Italy, and Spain. The comparable American weapon, AMRAAM, is produced by Raytheon. See David Cracknell, "Cohen Begs Britain Not to Purchase Euro Missile," *Sunday Telegraph* (London), May 14, 2000; and British Embassy press release, "Defence Procurement: The Rt. Hon. Geoffrey Hoon, Secretary of State for Defence," May 16, 2000, http://www.Britain-USA.com.

47. Data for 2003 from *The Military Balance, 2004–2005* (London: International Institute for Strategic Studies and Oxford University Press, October 2004).

48. "Ready, or Not: Europe's Not-So-Rapid-Reaction Force," *Economist*, May 24, 2003.

49. "A Secure Europe in a Better World: European Security Strategy" (Brussels: European Union, December 12, 2003), p. 13. See also Fraser Cameron, "The EU's Security Strategy," *Internationale Politik: Transatlantic Edition* 5, no. 1 (Spring 2004): 16–24. For analysis of the Solana paper, see John Van Oudenaren, "The Solana Security Paper," AICGS, June 2003, www.aicgs.org/c/solana.shtml.

50. Speech to the Bundestag, quoted in German Information Center, *The Week in Germany*, July 12, 2002, www.germany-info.org.

51. *New York Times*, March 28, 2003.

52. Peter Struck, German Minister of Defense, quoted in *The Week in Germany*, May 23, 2003, www.info-germany.org.

53. Speech by Joschka Fischer, Federal Minister for Foreign Affairs, at the 40th Munich Conference on Security Policy Munich, February 7, 2004, reprinted in www.germany-info.org.

54. Quoted, *Economist*, November 20, 2004.

55. French Defense Minister Michele Alliot-Marie, cited in Craig S. Smith, "For U.S. to Note, Europe Flexes Muscle in Afghanistan," *New York Times*, September 22, 2004.

56. The Kosovo Force (KFOR) entered Kosovo on June 12, 1999, under a United Nations mandate, two days after the adoption of U.N. Security Council Resolution 1244.

4. Globalization, Culture, and Identities in Crisis

1. Salman Rushdie, "America and the Anti-Americans," *New York Times*, February 4, 2002.
2. Quotation from *Le Monde*, cited in Sophie Meunier, "The French Exception," *Foreign Affairs* 79, no. 4 (July/August 2000): 107.
3. Larry Rohter, "Learn English, Says Chile, Thinking Upwardly Global," *New York Times*, December 29, 2004.
4. Robert Gilpin observes that political scientists tend to overlook the role of markets, while economists often neglect the political context of events and the important role of power. See *U.S. Power and the Multinational Corporation: The Political Economy of Direct Foreign Investment* (New York: Basic Books, 1975), pp. 4–5.
5. Samuel P. Huntington, *The Clash of Civilizations and the Remaking of World Order* (New York: Simon & Schuster, 1996).
6. Quoted in Salman Rushdie, "A Liberal Argument for Regime Change," *Washington Post*, November 1, 2002.
7. Among other definitions of globalization, Thomas Friedman describes it as "the integration of everything with everything else." He adds, "Globalization enables each of us, wherever we live, to reach around the world farther, faster and cheaper than ever before and at the same time allows the world to reach into each of us farther, faster, deeper, and cheaper than ever before." Friedman, "Techno Logic," *Foreign Policy* (March/April 2002): 64. Also Friedman, *The Lexus and the Olive Tree* (New York: Farrar, Straus & Giroux, 1999). One of the best books on globalization addresses its intellectual underpinnings, particularly the influence of Britain through the ideas of Keith Joseph and the policies of Margaret Thatcher. See Daniel A. Yergin and Joseph Stanislaw, *The Commanding Heights* (New York: Simon & Schuster, 1998).
8. Quoted by Fouad Ajami, "The New Faith," *Saisphere*, alumni magazine of Johns Hopkins University School of Advanced International Studies, Washington, D.C., 2000, p. 13.
9. David Rothkopf, "In Praise of Cultural Imperialism?" *Foreign Policy*, no. 107 (Summer 1997): 38–53, at 39. A more ambivalent treatment is that of Benjamin Barber, who emphasizes tensions between global and parochial values as increasingly central to world affairs. *Jihad versus McWorld* (New York: Times Books, 1995).

10. The term is quoted in William Drodziak, "L'Etat C'est Mouse," *Washington Post*, March 2, 1992.

11. See Daniel Benjamin and Steven Simon, *The Age of Sacred Terror* (New York: Random House, 2003), p. 62; and Bernard Lewis, *The Crisis of Islam* (New York: Modern Library, 2003), pp. 76–79.

12. Charles Krauthammer, "Who Needs Gold Medals?" *Washington Post*, February 20, 2002.

13. Data cited in *The Economist* (London), November 23, 2002.

14. Paul Kennedy, "The Eagle Has Landed," *Financial Times* (London), February 1, 2002.

15. Karsten Voight, a German foreign ministry official and influential figure in the Social Democratic Party, speaking in Washington on March 8, 2000, quoted in Peter Rodman, *Uneasy Giant: The Challenges to American Predominance* (Washington, D.C.: Nixon Center, June 2000), p. 1.

16. "Defector Says She Was Saddam's Mistress," interview by Claire Shipman of ABC News with Parisoula Lampsos, September 12, 2002, www.abcnews.com.

17. Barbara Crossette, "At the U.N. French Slips and English Stands Tall," *New York Times*, March 25, 2001.

18. Anthony Faiola, "English Camps Reflect S. Korean Ambitions," *Washington Post*, November 18, 2004, and Larry Rohter, "Learn English, Says Chile," *New York Times*, December 29, 2004.

19. See http://www.davidpbrown.co.uk/help/top-100-languages-by-population.html for data on the top 100 languages by population. This lists "first language" speakers in Chinese 885 million, Spanish 332 million, and English 322 million. Source: Joseph E. Grimes (ed.), *Ethnologue*, 13th ed. (Dallas: Summer Institute of Linguistics, 1996). Other sources differ, depending on definitions. E.g., the *Time Almanac 2005* (New York: Pearson Education, 2004) ranks Chinese with 1,075 million, followed by English with 514 million, as the world's top "widely spoken" languages.

20. Data from "A World Empire by Other Means," *The Economist* (London), December 22, 2001, pp. 65–67.

21. Pierre Defraigne, quoted in, "Charlemagne: The Galling Rise of English," *The Economist*, March 1, 2003, p. 30. Secondary school language teaching data can be found in this article.

22. David Ignatius, "France's Constructive Critic," *Washington Post*, February 22, 2002.

23. Philippe Van Parijs elaborates in "The Ground Floor of the World: On the Socio-Economic Consequences of Linguistic Globalization," *International Political Science Review* 21, no. 2 (2000): 217–33.

24. Sam Dillon, "U.S. Slips in Attracting the World's Best Students," *New York Times*, December 21, 2004.

25. "Globalization and Cinema," in *Correspondence: An International Review of Culture and Society* (New York: Committee on Intellectual Correspondence, published by the Council on Foreign Relations), no. 8 (Summer/Fall 2001), p. 1.

26. Keith Richburg, "Vive le Cinema! France Looks to Protect Its Film Industry's 'Cultural Exception,' " *Washington Post*, January 28, 2002.

27. Alan Riding, "A Global Culture War Pits Protectionists against Free Traders," *New York Times*, February 5, 2005.

28. During the first week of June 2004, the top five box office films in France were American (*Harry Potter and the Prisoner of Azkaban*, *The Day after Tomorrow*, *Troy*, *Kill Bill Vol. 2*, and *You Got Served*). Hollywood reporter.com, as reported in *International Herald Tribune*, June 14, 2004.

29. Guy Konopnicki, "French Cinema's American Obsession," abridged from *Marianne*, March 5–11, 2001, reprinted in *Correspondence* (Summer/Fall 2001): 9.

30. Films titles on display at the Sony multiplex, Berlin, Potsdamer Platz, June 17, 2000.

31. Data from Media Sales, Milan, Italy, www.mediasales.it, in Tyler Cowen, "Why Hollywood Rules the World (and Should We Care?)," in *Correspondence* (Summer/Fall 2001): 7.

32. Alan Riding, "Filmmakers Seek Protection from U.S. Dominance," *New York Times*, February 5, 2003.

33. Michael Medved, "That's Entertainment? Hollywood's Contribution to Anti-Americanism Abroad," *The National Interest*, no. 68 (Summer 2002): 6.

34. See, e.g., Celestine Bohlen, "Cultural Salvage in Wake of Afghan War," *New York Times*, April 15, 2002.

35. Marc Kaufman, "Afghanistan's Monument of Rubble," *Washington Post*, March 6, 2002, p. C8.

36. Dick Hebdige, *Subculture: The Meaning of Style* (London and New York: Routledge, 1979).

37. Samuel P. Huntington, "The Clash of Civilizations?" *Foreign Affairs* 72, no. 3 (Summer 1973): 22–49, at 27.

38. Louis Hebron and John F. Stack, Jr., summarize the negative view of the globalization of mass culture: "This foreign invasion and assimilation of cosmopolitan consumerism with its materialistic orientation, indulgent values, moral bankruptcy and fraternizing of nationalities is a prescription

of cultural genocide because of the process' potential to vulgarize and/or destroy the rich diversity of human civilizations." "The Globalization Process: Debunking the Myths," paper presented at the annual meeting of the International Studies Association, Chicago, February 20–24, 2001.

39. Quoted in ibid.

40. Richard Pells, "American Culture Goes Global, or Does It?" *Chronicle of Higher Education*, April 12, 2002, p. B8.

41. Neal Gabler, "The World Still Watches America," *New York Times*, January 9, 2003.

42. Selma Reuben Holo, *Beyond the Prado: Museums and Identity in Democratic Spain* (Washington, D.C.: Smithsonian Institution Press, 1999), p. 149.

43. Carol Vogel, "A Museum Visionary Envisions More," *New York Times*, April 27, 2005.

44. Andrew Solomon, "An Awakening after the Taliban," *New York Times*, March 10, 2002. After the ouster of the Taliban, the new minister of information and culture, Said Makhtoum Rahim, estimated that the Taliban had destroyed "about 80% of our cultural identity."

45. Michael Howard, "What's in a Name? How to Fight Terrorism," *Foreign Affairs* 81, no. 1 (January/February 2002): 8–13, at 13.

46. "Sondage Ifop," *Le Figaro*, April 2, 2002.

47. T. R. Reid, "After Shaky Start, London Bridge Reopens," *Washington Post*, February 23, 2002.

48. Robert Paarlberg, "The Global Food Fight," *Foreign Affairs* 79, no. 3 (May/June 2000): 24–38. Paarlberg's analysis of this issue is compelling, and he also notes that the de facto ban blocked corn imports from the United States worth roughly $200 million annually to U.S. farmers, pp. 27–28. Also, Europe Press Release, Memo/04/85, "Questions and Answers on the Regulation of GMOs in the EU," Brussels, April 15, 2004.

49. Lanham, Md.: Rowman & Littlefield, 2001.

50. David Brooks summarizes these ideas in his review of Cantor's book. See "Farewell to Greatness: America from Gilligan's Island to the X-Files," *Weekly Standard*, September 17, 2001, pp. 31–35.

51. Gallup poll data for "trust and confidence...in our federal government in Washington when it comes to handling [international/domestic] problems." Responses September 13–15, 2004: international problems: a great deal 18%; fair amount 45%. October 11–14, 2001: 36% and 47%. Domestic problems, September 13–15, 2004: 13% and 48%; October 11–14, 2001: 24% and 53%. Data reported in "Major Institutions," www.pollingreport.com/institut.htm; and Jeffrey M. Jones, "Ratings of

Government and Bush Remain High," Gallup News Service, October 31, 2001.

52. See David Hoffman, "Beyond Public Diplomacy," *Foreign Affairs* 81, no. 2 (March/April 2002): 83–95.

53. Described in Elisabetta Burba, "How Lebanon Reacted to the News," *Wall Street Journal Europe*, September 19, 2001. As another example, Osama bin Laden, in his video denunciations of the United States, appeared to be wearing a Timex Ironman Triathlon watch. See Edward Rothstein. "Damning (Yet Desiring) Mickey and the Big Mac: It Isn't Imperialism but Freedom That Makes Pop Culture So Appealing Even among America's Enemies," *New York Times*, March 2, 2002.

54. Quoted in "British Detail bin Laden Tie to U.S. Attacks," *New York Times*, October 5, 2001. Also see text of report issued by British government, "Responsibility for the Terrorist Atrocities in the United States, 11 September, 2001," reprinted in the same issue.

55. Fouad Ajami, "Arabs Have Nobody to Blame but Themselves," *Wall Street Journal*, October 16, 2001. Also see Ajami, *The Dream Palace of the Arabs: A Generation's Odyssey* (New York: Pantheon, 1998.)

56. Text of bin Laden Remarks. "Hypocrisy Rears Its Ugly Head," as broadcast by Al-Jazeera television on October 7, 2001. *Washington Post*, October 8, 2001.

57. David Rhode and J. C. Chivers, "Al-Qaeda's Grocery Lists and Manuals of Killing," *New York Times*, March 17, 2002, p. 18.

58. On this point, see Bernard Lewis, *What Went Wrong? Approaches to the Modern History of the Middle East* (New York: Oxford University Press, 2002).

59. Quoted in Daniel Pipes, "God and Mammon: Does Poverty Cause Militant Islam?" *The National Interest*, no. 66 (Winter 2001/2): 14–21 at 17.

60. The Egyptian study was conducted in 1980 by a respected Egyptian scholar, Said Eddin Ibrahim. In 2000, Ibrahim was jailed as a result of his vigorous efforts to promote democratic freedoms within Egypt and spent three years in prison before being freed. Daniel Pipes makes the case that militant Islam is not a response to poverty and has often surged in countries experiencing rapid economic growth. He concludes that militant Islam has far more to do with issues of identity than with economics. Ibid., p. 14.

61. Fouad Ajami, "Nowhere Man," *New York Times Magazine*, October 7, 2001.

62. *New York Times*, April 5 and 15, 2004.

63. These data, in a survey done by Gallup for *USA Today* and CNN, should be regarded with some caution. Although Gallup polled nearly

10,000 respondents in nine countries (Pakistan, Iran, Indonesia, Turkey, Lebanon, Morocco, Kuwait, Jordan, and Saudi Arabia), the percentages reported may not be reliable. Summary data for the entire group were not weighted by size of population; non-citizens were included; and the political cultures in most of the countries would make respondents wary of expressing their views candidly. See Richard Morin and Claudia Dean, "The Poll That Didn't Add Up: Spin on Data Blurs Findings from Gallup's Muslim Survey," *Washington Post*, March 23, 2002. Also see CNN.com, "Poll: Muslims Call U.S. 'Ruthless, Arrogant,'" February 26, 2002.

64. For a sample of these views, see "Three Years Later – The Arab and Iranian Media Commemorate 9/11," MEMRI (Middle East Research Institute), Special Report No. 33, September 9, 2004, www.memri.org.

65. An egregious example appeared in the Saudi government daily newspaper *Al-Riyadh*. In a two-part series, a columnist, Dr. Umayma Ahmad Al-Jalahma of King Faysal University in Al-Damman, wrote on the "Jewish Holiday of Purim," stating that, "For this holiday, the Jewish people must obtain human blood so that their clerics can prepare the holiday pastries." The article is translated in MEMRI, Special Dispatch – Saudi Arabia/Anti-Semitism, 3.13.02, no. 354, www.memri.org. The blood libel has also appeared in the Egyptian government dailies, *Al-Ahram* (October 28, 2000) and *Al-Akhbar* (October 20, 2000, and March 25, 2001), see MEMRI's Special Dispatches nos. 150 and 201. In turn, Egypt's ruling party newspaper has described the Holocaust as a "Zionist lie." Columns by Dr. Rif'at Sayyed Ahmad in *Al-Liwa Al-Islami* (Egypt), June 24 and July 1, 2004, quoted in MEMRI, no. 756, July 30, 2004.

66. Alexis de Tocqueville, *Democracy in America* (New York: Harper & Row, 1967), Author's Introduction, p. 14. Also see *The Old Regime and the Revolution*, ed. Francois Furet and Francoise Melonio (1856; rpt. Chicago: University of Chicago Press, 1998).

67. Seymour Martin Lipset, *Political Man* (Garden City, N.Y.: Doubleday, 1960), pp. 131ff.

68. "What We're Fighting For: A Letter from America," text of statement from a group of American scholars, *Chronicle of Higher Education*, posted February 12, 2002, http://chronicle.com/prm/weekly/documents/v48/i24/4824sep_11_letter.htm, accessed April 24, 2005.

69. Salman Rushdie, "America and the Anti-Americans," *New York Times*, February 4, 2002.

70. For example, in the autumn of 2001, demonstrations against the American intervention in Afghanistan quickly subsided as U.S. and anti-Taliban forces gained the upper hand and it became clear that much of the

Afghan population was celebrating its liberation from an oppressive regime.

71. Abd Al-Hamid Al-Bakkoush, "The U.S. and the Complexities of the Arab Mind," *Al-Hayat* (London), February 12, 2002. Quoted in MEMRI, no. 348, February 22, 2002, www.memri.org.

72. Sheikh Abd Al-Hamid Al-Ansari, "Following the 9/11 Commission, Do the Arabs Have the Courage to Reconsider Their Position?," in the London-based Arabic-language daily *Al-Hayat*, August 2, 2004, quoted in MEMRI, no. 757, August 3, 2004, www.memri.org/bin/opener_latest.cgi?ID=SD75704.

5. Iraq and the Middle East

1. Henry Kissinger, "Better Intelligence Reform," *Washington Post*, August 16, 2004, p. A17.

2. Quoted in David Remnick, "Going Nowhere," *New Yorker*, July 12, 2004, p. 81.

3. The words are those of Lebanese Druze leader Walid Jumblatt, in the *Daily Star* (Lebanon), quoted in MEMRI (Middle East Media Research Institute), Special Dispatch – Syria/Lebanon, February 7, 2003, no. 466, www.memri.org. But statements implicating Jews and Israel could also be found among the chattering classes in Paris, Brussels, London – and Washington. See Robert Kagan, "Politicians with Guts," *Washington Post*, January 31, 2003, p. A27.

4. These views, along with the arguments of Pat Buchanan in his magazine, the *American Conservative*, the words of Robert Novak ("Sharon's war") and writers in *The Nation* (Bush's "attack-Iraq chorus" in tandem with "far-right American Zionists"), and Gary Hart (invoking the dual loyalty canard), are cited in Lawrence F. Kaplan, "Toxic Talk on War," *Washington Post*, February 18, 2003, p. A25.

5. The Soviet Union was a co-sponsor of the Madrid talks, but its role was largely symbolic.

6. This section builds on my arguments and writing in "The Folly of Containment," *Commentary* 115, no. 4 (April 2003): 15–21; and in "The Neoconservative-Conspiracy Theory: Pure Myth," *Chronicle of Higher Education* 49, issue 34, May 2, 2003.

7. Carnegie Endowment for International Peace, *Iraq: What Next?* (Washington, D.C., January 2003).

8. John Mearsheimer and Stephen Walt, "An Unnecessary War," *Foreign Policy*, January/February 2003.

9. Jacques Chirac, quoted in *Washington Post*, February 22, 2003.

10. Kofi Annan, *Washington Post, February* 9, 2003.

11. Stanley Hoffmann, "The High and the Mighty," *American Prospect*, January 13, 2003.

12. The authors' use of the word "only" can be found in "'Realists' Are Not Alone in Opposing War in Iraq," *Chronicle of Higher Education*, November 15, 2002, p. B15, and in their working paper for the Kennedy School of Government at Harvard University, "Can Saddam Be Contained? History Says Yes," November 12, 2002. Chaim Kaufmann also argues that Saddam's behavior was not reckless. See "Threat Inflation and the Failure of the Marketplace of Ideas," *International Security* 29, no. 1 (Summer 2004): 5–48.

13. Quoted in David Glenn, " 'Realist' Foreign-Policy Scholars Denounce Push to Attack Iraq," *Chronicle of Higher Education*, September 26, 2002.

14. See, e.g., "Is There a Better Way to Go," *Washington Post*, February 9, 2002.

15. Joseph Cirincione and Dipali Mukhopadhyay, "Why Pollack Is Wrong: We Have Contained Saddam," Carnegie Non-Proliferation Project, February 21, 2003, http://www.ceip.org/files/nonprolif/templates/article.asp? NewsID=4379, accessed April 28, 2005.

16. *New York Times*, September 26, 2002.

17. Mearsheimer and Walt, "An Unnecessary War," p. 54.

18. This pattern has been extensively documented elsewhere. See, e.g., Richard Butler, *The Greatest Threat: Iraq, Weapons of Mass Destruction, and the Crisis of Global Security* (New York: Public Affairs, 2000); and Kenneth Pollack, *The Threatening Storm: The Case for Invading Iraq* (New York: Random, 2002).

19. Eason Jordan, "The News We Kept to Ourselves," *New York Times*, April 11, 2003.

20. "It was only by the end of May 2003, after the occupation, that I concluded they did not exist." Quoted in "The Importance of Inspections," Proliferation Brief, vol. 7, no. 11, July 26, 2004. Carnegie Endowment for International Peace, www.prolioferationnews.org, accessed April 25, 2005.

21. Quoted in Patrick Clawson, "Tighten the Finger on the Trigger," *Los Angeles Times*, December 5, 2002.

22. David Kay, who led the postwar effort to find Iraq's WMD, has estimated the number of those murdered by Saddam's regime at between 400,000 and one million. Lecture, Public Policy Institute, Georgetown University, March 25, 2004.

23. Kenneth Pollack provides evidence on these points. See *The Threatening Storm*, pp. 258–60 passim.

24. Quoted in ibid., p. 255.

25. See, e.g., Baram, "The Iraqi Invasion of Kuwait: Decision-Making in Baghdad," in Baram and Barry Rubin, eds., *Iraq's Road to War* (New York: St. Martin's Press, 1993), pp. 5–36.

26. Statement by David Kay on the Interim Progress Report on the Activities of the Iraq Survey Group (ISG) before the House Permanent Select Committee on Intelligence, the House Committee on Appropriations, Subcommittee on Defense, and the Senate Select Committee on Intelligence, October 2, 2003.

27. Testimony of David Kay before the Senate Armed Services Committee, January 28, 2004, http://www.cnn.com/2004/US/01/28/kay. transcript, accessed April 25, 2005.

28. Douglas Jehl, "Iraq Study Finds Desire for Arms, but Not Capacity," *New York Times*, September 17, 2004.

29. Quoted in Ruth Wedgwood, "A Nuclear Iraq," *New York Times*, September 30, 2004.

30. Director Tenet's testimony to Senate Intelligence Committee on October 2, 2002, declassified in a letter from the Central Intelligence Agency, Washington, D.C., October 7, 2002, to Senator Bob Graham, Chairman, Select Committee on Intelligence. *Congressional Record*, October 9, 2002, p. S10154.

31. *The 9/11 Commission Report: Final Report of the National Commission on Terrorist Attacks upon the United States* (New York: W. W. Norton, 2004), p. 66.

32. February 2003 taped statement by Osama bin Laden, quoted in *Wall Street Journal*, February 14, 2003.

33. See, e.g., U.S. Department of State, *Patterns of Global Terrorism 2002* (Washington, D.C., April 2003). On Abu Abbas, see "Tug-of-War over Hijack Mastermind," Washington, D.C., April 16, 2003, cbsnews.com.

34. See "A Year after the Iraq War: Mistrust of America in Europe Ever Higher, Muslim Anger Persists," Washington, D.C.: Pew Research Center for People & the Press, March 16, 2004, www.people-press.org.

35. Kanan Makiya, *Republic of Fear: The Inside Story of Saddam's Iraq* (Berkeley: University of California Press, 1989). Fearing retribution, the author initially published the book under the pseudonym of Samir al-Khalil.

36. Michael Mandelbaum, quoted by Thomas Friedman, in "52 to 48," *New York Times*, September 3, 2003. Also see the chapter on "Hama Rules" in Friedman, *From Beirut to Jerusalem* (New York: Farrar Straus Giroux, 1989).

37. A study of two dozen occupations since the Napoleonic era finds that occupations are likely to succeed only if they are lengthy, but that – paradoxically – long occupations tend to provoke nationalist reactions. See David M. Edelstein, "Occupational Hazards: Why Military Occupations Succeed or Fail," *International Security* 29, no. 1 (Summer 2004): 49–91.

38. Ian Buruma and Avishai Margalit, *Occidentalism: The West in the Eyes of Its Enemies* (New York: Penguin, 2004), and Buruma, "Killing Iraq with Kindness," *New York Times*, March 17, 2004. In Buruma's words, "the forceful imposition of even decent ideas in the claim of universalism tends to backfire – creating not converts but enemies who will do anything to defend their blood and soil."

39. See, e.g., Robert Jervis, *System Effects: Complexity in Political and Social Life* (Princeton, N.J.: Princeton University Press, 1997).

40. Saddam's beliefs are described in an oral history transcript by Joseph C. Wilson, the State Department official who was stationed in Baghdad and who met with the Iraqi dictator on August 6, 1990, just days after Saddam's invasion of Kuwait. The transcript is available from the Association for Diplomatic Studies in Arlington, Virginia, and cited in David Ignatius, "Saddam Hussein Revisited," *Washington Post*, September 14, 2004.

41. Text of Prime Minister Tony Blair's speech to his constituency, Sedgefield, England, March 5, 2004. Reprinted in *The Guardian* (London), http://politics.guardian.co.uk, March 6, 2004.

42. Robert Jervis offered a nuanced assessment in observing, "The war is hard to understand if the only objective was to disarm Saddam or even to remove him from power. . . . But if changing the Iraqi regime was expected to bring democracy and stability to the Middle East, discourage tyrants and energize reformers throughout the world, and demonstrate the American willingness to provide a high degree of world order . . . then as part of a larger project, the war makes sense." Jervis, "Understanding the Bush Doctrine," in Demetrios James Caraley, ed., *American Hegemony* (New York: Academy of Political Science, 2004), p. 24.

43. John Ruggie, former Assistant Secretary-General under Kofi Annan at the U.N., has made this argument, as has Martin Indyk, "The Iraq War Did Not Force Gadaffi's Hand," *Financial Times* (London), March 9, 2004.

44. A spokesman for the Italian prime minister reported this statement to the *London Daily Telegraph* in September 2003. Cited in Charles Krauthammer, "Why We Are Safer," *Washington Post*, January 9, 2004.

45. See, e.g., Remarks by President George W. Bush at the National Endowment for Democracy's 20th Anniversary Event, Washington, D.C., November 6, 2003; and Steven Simon and Dan Benjamin, *The Age of Sacred*

Terror: Radical Islam's War against America (New York: Random House, 2003.)

46. "Osama bin Laden's Message to the Iraqi People on Elections," MEMRI, Special Dispatch no. 837, December 30, 2004. In the message, bin Laden praised Zarqawi as the "commander of the al-Qaeda organization in the land of the Tigris and the Euphrates" and stated that "the comrades in the organization there must obey him." Also see "Zarqawi and Other Islamists to the Iraqi People: Elections and Democracy Are Heresy," MEMRI, Special Dispatch no. 856, February 1, 2005, www.memri.org.

47. Quoted in "Inquiry & Analysis – Iraq/Jihad & Terrorism Studies Project," MEMRI, no. 202, January 18, 2005, www.memri.org.

48. Jordan and Saudi Arabia even allowed U.S. special forces teams to launch operations from their territory into Iraq just before the war began on March 19, 2003. See Bob Woodward, *Plan of Attack* (New York: Simon & Schuster, 2004), also Woodward, "U.S. Aimed for Hussein as War Began," *Washington Post*, April 22, 2004.

49. Quoted in "EU Rejects Bin Laden's Offer," *Sydney Morning Herald*, April 15, 2004, www.smh.com.au.

50. Quoted in *Washington Post*, February 6, 2003.

51. Figures according to a report by the U.S. General Accounting Office, cited in Colum Lynch, "Volcker to Head U.N. Iraq Probe," *Washington Post*, April 17, 2004.

52. Calculations as reported in James Bone, "Saddam's Billions from Oil for Food Corruption," *The Times* (London), April 23, 2003.

53. Hisham Kassem, Head of the Egyptian Organization for Human Rights, quoted in David Remnick, "Going Nowhere," *The New Yorker*, July 12, 2004, p. 81.

54. Dennis Ross, *The Missing Peace: The Inside Story of the Fight for Middle East Peace* (New York: Farrar Straus Giroux, 2004).

55. Quoted in Danielle Pletka, "Arabs on the Verge of Democracy," *New York Times*, August 9, 2004.

6. Asia's American Pacifier

1. Quoted in Norimitsu Onishi, "Japan Says Its U.S. Alliance Helps Maintain Asian Peace," *New York Times*, October 17, 2003.

2. Quoted in Jane Perlez, "South Korean Says North Agrees U.S. Troops Should Stay," *New York Times*, September 11, 2000.

3. Quoted in Ayako Doi, "Asian Enmities: China and Japan Revert to Hostility, and Hope for Reconciliation Fades," *Washington Post*, August 29, 2004.

4. Data from "Trade (Imports, Exports and Trade Balance) with China," Foreign Trade Statistics, U.S. Census Bureau, www.census.gov/foreign-trade/balance.

5. Data from *The Economist*, January 17, 2004, p. 66, and February 14, 2004, p. 70. The IMF has estimated that the Chinese and Japanese treasuries hold $1.3 trillion in U.S. Treasury securities. Louis Uchitelle, "U.S. and Trade Partners Maintain Unhealthy Long-Term Relationship," *New York Times*, September 18, 2004.

6. Joseph S. Nye, Jr., "The Case for Deep Engagement," *Foreign Affairs* 74, no. 4 (July/August 1995): 90–102, at 102. At the time, Nye was Assistant Secretary of Defense for International Security Affairs.

7. E.g., Robert Art, *A Grand Strategy for America* (Ithaca, N.Y.: Cornell University Press, 2003).

8. E.g., Kenneth N. Waltz, "Globalization and Governance," *PS* (December 1999): 693–700; and Stephen M. Walt, "The Ties That Fray: Why Europe and America Are Drifting Apart," *National Interest*, no. 54 (Winter 1998/99): 3–11.

9. See John J. Mearsheimer, *The Tragedy of Great Power Politics* (New York: W. W. Norton, 2001).

10. E.g., Charles Kupchan, *The End of the American Era* (New York: Vintage, 2002); and "After Pax Americana: Benign Power, Regional Integration, and the Sources of a Stable Multipolarity," *International Security* 23, no. 2 (Fall 1998): 42–79.

11. Chalmers Johnson, *Blowback: The Costs and Consequences of the American Empire* (New York: Metropolitan Books, 2000), pp. ix and 228–29.

12. E.g., Edward A. Olsen, *Toward Normalizing U.S.–Korea Relations: In Due Course?* (Boulder, Colo.: L. Rienner, 2002); also see James T. Laney and Jason Shaplen, "How to Deal with North Korea," *Foreign Affairs* 82, no. 2 (March/April 2003): 16–30.

13. Morton Abramowitz and Steven Bosworth, "Adjusting to the New Asia," *Foreign Affairs* 82, no. 4 (July/August 2003): 119–31, at 131.

14. Victor Cha makes this point in "Abandonment, Entrapment, and Neoclassical Realism in Asia: The United States, Japan, and Korea," *International Studies Quarterly* 44, no. 2 (June 2000): 261–91.

15. See Aaron L. Friedberg, "Will Europe's Past Be Asia's Future?" *Survival* 42, no. 3 (Autumn 2000): 147–59.

16. Josef Joffe, "Europe's American Pacifier," *Foreign Policy* (Spring 1984).

17. For a contrary view, see Amitav Acharya, *Regionalism and Multilateralism: Essays on Cooperative Security in the Asia Pacific* (Singapore: Times Academic Press, 2002).

18. Quoted in Jane Perlez, "South Korean Says North Agrees U.S. Troops Should Stay," *New York Times*, September 11, 2000, p. A3. On the delicate triangular relationship of the United States, Korea, and Japan, see Victor D. Cha, *Alignment Despite Antagonism: The U.S.-Korea-Japan Security Triangle* (Stanford: Stanford University Press, 1999), and "The Continuity behind the Change in Korea," *Orbis* 44, no. 4 (Fall 2000): 571–84.

19. Victor Cha makes a compelling case for this conclusion in "Mr. Kim Has Our Attention. But He Won't Be Able to Keep It," *Washington Post* Outlook, May 4, 2003, pp. B1, B5. For an account of North Korea's record of broken agreements, see Nicholas Eberstadt, "La Grande Illusion, Korean Style," Nautilus Institute: DBPK Briefing Book, February 12, 2004, full text available at: http://www.aei.org/news19917, accessed April 25, 2005.

20. In August 2004, South Korea acknowledged having conducted secret experiments that could be used in making fissile material for nuclear weapons. However, the South Korean Foreign Minister subsequently reaffirmed Seoul's intention not to develop or possess nuclear weapons. See James Brooke, "6-Nation North Korean Nuclear Talks in Doubt," *New York Times*, September 26, 2004.

21. On the likelihood of such a nuclear arms race, see James E. Goodby, "Negotiating with a Nation That's Really Gone Nuclear," *Washington Post* Outlook, February 15, 2004, p. B4.

22. The Iraq troop measure was approved in February 2004 by a vote of 155 in favor and 50 opposed, with seven abstentions. The initial U.S. announcement of pending force reductions took place in mid-2003, and the specific numbers were made public in June 2004. Agreement to stretch out the force withdrawals was reached in October 2004. See "U.S. to Slow Pullout of Troops from S. Korea," *Washington Post*, October 6, 2004.

23. Quoted in Norimitsu Onishi, "Japan Says Its U.S. Alliance Helps Maintain Asian Peace," *New York Times*, October 17, 2003.

24. Cited in James Brooke, "Japan's New Military Focus: China and North Korea Threats," *New York Times*, December 11, 2004.

25. On the assertive Chinese posture, see Edward Friedman, "Lone Eagle, Lone Dragon? How the Cold War Did Not End for China," in Robert J. Lieber, ed., *Eagle Rules?*, pp. 194–213. For examples of how Japan has reacted by adopting a tougher stance toward China and North Korea and by maintaining close ties with the United States, see Michael J. Green, "The Forgotten Player," *National Interest*, no. 60 (Summer 2000): 45–48; and Michael J. Green and Benjamin L. Self, "Japan's Changing China Policy: From Commercial Liberalism to Reluctant Realism," *Survival* 38,

no. 2 (Summer 1996): 35–58; also "Japan and China Eye Each Other Warily – As Usual," *The Economist*, September 2, 2000, p. 35.

26. Japan has committed to purchase two missile defense systems from the United States: the land-based Patriot-3 and the Aegis cruiser equipped with the Standard missile. Deployment is to take place in 2007. See James Brooke, "Japan Seeks Shield for North Korean Missiles," *New York Times*, August 30, 2003; and "Japan's Push for Missile Defense," *Strategic Comments* (London: International Institute for Strategic Studies), vol. 9, issue 8 (October 2003).

27. Japanese officials plan to open a commercial nuclear fuel reprocessing plant at Rokkasho in Northern Japan in 2006. The operation will process 800 tons of spent reactor fuel per year and produce as much as eight tons of plutonium that will be mixed with uranium for Japan's light water reactors. However, the plutonium could also be recovered for use in nuclear weapons. See Joseph Cirincione and Jon Wolfsdahl, "Producing Plutonium at Rokkasho-mura," Carnegie Endowment for International Peace, Washington, D.C., October 2004, http://www.carnegieendowment.org/npp/publications/index.cfm?fa=view&id=15955, accessed April 25, 2005.

28. The statement occurred during an argumentative five-hour meeting involving the Chinese Military Commission and an American diplomat, Chas Freeman, and accounts of it subsequently appeared in the *New York Times*. According to Ambassador Freeman, who insists the comment was not a threat to bomb Los Angeles, the Chinese official said, "And finally, you do not have the strategic leverage that you had in the 1950s when you threatened nuclear strikes on us. You were able to do that because we could not hit back. But if you hit us now, we can hit back. So you will not make those threats. In the end you care more about Los Angeles than you do about Taipei." See Carnegie Non-Proliferation Project, "Did China Threaten to Bomb Los Angeles?" *Proliferation Brief* 4, no. 4 (March 21, 2001), Carnegie Endowment for International Peace, Washington, D.C., www.ceip.org.

29. Bush was interviewed on ABC Television on April 24, 2001. See, e.g., www.cnn.com/2001/ALLPOLITICS/04/25/bush.taiwan.03, accessed April 26, 2005.

30. In December 2003, the Seoul National University announced that Chinese had superseded English as the most popular liberal arts major. See Barbara Demick, "Who Needs English?" *Los Angeles Times*, March 29, 2004.

31. The issue is described at length in James Brooke, "China Fears Once and Future Kingdom," *New York Times*, August 25, 2004. Also Edward Cody,

"China Gives No Ground in Spats over History," *Washington Post*, September 22, 2004.

32. U.S. data from "Trade (Imports, Exports and Trade Balance) with China," Foreign Trade Statistics, U.S. Census Bureau, www.census.gov/foreigntrade/balance. China-Russia data from interfax.com.

33. Erich Weede observes that while the rise of China implies security risks, there are also positive opportunities because of the "pacifying impact of free trade and globalization and prospects for democratization." He finds conceivable a long-run "capitalist peace" among China, Russia, and the West. See Weede, "China and Russia: On the Rise and Decline of Two Nations," *International Interactions* 29 (2003): 343–63.

34. C. Raja Mohan, "'Old' Europe, Make Way for New Delhi," *Wall Street Journal*, December 15, 2004.

35. Indian Foreign Minister Jaswant Singh, quoted in Jim Hoagland, "Staying on in Central Asia," *Washington Post*, January 20, 2002, p. B7. Also see interview with General Pervez Musharraf by Judith Miller, "Pakistani Leader Wants U.S. Air Power to Support Bigger Afghan Peace Force," *New York Times*, January 20, 2002.

36. Hoagland, "Staying On."

37. Joseph S. Nye, Jr., "The Case for Deep Engagement," *Foreign Affairs* 74, no. 4 (July/August 1995): 90–102, at 91.

38. Victor Cha makes this point insightfully, and the elaboration of it here draws in part on his assessment. See *Financial Times*, October 22, 2003.

7. Why They Hate Us and Why They Love Us

1. Quoted in Henri Astier, *Times Literary Supplement* (London), January 10, 2003.

2. Ibid.

3. Quoted, *The Economist*, February 1, 2003.

4. "Yankee Go Home but Take Me with You," paper by Jairam Ramesh, Secretary, Economic Affairs Department, All-India Congress Committee, presented to the Roundtable on Indo-American Relations organized by the Council on Foreign Relations and the Asia Society, New York, November 1, 1999, http://www.jairam-ramesh.com/publications/publications.html, accessed April 27, 2005.

5. "Bin Laden's Sermon for the Feast of the Sacrifice," quoted in MEMRI, memri@memri.org, Special Dispatch – Jihad and Terrorism Studies, March 5, 2003, no. 476.

6. Arne Perras, editorial in *Sueddeutsche Zeitung* (Munich), August 1, 2003.

7. Fouad Ajami, "The Falseness of Anti-Americanism," *Foreign Policy*, no. 118 (September–October 2003): 52–61.

8. Alan B. Krueger and Jitka Maleckova, "Does Poverty Cause Terrorism?" *New Republic* (June 24, 2002): 27–33, at 32.

9. E.g., Olivier Roy notes that al-Qaeda militants in Europe were cultural outcasts both in their own societies and in the host countries, but all were in some way Westernized, were trained in scientific or technical fields, and spoke a Western language. See "Euro Islam: The Jihad Within," *National Interest*, no. 71 (Spring 2003): 70.

10. *The Sociology and Psychology of Terrorism: Who Becomes a Terrorist and Why?* (Washington, D.C.: Federal Research Division, Library of Congress, September 1999). This report and Maxwell Taylor's 1988 book, *The Terrorist*, are discussed in Krueger and Maleckova, "Does Poverty Cause Terrorism?" p. 32.

11. Charles A. Russell and Bowman H. Miller evaluated eighteen revolutionary groups, including the German Baader-Meinhof Gang, Italy's Red Brigades, and the Japanese Red Army. They concluded that "the vast majority of those individuals involved in terrorist activities as cadres or leaders are quite well educated. In fact, approximately two-thirds of those identified terrorists are persons with some university training, [and] well over two-thirds of these individuals came from the middle or upper classes in their respective nations or areas." In Lawrence Z. Freedman and Yonah Alexander, eds., *Perspectives on Terrorism* (Wilmington, Del.: Scholarly Resources, 1983). See also Russell and Miller, "Profile of a Terrorist," *Terrorism: An International Journal* 1, no. 1 (1977): 17–34.

12. The "Bojinka" plan to blow up eleven or twelve U.S. aircraft flying from East Asia to the United States was uncovered in January 1995 when Philippine police found a bomb-making laboratory in a Manila apartment. See Phillip A. Karber, "Re-Constructing Global Aviation in the Era of the Civilian Aircraft as a Weapon of Destruction," *Harvard Journal of International Law and Public Policy* 25, no. 2 (Spring 2003): 789. Also see *Report of the Joint Inquiry into the Terrorist Attacks of September 11, 2001* (Washington, D.C.: 107th Congress, 2nd Session, House Permanent Select Committee on Intelligence, H. Report No. 107–792); and Senate Select Committee on Intelligence, S. Report No. 107–351, December 2002, pp. 129–92.

13. I have elaborated on these features in chapter 4 above.

14. *Al-Quds* (newspaper of the Palestinian Authority), December 15, 2003, quoted in the Middle East Media Research Institute (MEMRI), "Arab Media Reaction to Saddam's Arrest: Part I," Special Dispatch – Iraq,

December 16, 2003, no. 628, http://memri.org/bin/articles.cgi?Page= archives&Area=sd&ID = SP62803, accessed on April 27, 2005.

15. Michael Scott Doran, "Somebody Else's Civil War," *Foreign Affairs* 81, no. 1 (January/February 2002): 22–42, at 27–28.

16. Portions of this section are adapted from my essay, "The Neoconservative-Conspiracy Theory: Pure Myth," *Chronicle of Higher Education* 49, issue 34 (May 2, 2003).

17. For example, the Saudi Interior Minister, Prince Nayef ibn Add Al-Aziz, told a Kuwaiti newspaper that the Zionists were behind the attacks on the World Trade Center and Pentagon. An English translation of this assertion was then circulated in an on-line magazine published by the Saudi royal family. See Jaap van Wesel, "MEMRI Games," *The Jerusalem Report*, December 29, 2003, p. 22.

18. Gallup poll conducted in 2002, cited in *Washington Post*, December 23, 2003.

19. Anne Applebaum, "Germans as Victims," *Washington Post*, October 15, 2003.

20. (Carnot USA Books, 2002). Published in France as *11 Septembre 2001: L'effroyable imposture* (Paris: Editions Carnot, 2002).

21. Scott Wilson, "U.S. Troops Kill 2 Iraqis after Ambush," *Washington Post*, May 23, 2003.

22. Michael Lind, "The Weird Men behind George W. Bush's War," *New Statesman* (London), April 7, 2003, and "How Neoconservatives Conquered Washington – and Launched a War," Salon.com, April 9, 2003.

23. Eric Alterman, "Can We Talk?" *The Nation*, April 21, 2003.

24. Lind, "The Weird Men."

25. Edward Said, "The Academy of Lagado," *London Review of Books* 25, no. 8 (April 17, 2003).

26. Lind, "The Weird Men."

27. William Pfaff, "The Neoconservative Agenda: Which Country Is Next on the List?" *International Herald Tribune*, April 10, 2003.

28. Patrick J. Buchanan, "Whose War?" *American Conservative*, March 24, 2003, and Buchanan, "To Baghdad and Beyond," *American Conservative*, April 21, 2003. Also Alterman, "Can We Talk?"

29. "Author of Saudi Blood Libel: 'U.S. War on Iraq Timed to Coincide with Purim,'" Middle East Media Research Institute, Special Dispatch – Saudi Arabia/Arab Anti-Semitism, April 11, 2003, no. 494, www.memri.org. The speech was given at the Zayed Center for Coordination and Follow-Up, where previous speakers had included former Vice President Al Gore, former Secretary of State James Baker, and former President Jimmy Carter.

30. Alterman, "Can We Talk?"

31. Lind, "The Weird Men" and "How Neoconservatives Conquered Washington."

32. Lind, "How Neoconservatives Conquered Washington."

33. Buchanan, "Whose War?"

34. By contrast, Ivo Daalder and James Lindsay, moderate Democrats who are critics of Bush foreign policy, nonetheless take Bush seriously as someone who has a coherent vision of grand strategy and should not be underestimated. See their book, *America Unbound: The Bush Revolution in Foreign Policy* (Washington, D.C.: Brookings, 2003).

35. "Resources of Hope," report of a roundtable organized by *Al-Ahram Weekly* (Cairo), reported by Amina Elbendary, Al-Ahram Weekly Online, March 27–April 2, 2003 (issue no. 631), http://weekly.ahram.org.eg/2003/631/focus.htm, accessed April 27, 2005.

36. See, e.g., Robert Jervis, "Understanding the Bush Doctrine," *Political Science Quarterly* 118, no. 3 (2003): 365–88.

37. E.g., John Lewis Gaddis, "A Grand Strategy of Transformation" *Foreign Policy*, no. 133 (November/December 2002): 50–57.

38. *Views of a Changing World, June 2003* (Washington, D.C.: Pew Research Center for the People and the Press, 2003). The study was based on surveys in twenty-one countries conducted from April 28 to May 15, 2003, in Europe, the United States, the Middle East, and elsewhere.

39. Fouad Ajami provides an incisive critique of the assumptions on which these criticisms are based. See "The Falseness of Anti-Americanism."

40. Data cited in *The Economist*, February 1, 2003, p. 46.

41. Quoted in Edward Rothstein, "An Open Mind among Growing Ideologues," *New York Times*, January 4, 2002. For a comprehensive presentation of Aron's views, see his now classic book, *The Opium of the Intellectuals* (Garden City, N.Y.: Doubleday, 1957).

42. See, esp., the analysis of French anti-Americanism and its origins in Philippe Roger, *L'ennemi americain: Geneologie de l'antiamericanism francais* (Paris: Seuil 2002), Jean-Francois Revel, *L'obsession anti-americaine* (Paris: Plon, 2002), and the review of these works by Walter Russell Mead, *Foreign Affairs* 8, no. 2 (March/April 2003): 139–42. Philippe Roger's book has been published in English as *The American Enemy: The History of French Anti-Americanism* (Chicago: University of Chicago Press, 2005).

43. Quoted in David Brooks, "Among the Bourgeoisophobes," *Weekly Standard*, April 15, 2002, p. 21.

44. See, e.g., Philip Zelikow, "The Transformation of National Security," *National Interest*, no. 71 (Spring 2003): 17–28, at 18.

45. Philippe Roger makes this point as well. See Mead, review in *Foreign Affairs* (March/April 2003). A good insight about the link between anti-Americanism and anti-Semitism is provided by Michael Mousseau: "[J]ust as the Jews symbolized emerging market norms in Europe a century ago, today, with modern technology, America and Western culture symbolizes the dreaded market norms linked with globalization." See "Market Civilization and the Clash with Terror," *International Security* 27, no. 3 (Winter 2002/3): 5–29, at 19.

46. Ajami, "The Falseness of Anti-Americanism."

47. *The Economist* (London), "Blair, the BBC and the War," July 26, 2003.

48. This assessment appeared in the French newspaper *La Croix* in December 2003.

49. *Daily Mirror* (London), January 29, 2003.

50. Margaret Drabble, "I Loathe America and What It Has Done to the Rest of the World," *The Daily Telegraph* (London), May 8, 2003.

51. *The Guardian* (London), November 18, 2003.

52. March 26, 2003. The author is a French philosopher and writer.

53. Quoted in Takis Michas, "America the Despised," *National Interest* (Spring 2002): 101–2.

54. As reported for the year 2003 by the E.U. Environmental Commissioner, only Sweden and Britain were able to meet yearly Kyoto emission targets, while the remaining thirteen of then fifteen members of the E.U. were not. See *Washington Post*, December 11, 2003.

55. For example, on the proposition that the E.U. will emerge within the decade to counterbalance the United States, see Charles Kupchan, *The End of the American Era* (New York: Vintage, 2002). For predictions of balancing, see, e.g., Kenneth N. Waltz, "The Emerging Structure of International Politics," *International Security* 17, no. 4 (Spring 1993): 5–51; Robert S. Pape, "The World Pushes Back," *Boston Globe*, March 23, 2003; Stephen Walt, Interview, "Opposing War Is Not Appeasement," www.tompaine.com/feature.cfm/ID/7431, accessed April 27, 2005; and Christopher Layne, "America as European Hegemon," *National Interest*, no. 72 (Summer 2003): 17–28.

56. I elaborate on this in "Are Realists Realistic about Foreign Policy?" paper delivered at the 2003 Annual Meeting of the American Political Science Association, Philadelphia, August 28–31, 2003.

57. Keir Lieber and Gerard Alexander, "Waiting for Balancing: Why the World Isn't Pushing Back," *International Security* 30, no. 1 (Summer 2005).

58. The leaders of eight Western European countries (Britain, Spain, Italy, Portugal, Denmark, Poland, Hungary, and the Czech Republic) signed a

support letter written by the British and Spanish Prime Ministers, Tony Blair and Jose Maria Aznar, and the heads of ten East European countries of the Vilnius group (Romania, Latvia, Lithuania, Estonia, Bulgaria, Albania, Croatia, Slovenia, Slovakia, and Macedonia) signed a similar statement.

59. Since the end of the Cold War, Kenneth Waltz has predicted the demise of NATO and warned that with the end of the Soviet threat, former friends and foes of the United States would seek to balance against it. See Waltz, "The Emerging Structure of International Politics," pp. 75–76.

60. During the last decade of the Cold War, Josef Joffe made a similar point in his widely cited article, "Europe's American Pacifier," *Foreign Policy* (Spring 1984).

61. NATO assumed command of the ISAF (International Security and Assistance Force) in August 2003. See, e.g., *Le Figaro* (Paris), Internet edition, August 11, 2003: "After playing a passive deterrent role for a half-century, the Atlantic alliance has certainly never been as active since the disappearance of the Soviet Union."

62. Stephen Peter Rosen, "An Empire If You Can Keep It," *National Interest*, no. 71 (Spring 2003): 54. Also see John Owen, "Transnational Liberalism and U.S. Primacy," *International Security* 26, no. 3 (Winter 2001–2): 117–52, at 121.

63. Hans-Ulrich Klose, Deputy Chairman of the Foreign Relations Committee of the Bundestag, remarks to a roundtable of the Friedrich Ebert Foundation, Washington, D.C., September 30, 2003.

8. Postscript: The Future of the American Era

1. This introductory discussion of progress and problems expands on my earlier contribution to "Defending and Advancing Freedom: A Symposium," *Commentary* 120, no. 4 (November 2005): 44–46. Parts of this chapter appear in "The U.S. and the Middle East: Five Years After 9/11," *Internationale Politik* (Berlin), September 2006.

2. Max Boot, in a thorough and largely positive assessment of the Iraq situation, provides sharp criticism of policy failures in the immediate aftermath of the fall of Baghdad and places much of the responsibility on Secretary of Defense Donald Rumsfeld and the military commander, General Tommy Franks, for their indifference to nation-building and post-conflict planning. See "Guess What? We're Winning," *American Interest* I, no. 3 (Spring 2003).

3. John Lewis Gaddis, "After Containment: The Legacy of George Kennan in the Age of Terrorism," *The New Republic*, April 25, 2005, pp. 27–31, at 28.

4. After the fall of Baghdad in April 2003, the U.S. Joint Forces Command undertook a study of the inner workings of Saddam Hussein's regime based on interviews with captured senior Iraqi military and political leaders and official Iraqi documents. The study was partially declassified in late February 2006 and its key findings are presented in Kevin Woods, James Lacey, and Williamson Murray, "Saddam's Delusions: The View from the Inside," *Foreign Affairs* 85, no. 3 (May/June 2006): 2–26. For the full report, see *Iraqi Perspectives Project: A View of Operation Iraqi Freedom from Saddam's Senior Leadership*, available at www.foreignaffairs.org/special/iraq/ipp.pdf.

5. Kevin Woods, James Lacey, and Williamson Murray, "Saddam's Delusions," *loc. cit.*, p. 9.

6. *Loc. cit.*, p. 11.

7. *Loc. cit.*, p. 12.

8. *Loc. cit.*, p. 26.

9. *Loc. cit.*, p. 6n.

10. See "Comprehensive Report of the Special Advisor to the DCI on Iraq's WMD (Duelfer report) September 30, 2004. Full text at www.cia.gov/cia/reports/iraq_wmd_2004/index.html. Also see "Tapes Reveal WMD Plans by Saddam," *Washington Times*, March 13, 2006; and Max Boot, "Guess What? We're Winning," p. 56.

11. The quote is from Iraqi documents. See *Iraqi Perspectives Project*, p. 54.

12. "Saddam's Delusions," p. 16.

13. "Iran's New President Says Israel 'Must Be Wiped Off the Map,'" *New York Times*, October 27, 2005.

14. Nazila Fathi, "Senior Iran Cleric Tells Sudan That Nuclear Aid Is Available," New York Times, April 26, 2006.

15. In June 2004, the UN Security Council established a mandate for the U.S.-led multinational force in Iraq, and in November 2005 it renewed the mandate. See "U.N. Extends Mandate in Iraq for U.S. Troops," *New York Times*, November 9, 2005.

16. "Text of President Clinton's address to Joint Chefs of Staff and Pentagon staff," February 17, 1998. Transcript: http://www.cnn.com/ALLPOLITICS/1998/02/17/transcripts/clinton.iraq/. Accessed May 8, 2006.

17. "UN Cuts Sudan Food Aid Due to Lack of Funds," Reuters and MSNBC.com, April 28, 2006. http://www.msnbc.com/id/12530891.

18. Stephen G. Brooks and William C. Wohlforth, "International Relations Theory and the Case Against Unilateralism," *Perspectives on Politics* 3, no. 3 (September 2005): 509–24.

19. Peter Berkowitz, "Laws of Nations," *Policy Review*, April/May 2005, pp. 71–80.

20. U.S. Department of Defense, Quadrennial Defense Review Report, February 6, 2006. http://www.defenselink.mil/pubs/pdfs/QDR20060203.pdf. Accessed May 2, 2006.

21. "9/11 Panel Gives Administration Failing Grades," National Public Radio, *Day to Day*, December 5, 2005. Kean and Hamilton were speaking as co-chairs of the 9/11 Public Discourse Project, which continued as a private group for a year following the issuing of the official 9/11 Commission's report. See www.npr.org/templates/story/story.php?storyId = 5039199.

22. Lugar Survey on Nuclear Proliferation, June 2005, text at: http://lugar.senate.gov/reports/NPSurvey.pdf.

23. *The National Security Strategy of the United States of America*, March 2006, p. 23, http://www.whitehouse.gov/nsc/nss/2006. Accessed May 3, 2006.

24. *Ibid.*, p. 1.

25. *Ibid.*, pp. 8 and 23.

26. Olivier Roy, "Why Do They Hate Us? Not Because of Iraq," *New York Times*, July 22, 2005.

27. Jeffrey Herf, *Reactionary Modernism: Technology, Culture, and Politics in Weimar and the Third Reich* (NY: Cambridge University Press, 1994); and "Historic Transgressions: The Uses and Abuses of German History," *International Politik* (Berlin), Transatlantic Edition, Vol. 7 (Spring 2006): 47–53, at 48–49.

28. See Paul Berman, *Terror and Liberalism* (New York: Norton, 2003). Other authors have identified early intellectual and organizational ties between Soviet totalitarianism and the Muslim Brotherhood in the1920s and '30s. See Laurent Murawiec, *The Mind of Jihad* (Washington, D.C.: Prepared for the Director of Net Assessment, U.S. Department of Defense; Hudson Institute, 2005).

29. Herf, "Historic Transgressions," p. 49.

30. Middle East Media Research Institute (MEMRI). Special Dispatch – Iran / Antisemitism Documentation Project, No. 1110, February 24, 2006, www.memri.org/bin/opener_latest.cgi?ID = SD110106.

31. "Syrian Gov't Daily Suggests Israel Created Avian Flu Virus," MEMRI, Special Dispatch – Syria, No. 1094, February 16, 2006, www.memri.org/bin/opener_latest.cgi?ID = SD109406.

32. Especially John Mearsheimer and Stephen Walt, "The Israel Lobby," *London Review of Books* 28, no. 6, 23 March 2006. And see rebuttals, e.g., Jeffrey Herf and Andrei S. Markovits, letter, *London Review of Books* 28, no. 7, April 6, 2006; Alan Dershowitz, "Debunking the Newest – and Oldest – Jewish Conspiracy: A Reply to the Mearsheimer-Walt," Working Paper, Harvard Law School, April 2006, http://www.ksg.harvard.edu/research/working_papers/facultyresponses.htm. Accessed June 1, 2006;

Eliot A. Cohen, "Yes, It's Anti-Semitic," *Washington Post*, April 5, 2006.

33. Mearsheimer and Walt make substantial use of the work of Israeli revisionist historian Benny Morris, quoting him in corroboration of their remarks. But Morris himself has since written that, "...their work is a travesty of the history that I have studied and written for the last two decades." He adds, "...the 'facts' presented by Mearsheimer and Walt suggest a fundamental ignorance of the history with which they deal, and...the 'evidence' they deploy is so tendentious as to be evidence only of an acute bias." Benny Morris, "The Ignorance at the Heart of an Innuendo: And Now for Some Facts," *The New Republic*, May 8, 2006. See also the critique by Marc Landy, "Zealous Realisms," *The Forum* 4, no. 1 (2006), Berkeley Electronic Press.

34. Text of bin Laden Remarks. "Hypocrisy Rears Its Ugly Head," as broadcast by Al-Jazeera television on October 7, 2001. *Washington Post*, October 8, 2001.

35. See especially Bernard Lewis, *What Went Wrong?: Western Impact and Middle Eastern Response* (New York: Oxford University Press, 2002), and Fouad Ajami, "The Century's Solitude," *Foreign Affairs*, Nov/Dec 2001: 2–16.

36. Olivier Roy, "Why Do They Hate Us?"

37. Mearsheimer and Walt, "The Israel Lobby."

38. National Thermometer poll conducted by Quinnipiac University Polling Institute. Voters were asked to rate foreign countries and governing organizations on a scale of zero to 100. Britain received the highest mean score at 76.4, followed by Canada 70.9, Israel 61.8, Mexico 54.9, India 52.1, the United Nations 50.6, Russia 47.1, France 45.9, China 41.5, etc. See "Americans Prefer Russia to France, Poll Shows," Associated Press, March 13, 2005. Sample size of 1900 respondents, queried about their views of 15 countries and organizations.

39. "American Attitudes Hold Steady in Face of Foreign Crises," August 17, 2006, http://people-press.org/reports/display.php3?Report ID = 285. Accessed August 29, 2006; and "Most in U.S. See Israel as Friendly," *Wall Street Journal Online*, August 30, 2006, WSJ.com.

40. "Hamas Deputy Marzouk: Non-Recognition of Israel a Hamas Founding Principle," MEMRI Special Dispatch Series – No. 1158, May 9, 2006, http://memri.org/bin/articles.cgi?Page = archives&Area = sd&ID = SP115806. Accessed June 22, 2006.

41. Excerpts from "The Covenant of the Islamic Resistance Movement – Hamas," MEMRI Special Dispatch – Jihad & Terrorism Studies

Project/Palestinian Authority, February 15, 2006, No. 1092, http://memri. org/bin/articles.cgi?Page = archives&Area = sd&ID = SP109206. Accessed June 21, 2006.

42. See, e.g., poll of Arab public opinion by James Zogby, cited in Robert Satloff, "Hamas's Rise and Israel's Choice," Washington Institute for Near East Policy, PolicyWatch #1072: Special Forum Report, January 26, 2006, http://www.washingtoninstitute.org/templateC05.php?CID = 2436. Accessed June 22, 2006.

43. Josef Joffe, "A World without Israel," *Foreign Policy* (Jan/Feb 2005): 36–42.

44. Estimate for Europe from Tore Bjoergo, a terrorism expert at the Norwegian Police University College, cited in Paul Haven, "Europe Tries to Prevent the Next Attack," Associated Press, Monday, May 29, 2006, http://www.washingtonpost.com/wp-dyn/content/article/2006/05/29/AR2-006052900478_pf.html. Accessed May 31, 2006.

45. Alain Marsaud, former chief counterterrorism coordinator in the 1980s, quoted in, "Europe, Too, Takes Harder Line in Handling Terrorism Suspects," *New York Times*, April 17, 2006.

46. Estimate for France from Louis Caprioli, the former assistant director of the DST, cited in Haven, "Europe Tries to Prevent the Next Attack," Associated Press, Monday, May 29, 2006, http://www.washingtonpost.com/wp-dyn/content/article/2006/05/29/AR2006052900478_pf.html. Accessed May 31, 2006.

47. Quoted in *The Atlantic Times: A Monthly Newspaper from Germany* 2, no. 12, December 2005, http://www.atlantic-times.com/archive_detail. php?recordID = 360. Accessed May 10, 2006.

48. See especially Michael Mandelbaum's discussion of the United States as the world's key provider of public goods, especially in the realm of security and economics, *The Case for Goliath* (New York: Public Affairs, 2005).

49. Quoted in "The Past's Long Shadow," *The Economist*, February 18, 2006.

50. Quoted in "Chinese General: Threatens Use of A-Bombs If U.S. Intrudes," *New York Times*, July 15, 2005.

51. China possesses only 18 missiles capable of reaching the United States. Their single warheads are stored separately, and before the missiles can be launched they need to be armed and loaded with volatile liquid fuel. In the event of a grave crisis, they could readily be destroyed in an American first strike. See Keir A. Lieber and Daryl G. Press, "The End of MAD? The Nuclear Dimension of U.S. Primacy," *International Security* 30, no. 4 (Spring 2006): 7–44 at 8. The authors also find that the United States should be able to maintain this first strike capability for a decade or more.

See Lieber and Press, "The Rise of U.S. Nuclear Primacy," *Foreign Affairs* 85, no. 2 (March/April 2006): 42–54, at 49–50.

52. Aaron L. Friedberg, "The Future of U.S.-China Relations: Is Conflict Inevitable?" *International Security* 30, no. 2 (Fall 2005): 7–45.

53. Husain Haqqani and Kenneth Ballen, "Our Friends the Pakistanis," *Wall Street Journal*, December 19, 2005.

54. "Huge Crowds in India Rally Against Bush Visit," *International Herald Tribune*, March 2, 2006.

55. E.g., Stephen M. Walt, *Taming American Power: The Global Response to U.S. Primacy* (New York: Norton, 2005); Anatol Lieven, *America Right or Wrong: An Anatomy of American Nationalism* (New York: Oxford University Press, 2005); John Ikenberry, "America's Imperial Ambition," *Foreign Affairs, September/October 2002;* Francis Fukuyama, *America at the Crossroads: Democracy, Power and the Neoconservative Legacy* (New Haven: Yale University Press, 2006); Clyde Prestowitz, *Rogue Nation: American Unilateralism and the Failure of Good Intentions* (New York: Basic Books, 2003); Charles A. Kupchan, *The End of the American Era: U.S. Foreign Policy and the Geopolitics of the Twenty-first Century* (New York: Knopf, 2002).

56. See especially Stephen G. Brooks and William C. Wohlforth, "Hard Times for Soft Balancing," *International Security* 30, no. 1 (Summer 2003): 72–108; and Keir A. Lieber and Gerard Alexander, "Waiting for Balancing: Why the World Is Not Pushing Back," *International Security* 30, no. 1 (Summer 2003): 109–39. Also see the exchange between Robert J. Art and these authors, "Correspondence: Striking the Balance," *International Security* 30, no. 3 (Winter 2005/06): 177–96.

57. Richard Betts, "The Political Support System for American Primacy," *International Affairs* (London) 81, no. 1, 2005: 1–14 at 1, 11.

58. "Networked readiness index" data from World Economic Forum, *The Economist*, April 1, 2006.

59. OECD data cited in *Atlantic Times* 2, no. 10, October 2005.

60. Data from the World Economic Forum, cited in *The Economist*, October 1, 2005, p. 96.

61. Oxford, Cambridge, and Tokyo were the only foreign universities in the top 20; France lacked a single entry in the top 40. Data from Jiao Tong University, Shanghai, based on academic and research performance, including Nobel prizes and articles in respected publications. See *Economist*, September 10, 2005.

62. Comparative data from a study by Peter Katzenstein and Robert Keohane, "Anti-Americanism in World Politics," reported in the *Economist*, December 17, 2005, p. 62. As of 2006, McDonald's had 1035 restaurants in

France and a total of 6,276 in Europe. See John Tagliabue, "A McDonald's Ally in Paris," *New York Times*, June 20, 2006.

63. Michael Howard, "The Forgotten Dimensions of Strategy," *Foreign Affairs*, Summer 1979.

64. Nell Henderson, "Greenspan Renews Warning on Budget Deficits," Washington Post, April 21, 2005.

65. For example, in his acceptance speech to the 2004 Democratic National Convention, the party's presidential nominee, Senator John Kerry, stated, "I will never give any nation or any institution a veto over our national security." Text, "We Have It in Our Power to Change the World Again," New York Times, July 29, 2004.

Index